THE SOCIAL BRAIN

The Psychology of Successful Groups

Tracey Camilleri, Samantha Rockey
& Robin Dunbar

Cornerstone Press

1 3 5 7 9 10 8 6 4 2

Cornerstone Press
20 Vauxhall Bridge Road
London SW1V 2SA

Cornerstone Press is part of the Penguin Random House group of companies
whose addresses can be found at global.penguinrandomhouse.com

Copyright © Tracey Camilleri, Samantha Rockey, Robin Dunbar 2023

Tracey Camilleri, Samantha Rockey and Robin Dunbar have asserted their right to be identified
as the authors of this Work in accordance with the Copyright, Designs and Patents Act 1988.

First published by Cornerstone Press in 2023

www.penguin.co.uk

A CIP catalogue record for this book is available from the British Library.

ISBN 9781847943606 (Hardback)
ISBN 9781847943613 (Trade paperback)

Typeset in 12/14.75pt Dante MT Std by Jouve (UK), Milton Keynes
Printed and bound in Great Britain by Clays Ltd, Elcograf S.p.A.

The authorised representative in the EEA is Penguin Random House Ireland,
Morrison Chambers, 32 Nassau Street, Dublin D02 YH68

www.greenpenguin.co.uk

MIX
Paper from
responsible sources
FSC® C018179

Penguin Random House is committed to a
sustainable future for our business, our readers
and our planet. This book is made from Forest
Stewardship Council® certified paper.

To the three small groups at the centre of our circles – the Camilleri, Dunbar and Rockey families – with love.

Contents

Preface   ix

1. Introduction   1
2. Leading by Numbers   17
3. A Sense of Belonging   49
4. Bonding   79
5. The Medium and the Message   109
6. The Size of Trust   136
7. Social Space, Social Time   159
8. The Social Brain at Work   186

   Afterword   223
   Acknowledgements   227
   Notes   229
   Appendix: List of Contributors   247
   Index   251

The Thrive Model ™ Environments for Performance, Innovation and Impact

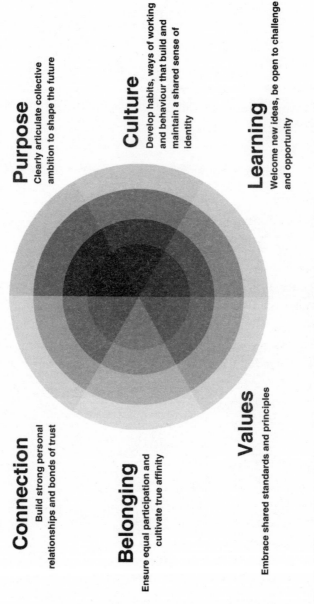

Purpose
Clearly articulate collective ambition to shape the future

Culture
Develop habits, ways of working and behaviour that build and maintain a shared sense of identity

Learning
Welcome new ideas, be open to challenge and opportunity

Values
Embrace shared standards and principles

Connection
Build strong personal relationships and bonds of trust

Belonging
Ensure equal participation and cultivate true affinity

The Thrive Model™ sets out the six elements of optimal group performance and well-being (shown here as quadrants of a circle) that are analysed in the following chapters. The more developed each element is – in other words, the closer to the centre of the circle – the stronger that group will be.

Preface

This book arose out of a meeting of minds in Oxford between three people with different experiences, backgrounds and professional orientations. Tracey Camilleri has spent twenty years at Oxford Saïd Business School as an Associate Fellow with a focus on designing and directing leadership programmes for business and government. Samantha Rockey has looked at human development from an alternative perspective, having spent most of her career in a global corporation, responsible for learning, team effectiveness, culture and performance. Tracey and Samantha have pooled their experience to advise some of the leading companies in the world, putting this research into practice. Both have witnessed first-hand the challenges of leading organisations to optimise their social potential – and the perils of ignoring these forces. They have developed insights into what leaders can achieve by working both with the grain of our natural, evolved behaviour and, crucially, where they need to work against it. Robin Dunbar, Professor of Evolutionary Psychology at Oxford University, is perhaps best known for the Dunbar Number. His award-winning research has been foundational to the understanding of human connection and social dynamics. Robin's lifetime focus constitutes the scientific ballast for the book, providing an understanding of the ebb and flow of human behaviour that often takes place beneath the horizon of consciousness, unnoticed and unmeasured but always significant.

Tracey first became interested in the ways in which groups bond early in her career when she worked as a schoolteacher and sought to help students collaborate, express themselves, take risks, and be open to new ideas. But it has been her work as Director of the Oxford Strategic Leadership Programme – a six-day, flagship leadership development course that has been running twice a year since

1982 – that has helped crystallise her ideas. In particular, she was fascinated to discover early on in the programme's history that while its intimate honeycomb tutorial structure yielded transformational results on an individual basis, it sometimes proved difficult for those involved to roll out the strategies they had learned at scale and in large organisations. Pinpointing how groups function best – and what size those groups should be – therefore became a fundamental preoccupation for her.

Samantha's background has been similarly diverse. She started out working on development planning and policy in her home country of South Africa in the early post-apartheid years. Here she quickly realised that the policy decisions and ambitions of the new government would be stymied if the right organisational culture and leadership were not in place. She then worked for the global brewing giant SABMiller for nearly eighteen years. Her focus on the intricacies of human behaviour and social dynamics within an organisation proved invaluable when she joined the Saïd Business School and teamed up with Tracey to establish their leadership and organisational development consultancy Thompson Harrison. Here she has focused on understanding the 'cultural magic' that makes an organisation feel truly human, and creates a sense of connection and belonging.

Robin spent the better part of two decades studying the behaviour of wild monkeys and antelope in Africa, and focusing on social evolution: why species have the particular societies that they do. During that period, humans were, at best, only a very superficial interest for him. However, his immersion during the first two decades of his life in four very different human cultures in the richly diverse environment of East Africa turned out to be an important catalyst for developing the sensitivities needed for careful observation of human as well as animal social worlds. Much of what happens in the lives of wild monkeys and apes is fleeting, and easily missed. Yet it is in the seemingly casual encounters between the members of a group that the subtleties of the primate social world are most clearly revealed. This world is very different from those of all other birds and mammals. It has an intimacy to it and an important element of continuity over time that engenders obligations and commitments of a kind very familiar from our own human society. Without knowing the dynamics of the relationships involved, without being there at a particular moment and realising what is going on, the casual observer can never hope to have any appreciation of the subtlety of primate social life. Blink, and you will have missed it. Refining an ability to spot tell-tale signs in the animal kingdom paid dividends when he later turned his attention to studying human behaviour. The nature of human social relationships, and the structure and dynamics of human social groups, then dominated the second half of his research career.

Robin's research and Samantha's and Tracey's experience demonstrate the vital importance of understanding the intricate workings of social groups. Organisations are groups of individual human beings, hopefully united by a shared purpose, who happen to have come together at a particular moment in time, often for very different individual reasons. The organisation itself doesn't decide anything. Individuals do that. But the structure of organisations shapes how those decisions are expressed. Many organisations, particularly large ones, ignore the fact that our psychology, as humans, is designed to cope with a very small-scale social world. And, as a consequence, they struggle to function well.

Through working and talking together, we found that we shared a fascination for the unexplored social power of organisations, the preconditions for human thriving in groups and, importantly, what can change and what remains constant about the ways in which we behave together.

In this book, we argue that our inherited biology, rumbling beneath the surface of our seemingly rational work lives, deserves greater understanding. Everything in biology is a continuum with multiple dimensions. There are no absolutes, but there are nonetheless enduring evolutionary forces that influence each one of us every day. Entranced as we are by the new, the fact is that much of our social behaviour has not changed since the time of our ancient ancestors. We have non-negotiable constraints linked to brain size, time and underlying hormonal responses. Our ability to scale relationships is limited simply by the size of our brains, for example. Yet we also have clear opportunities: we can quite easily strengthen our social connections and trusted networks through certain types of shared experience. Those who lead organisations – and in fact those at any level within them – need to find ways to work both with and against the grain of our inherited tendencies. Through a greater understanding of our 'hardwired' motivations and responses, leaders can improve the chances for people to thrive within their organisations. Over the years, Samantha and Tracey have worked with a number of enlightened people leading groups in a variety of settings – from corporations through to music groups and sports teams. Conversations with these people have informed the evolution of this book and have provided practical stories and examples to bring alive the science.

The social lives of institutions are their lifeblood. Hard to measure and easy to overlook, corporate culture and ethos are nonetheless governed and regulated by the social brains of each individual member. In the following pages, we provide the science and some lived examples of that social brain in action. We also advance some ideas about what leaders can do to increase levels of happiness and a sense of belonging in their organisations.

Oxford, September 2022

Introduction

'Tell me about it if it's something human.'

'Home Burial' by Robert Frost[1]

It is a leader's job to create an environment within which people can thrive both as individuals and as a collective. This is as true for a hockey team as it is for a multinational insurance company. It may sound easy, but it's not.

Many people in positions of leadership end up there not by conscious design or focused ambition but simply because one thing led to another. The fact of your being the leader does not usher in the means to lead. People look to you for answers but at times you don't feel you even have the right questions. There is a constant pressure for growth, the responsibility for which lies at your door. The external context changes so fast that it feels as though you are running to stand still. Resources are constrained – particularly the precious resources of your time, energy and attention. Despite good intentions, there are too many people who need your focus to be able to manage relationships well. At times you have to cut off and be transactional simply to get through managing the day to day, let alone having time to think about the future. Time to think, in fact, is rare. The last thing you need is another model, another new leadership initiative, another book.

This book, however, doesn't focus on the new but instead explores what is unchanging in the way human beings behave. It brings the science of our inherited biology together with the practice and politics of life in organisations. All human beings are governed by the same social gifts, needs and dynamics, whether at home or at work. Yet, busy as we are with the surface, we pay scant attention to what is rumbling beneath all of our interactions. The drivers of human behaviour, our hormonal responses and wellsprings of group dynamics are challenging to measure and difficult to see. They are hidden in plain sight.

We bring hard numbers to this soft relational space. We suggest simple things that leaders can do to get the best from people, for themselves and for the organisations to which they belong. We examine how leaders can provide containment for people so that they feel they are respected, that they have a place and they belong. Happy, productive employees need to have meaningful work, to feel they can progress and grow. Having good relationships at work, feeling challenged but not fearful in a fair system are also key components of this notion of thriving (see the model in Chapter Eight). Everyone feels seen and heard. Everyone has a sense of autonomy.

Does that sound idealistic and exhausting? The good news is that, within a safe environment designed for human thriving, governed by a clear purpose and underpinned by shared values, people largely can do most of this for themselves and each other. Good leadership creates great followers. This book advocates leaders doing less but understanding more. By mostly going with the natural flow (trees don't need incentives to come into leaf!) and occasionally against it when it leads to clannishness or narrow thinking, leaders can free themselves to focus on the future – which is, after all, the proper territory of leadership.

We seek to explain the social processes that play a central role in the way people in organisations work. Our aim is to discuss the issues of scale, trust, bonding, identity, communication, environment, resilience and ultimately leadership that underpin effective organisations. These form a web of interlocking forces that, when we combine them in the right order and quantity, set the world of work on fire. Each chapter traces not only the science behind human behaviour but also some practical examples drawn from direct experience running the Oxford Strategic Leadership Programme (OSLP) for ten years, working in a FTSE top ten company, as well as examples drawn from interviews with leaders, practitioners, academics and experts (a list of those we interviewed is given in the Appendix at the back of this book). Taking a leaf from the fundamental premise of the OSLP – that leaders need to explore their own leadership through multiple lenses – we turn to historians, conductors, theatre directors, city planners, barristers, social entrepreneurs, philosophers, civil servants, designers, campaigners for social justice, elected officials and others, to provide fresh perspectives. No two organisations are exactly the same and we offer no one-size-fits-all panacea, no easy solutions, no magic mantras. Instead, our aim is to provoke useful conversations and opportunities for reflection for those who wish to lead organisations into a future in which people – and hence the organisations of which they are a part – thrive. We also provide some practical, actionable suggestions for those in positions of leadership in Chapter Eight.

We still live in a lean management world where the unmeasured is frequently thought of as unimportant. In this book, the opposite case is made: that it is precisely the conventionally unmeasurable that is actually the most important factor that determines how well an organisation performs. This viewpoint reflects one simple fact: an organisation is not a machine – it is a collection of individual human beings, and it simultaneously benefits and suffers from both the cleverness and the limitations to which the human social world is prone. It is a world built on normal, everyday human relationships, and it will work so much the better for us if we approach its design and management from a human-level perspective. Management practices that have dominated thinking for the last century or so have invariably imagined organisations as akin to a clockwork mechanism. Improving the efficiency of an organisation is simply a matter of pressing the right buttons. It is a view that derives largely from the early-twentieth-century behaviourists, who argued that human behaviour is infinitely malleable. Efficiency is merely a question of the push and pull of reward and persuasion.

This view, however, ignores the fact that all human organisations are social by nature, and our social propensities have very deep evolutionary roots. To overlook the most salient feature of our world is to sail against the wind of history. That is never the smartest thing to do, for, as the philosopher George Santayana famously observed, those who 'cannot remember the past are condemned to repeat it'.[2] By incorporating a better understanding of human nature and its origins, we inevitably have a better chance of playing to its strengths and avoiding the consequences of its weaknesses. If leaders are able to manage their organisations' 'shared tensions, anxieties and relationships', the outcome is a 'capacity for realistic hard work'.[3]

At the heart of these natural tensions and dynamics lies a set of oppositions: between conservatism and change; between, on the one hand, Robin's research into what stays constant in our inherited human behaviour and, on the other, the ever-present need to shape our futures – to adapt, to learn and transform. Humans have a natural tendency towards homophily in their social relationships, for example. They naturally seek out those who share interests and experiences. Homophily, defined broadly as a shared set of cultural values, can, under appropriate circumstances, be beneficial in fast-tracking friendship and connection. But it can also present challenges for organisations: groupthink, complacency, in-groups versus out-groups, narrow-mindedness and poor decision-making can all easily result from it. Good leaders will sense when the tendency to homophily is proving helpful and when it threatens to be disruptive. Working both with and against the grain of this tendency, to provide containment for this fluctuating dynamic, is part of the art of leadership.

In writing this book, our own small group dynamic has sometimes seen our positions begin to polarise. Robin has allied more with the 'pull of biology', emphasising what can only change slowly through the eons of human evolution, whereas Tracey and Samantha have wanted to explore the possibilities of more radical, quick-fire organisational transformation. It took us some time to appreciate these opposing dynamics. Open discussions between us contained positions that sometimes felt quite hard to reconcile. Once made conscious and articulated, however, we invariably found a way forward to complete our project happily together.

In turn, the question of containment relates crucially to matters of scale. Things easily become too big to manage or remain too small to generate much meaning. Here Robin's life's work and his research behind the Dunbar Number and the Dunbar Graph have given Tracey and Samantha's practical experience real scientific corroboration.

This connection started with a specific example: one iteration of the OSLP several years ago. The programme was riding particularly high, with a long waiting list of applicants wanting to join. Pressure mounted to increase the returns by admitting an ever-larger number of attendees. The suggestion was that the programme should be expanded to accommodate forty people (five more than before). Tracey, and the tutors who led the small groups were not entirely sure that this was the right thing to do, but they agreed to the proposal, assuming that the small number of extra individuals involved would not make much difference.

Unfortunately, it did. When the group had been smaller, its members, who had started out as an assortment of strangers from as many as twenty different countries, came to feel a sense of shared identity. When the group grew in size, that togetherness never took root. Participants appeared to conclude that there was simply not the time nor the space in one week to connect with everybody and so opted to stick with those from their own sectors or part of the world – their obvious 'kith and kin'. At social events, they formed factions rather than mingling freely. In plenary sessions, the quieter voices tended to give up: one side of the room was too far away from the other even to hear what was said, let alone to respond. An 'us' and 'them' dynamic developed.

Those running the programme found it hard work, too, and enjoyed it much less than they had previously. With smaller tutor groups, there had been the opportunity and time for each person to tell their story. With the greater number, tutors now found themselves having to cut short valuable airtime. They also discovered that discussions became less nuanced and that participants were less able to benefit from the wisdom of others. Tracey, who had always made a point of having one-on-one conversations with everybody involved at some point during the programme, now felt she simply didn't have the time.

In short, the relational and conversational nature of the programme was compromised. Somehow the powerful sense of group presence and engagement that had once existed had been lost. One evening after dinner, the tutors were surprised to learn that someone had organised for only half the group to go to a pub. His explanation was that there were too many people for one establishment to accommodate, and that, in any case, 'some people don't drink . . . and some want to talk to their children online from their rooms'. Fault lines had opened up. People were being pigeonholed before they had the chance to get to know one another.

The week worked – just. But it was work, instead of the usual exhilarating week of reciprocal learning. The feedback was OK, the financials looked good, but there were niggling criticisms about the venue, about pre-programme processes, logistics, the temperature of the rooms – small things that, when we'd had a more robust, personal connection, simply hadn't arisen. Afterwards, there was far less inclination among people to reconnect. The strong alumni relationships we'd seen spring up previously were much less in evidence.

The experiment was tried once more – with the same result. We were perplexed but felt intuitively that it must have something to do with the precise size of the group within the given time constraints. Why should increasing the numbers by a handful of people have made such a difference? Had this been a one-off, we would perhaps have blamed the programme itself. But the fact that it had previously worked so well and – more importantly – that those involved in it had had similar experiences in other environments where the group size had changed gave us pause for thought. We began to wonder whether we'd broken some immutable law. Perhaps there was a group size we could not go beyond without undermining the programme's effectiveness. Indeed, perhaps the reason why it had previously been so successful was closely tied up with how many people had been involved. That led us to Robin. He had often been a contributor to Tracey's leadership courses at the Saïd Business School and had found an intuitively receptive audience when describing how all humans are constrained by three fundamental factors: size of brain, hormonal response and time. In the simplest terms, the Dunbar Number is the natural limit on the extent of meaningful social relationships that an individual can manage at any one time. That number is 150. Robin's research also explores the social significance of other constituent numbers via the Dunbar Graph (see Chapter Two). So here, through his work – we had a scientific hypothesis and the start of a set of conversations that helped us to understand the expanded programme's struggle and why the smaller group worked. The cognitive load of building relationships with the larger group within the confines of a week, taken on top of the existing relationships held in mind by each of the participants, was simply too great. We requested that we return to our smaller programme model and, since then, the programme has thrived.

This book thus comes with a warning. The psychological bases of our behaviour, and the biological drivers that underpin these, present both promise and pitfalls. They provide insights into how organisations function – or might function better – but, at the same time, they reveal potential cracks in the superstructure that can have destructive consequences if we do not adapt our systems to take them into account. These cracks are created by the natural forces of human nature – the way our minds and behaviour have been adapted by evolution to the particular, rather small, scale of our natural social world. The questions of scale, of the basis for friendships and of the ways to develop a sense of belonging, which we trace in the following chapters, present both problems and real, practical opportunities – some of them simple and easy to exploit, others much less so. These insights are helpful in the creation of a common culture and a common story that can contain, but not constrain, groups of people. Particularly in times of stress or fragility, understanding the basis of natural friendships and relationships is of vital importance.

Uncovering the Science

The Social Brain Hypothesis is the idea that a species' brain size and available time determines, or more correctly constrains, the size of that species' social groups (for humans, as we have seen, the maximum natural level is 150 people). Humans are hardwired for connection and being part of a social group is critical. Given the constraints we discussed earlier (time, size of brain and hormonal response), the wellbeing of a group is dependent upon the following three principles:

- The first principle is that group size is a strong determinant of a group's wellbeing. People flourish in situations where they know people and are known themselves.
- The second follows from the first. The quality of relationships diminishes as the size of the group increases. Sixty per cent of our social time is spent with just fifteen people – this fact alone requires us to be choosy about who those people are.
- The third principle is concerned with our changing hormonal responses and how these can affect our equilibrium. Too much cortisol caused by fear and stress contributes to a range of negative outcomes. By contrast, neurotransmitters such as endorphins create feelings of safety. The origin of this positive hormonal response is what evolutionary biologists refer to as 'social grooming', awkward as contemporary resonances of the phrase may be. This is an activity that in monkeys and apes involves leafing through each other's fur but which humans, with their lack of fur, have adapted into the various forms of stroking, hugging and caressing that we use continuously in our closer

relationships. The stroking stimulates highly specialised neural sensors in the skin that send a signal to the brain which triggers the release of endorphins, the neurobiological underpinning of social bonding. Beyond our intimate relationships we have adopted a number of social practices, from handshakes, eating a meal together to sharing experiences, that turn out to produce the same hormonal response.

These three principles are fundamental to humans – they are hard-wired into our biology. We ignore them at our peril.

Some people instinctively understand the lessons of the Social Brain Hypothesis. Willard (Bill) Gore was one of these. Having worked for a major multinational, he went on to set up W. L. Gore and Associates with his wife Vieve Gore in 1958. The Gores were committed to a team-based organisation and as the company grew, Bill concluded that 150-person units were optimal. Many years later, he reflected on this:

> We . . . found that when we exceed 150 Associates per plant the Commitment principle and the one-on-one system tend not to work well because there are too many Associates who do not know each other. This is why we seek to limit our plant size to about 150 people or, with shifts, at most to 200 people. Our experience: Dividing plants up at an appropriate point will increase opportunities of the parts over those of the former whole. There is no exact formula for the appropriate time of dividing a growing organizational unit into new parts. There are, however, a few early indicators like a 'critical mass' of market segments, of technology, of products, of Associates in a certain area or of communication problems which help make that decision before the maximum of 150 to 200 Associates is reached. Several plants of about 150 persons may be located as a CLUSTER in a geographical proximity and benefit by sharing certain kinds of specialized skills, equipment, and so on, without the loss of the person-to-person relationships.[4]

The unique 'relatively flat structure' nature of the Gore management structure contrasted starkly with the more conventional hierarchical management structures adopted by most large organisations at the time. Many think it lay at the heart of the company's success.

Unfortunately, far too many organisations – from businesses to schools to hospitals and government departments – have ignored the Gore lesson: Scale poses major challenges. As organisations succeed, they grow; in consequence, they inevitably develop fracture lines and inefficiencies that are a corollary of our limited abilities as humans to monitor and manage large numbers of relationships. As a result, many forever teeter on the edge of structural collapse, with a left hand that has no idea what the right hand is doing.

And, of course, it's not just the size of a group, or the layers that make it up, that pose challenges. Ensuring that groups bond – and giving them the time to do so – is also essential. There's no point establishing the 'ideal' size of group if its members don't gel properly with each other. Conversely, there is also little purpose in establishing a small group in the hope that it will bond when its very size limits what it is able to achieve. Creating effective groups and teams demands a careful balancing of the three principles we've just outlined with a clear sense of what these groups and teams are there to achieve.

This should remind us that large organisations are not part of our natural make-up as humans. For most of the 8 million years of our evolutionary history since parting company with the African great apes (chimpanzees and gorillas), we have lived in very small groups of just thirty to fifty individuals (see p. 11). It was only at the end of the last Ice Age, a mere 10,000 years ago, that our species started to live in permanent villages. And not until around 4,000 years ago would any of these settlements have contained more than 10,000 people. That represents a mere tenth of 1 per cent of our evolutionary history since our lineage parted company with the great apes. Our psychology and our behaviour are adapted to managing a very, very small-scale world, and not the metropolises and mega-organisations within which we now live and work. In the tension between who we are and where we now find ourselves lie the dilemmas and stresses that face every human organisation in the contemporary world – and the focus of this book.

Human Evolution in a Nutshell

Humans have only had to grapple with the stresses and complexities of living in large societies for less than 8,000 years (Figure 1.1). In the grand scheme of our evolutionary history, this is the blink of an eye: the earliest members of our lineage first appeared around 6–8 million years ago. These early species, known collectively as Australopithecines, were distinguished from the great apes only by the fact that they walked upright on two legs rather than on all fours. They were chimpanzee-sized with brains no bigger than those of modern great apes. Between about 4.5 and 1.5 million years ago, there were around a dozen different species, all confined to Africa.

Around 2.5 million years ago, a new lineage emerged out of the Australopithecines. They launched the *Homo* family to which modern humans belong. They were recognisably more human in body size and shape, but still with very modest-sized brains. They were more nomadic than their predecessors and were the first members of the human lineage to emigrate from Africa, reaching as far as China and the islands of Indonesia where they survived until as recently as 60,000 years ago.

Around 500,000 years ago, a new lineage arose out of the African members of this family, forming the root for a family of archaic humans that included the Heidelberg Folk and the Neanderthals (who colonised Africa and southern Europe as far east as the Caucasus and modern Iran) and the Denisovans (who colonised central Asia as far east as modern-day China). Archaic humans had much larger brains than the earlier species, were heavily built and heavy-boned, and relied more on meat (which they hunted with spears by the dangerous method of surrounding large mammals like early horses and even mammoths). Although the Heidelbergs disappeared around 200,000 years ago, the Neanderthals survived in Europe until around 40,000 years ago, with the Denisovans probably surviving in southern China quite a bit later than this.

Modern humans (our own species, *Homo sapiens*) emerged out of the Heidelberg stock around 250,000 years ago, probably in north-east Africa. They had a much lighter body build, larger brains and developed more sophisticated culture and tools. They relied less heavily on meat than the Neanderthals, and hunted mainly smaller birds and mammals using bows and arrows rather than spears. Recognisably human language evolved during this phase, along with pictorial art (cave paintings), sculpture (Venus figurines), and sophisticated tools (needles, awls, arrowheads). Community size now approached the modern value of 150. But people still lived in dispersed communities, much as modern hunter-gatherers do. Their communities of family and friends rarely lived together in the same place, but instead lived in small 'camp groups' of thirty to fifty individuals that often exchanged members.

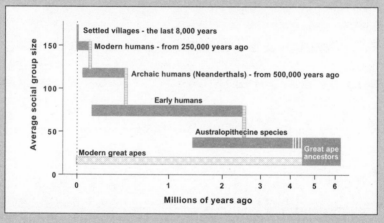

The History of Our Lineage

Figure 1.1. A timeline for the evolution of our species. We first emerge as a distinct lineage from our great ape ancestors around 6–8 million years ago. Successive phases of evolution witness a series of new lineages emerging that replace the older ones, culminating in the appearance of our own species around 250,000 years ago.

Little changed until the end of the last Ice Age around 10,000 years ago, when some of these hunter-gatherer groups began to live together in more permanent settlements. Even so, it was not until

around 8,000 years ago that we see villages of several hundred individuals, and it is not until 5,000 years ago that we find cities of 7,000–
10,000 people. The sea change brought about by living in permanent
villages marked a distinct phase shift in the levels of structural stress
that people had to cope with.

Prior to this, these kinds of stresses were minimised by living in
small mobile groups: if the stresses became too much, families were
free to leave and find a more congenial group with whom to live. Permanent settlements made this solution impossible, and novel solutions were required to mitigate the stresses. To solve this problem,
new forms of social organisation appeared such as warrior grades,
priests, temples, moral codes and formal marital arrangements. In
short, we have been exposed to the stresses of large organisations
only for the last few thousand years. While we have managed to
cope, our solutions are at best sticking plasters designed for villages
of a few hundred people, not organisations that number tens of
thousands.

This seems a particularly opportune time to undertake the challenge of examining afresh how to structure our organisations. If
the Covid-19 pandemic taught us one thing, it is the vital importance of the group to our wellbeing and ability to achieve. Isolated in
our houses, constrained into tight localities – our streets, apartment
blocks or villages – we experienced what it is to know our neighbours, to live virtually cheek by jowl with our once far-flung families, to connect living room to living room with our co-workers, to
become familiar with the insides of their houses through Zoom. We
suddenly became members of local WhatsApp groups, went shop-
ping for our neighbours, noticed the first butterfly in the park and
the birdsong in the garden, shared tomato plants on our windowsills
and, in remembering ourselves, focused closely on what means most
to us, yearning for a more human, communal future. Sue Wixley,
community activist, described the shift during Covid: 'So many

people wanted to volunteer. There was an outpouring of generosity and support. I have worked for charities my whole life and I was amazed at how proactive people were – on the mutual help website, people were offering to do the most extraordinary things. There was a huge spike in offers of help.'

At the same time, we also experienced the loneliness of being sequestered away from our natural communities. The pandemic was a melancholy laboratory for rediscovering what we value in each other. As we came to terms with virtual and hybrid work lives, we became acutely aware that the people in organisations are not simply cogs in a machine. How many of those recruited during the dystopian days of lockdown chose to move on before they even got to meet their colleagues in person, never mind bond with them? How many of them might have stayed longer – or might have made more lasting contributions while they were there – had they been able to find colleagues with whom they shared interests or experiences, and been able to feel part of a community?

Now is an opportune time to think about what we want from our work and why some of our previous ways of organising ourselves have proved so problematic. If relationships are the fundamental building blocks of healthy human groups, then we need to look anew at how we see the shape of organisations and, particularly, how we grow them. We have been apt to think of workers as a generic category, but in reality, they are individuals and we should think of them as such – seeing each in the context of the natural limits on their relational reach. Robin's research shows that, in our everyday social world, we devote 40 per cent of our social time to just five people and that these five are fairly constant over time; they provide a degree of stability for us in an ever-changing world, a source of support and advice. We devote a further 20 per cent of our time to an additional ten people who provide us with the more pleasurable, but equally important, benefits of sociality; theirs is a more dynamic social environment, changing as place, project, interests and context evolve. Work groups exhibit the same kinds of pattern and dynamics. In the context of work (and home!), the fifteen people in these two circles need to be the right people – and especially so for leaders.

The time is ripe for considering more keenly the ways in which we have worked, and how we continue to work, to scrutinise those habits we take for granted and those we need to rethink. The shape of working life has gone through a revolution and people are looking for more balance and meaning from their work than ever before. The old, unquestioning submission to a long commute, or the leap-on-a-plane-at-the-drop-of-a-hat mindset, the sterile hot-desking environment that many have endured, have come to be questioned during the Covid-19 pandemic. Working from home, at least part of the time, has entered into everyone's consciousness. The long, boring Monday-morning meetings – where the same old suspects monopolise the floor and little is accomplished – have mercifully come under scrutiny. It's a moment for stopping old habits and questioning traditional ways of structuring work. People in organisations need to find better ways of coming together: businesses are, by their nature, social enterprises. Those who ignore this imperative risk their organisations slipping over the narrow divide between effective productivity and terminal tailspin. Recognising this, thoughtful leaders will put greater effort into those precious face-to-face interactions in order to get more out of them, but in a more focused and productive way.

As we re-examine our old ways of working, we see how individual insights illuminate the three principles of group behaviour, and we assess how they can be best applied. How can leaders be more deliberate about the way in which they build groups and scale their organisations? How can they create environments within which friendship, trust and relational bonds flourish? What means are at their disposal to invigorate the social life of the group in order to mobilise more naturally towards a shared purpose?

In many respects, then, our interest here lies in what does not change in human psychology, of considering ourselves instead in the light of the glories and shortfalls of our human biology. That biology is explicitly social. It underpins the business of societies as well as the organisation of businesses – organisations made up of individuals who, one way or another, work together on a common task, not individuals acting in isolation. The central question is: how can we more effectively exploit natural human social behaviour to create organisations that perform better in terms of our traditional metrics because they are built on our natural psychology, honed by a million or more years of evolution, and, at the same time, also create more satisfying social environments for those who work in them?

It is not a leader's job to micromanage an organisation, but rather to design a structure within which it can become a self-correcting, learning community that changes as it develops. In this way it becomes what the psychoanalyst Wilfred Bion termed 'a mature work group'.[5] The balanced approach that leaders must strike to achieve this rests between knowledge and ignorance, control and spontaneous development, between stepping in and standing back. The locus of leadership lies in these tensions and in the relationship that any leader has with themselves, with those they lead and with the changing context in which they have to work. Leadership is never binary. And it is never stationary. It is not about mastery or providing solutions. Rather, it is an exercise of the moral imagination, a desire to enable the maximum human capability of whatever stripe to thrive and grow in the organisation and, ultimately, to help people to set sail in a direction that has meaning for them, for their stakeholders and for society.

2.

Leading by Numbers

'People can be themselves only in small comprehensible groups. Therefore, we must learn to think in terms of an articulated structure that can cope with a multiplicity of small-scale units.'

E. F. Schumacher[1]

The conductor Peter Hanke has long been fascinated by how leadership capabilities in business and music overlap. He directs a school for young conductors and invites business leaders to participate in workshops with young musicians and singers so they can learn from each other. Peter reflected on our question of whether groups could get 'too big to function' with reference to his experience of leading an orchestra: 'I have conducted large orchestras of over 150 in my career, but it is not very satisfying,' he observed. 'Musicians in such a large ensemble probably don't even know one another's name, and the unspoken value that the conductor ought to have a direct relationship with each musician is unsolvable. Moreover, they end up being spaced too far apart to be able to hear each other properly. As a result, they fail to connect in their music-making by their own professional intuition and need to be "managed" more than is ideal for the music-making.'

It's not surprising, therefore, that most orchestras comprise about 100 players. And even then the dynamics of the group change according to its size. When a large-scale orchestra is involved, section leaders are needed for the sub-groups of instruments, each typically around the fifteen to sixteen mark in size. The role of the conductor becomes one of logistics, mastery, planning – the personal, relational, inspirational role is not possible with so many. You can't work on intonation in the oboes, for example, if you have ninety-eight non-oboists drumming their fingers waiting for you to finish. Peter goes on: 'As the conductor at a scale beyond 100, you feel quite isolated. Relations with the musicians become weak: you become more like a field marshal than a conductor. Leaders are lonely; they always have been, but with such a large group that feeling is extreme, and you need to compensate for the lack of intimacy with a high level of energy and performing charisma. In some musical formats scaling up is OK – like opera or large oratorios – but here the musical leadership functions are a bit different, orchestra is on its own, soloists on stage forming a group, dancers, chorus etc are divisions of the organisation – and very importantly, they rehearse on their own before everybody gets together. Conducting becomes a grand scheme timing and complexity facilitation, and everybody knows it has to be like this.'

At the other end of the scale, there is a tipping point beyond which a conductor is no longer required – but that tipping point comes at a very small group size. 'The maximum number of musicians you can have without a leader, formal or informal, is five, no question,' Peter observes. Chamber music, rock bands, madrigal groups – all work with four or five members, no more. It's a powerful number, ideal for specialist teamwork. With four or five members, there's little danger of sub-groups emerging. If there's disagreement, people will probably split two to two, or three to two; it's unlikely that one person will be left isolated. The minute you get beyond five, someone has to take the lead. By the time you reach fifteen, you need a conductor or clearly defined formal leadership like a concert master or leading solo players facilitating and taking charge for efficacy in rehearsal as well as taking necessary artistic choices. At fifty, sub-groups kick in and you get a hierarchy of small groupings – brass, woodwind, strings etc. As Peter argues, it's essential to precisely establish the right kind of governing framework for every size of group. 'There are famous examples of orchestras working conductor-less by principle and here the leadership is more subtle, informal and hidden in more complex organisational dynamics.'

When we think about teams and groups, we think about their functions and responsibilities and about developing their value to us and the talents of those involved. Only rarely do we stop to think about their size. Can a department be too big to function well? Can a team be the wrong size to cope with the task assigned to it? To what extent can the toxic cultures that sometimes grow up in organisations – the 'us and them' mentality – be explained by the size of the groups within them? At what point does a conversation become unmanageable? Just as the mathematician Benoit Mandelbrot[2] saw clouds as atomised, composite structures, made up of 'billows upon billows', is there a benefit in focusing more clearly on the component clusters and micro-groups within our organisations?

Organisations are adept at measuring financial costs but less good at measuring the more intangible costs of lost human capital – the energy, talent, loyalty and discretionary effort that leak from the hulls of huge corporate tankers. We may know what our profits are, but not what they might have been had the trust and daring of each individual in the organisation been recognised, developed and mobilised. We may calculate the cost of overheads, but we overlook the extra layers of middle management, the policing of policy, the normative assessment, workplace support, absenteeism, churn and waste that are in part the result of diminished levels of trust. Above all, in pursuing the next objective or idea, we ignore the constants of human nature and human interaction.

This chapter explains why Peter Hanke's observations on the sizes of music groups reveal important truths about organisations more generally and about the best ways to structure them. Central to an understanding of the dynamics involved here is what has become known as the Dunbar Number.[3]

The Dunbar Number

In the simplest terms, the Dunbar Number is the natural limit on the number of meaningful social relationships that an individual

How the Dunbar Number Was Discovered

Dunbar's Number did not come out of the blue. It was, in fact, predicted from the size of the human brain using an equation relating typical group size and brain size in monkey and ape species.[4] This relationship between brain size and group size is known as the Social Brain Hypothesis.[5] Monkeys and apes differ from all other birds and mammals in that they live in large, cohesive, stable social groups based on bonded relationships (individuals have personalised friendships with each other). Such relationships depend on sophisticated

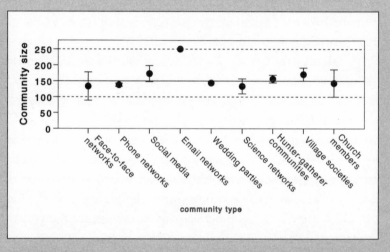

Network Size

Figure 2.1. Mean (± one standard deviation) for natural community size estimated from network size (personal social networks of friends and family), number of people called over a year in mobile phone datasets, the size of communities in online social media platforms, email lists, US wedding guest lists, science networks (co-author networks and sub-discipline sizes), hunter-gatherer community sizes, historical village sizes in Europe during the eleventh to eighteenth centuries, and church congregation sizes. The dashed lines indicate the confidence intervals around the predicted value of 150 (the range within which 95 per cent of all estimates would be expected to fall). Source: Dunbar (2020)[6]

psychological abilities that allow animals to figure out how others will behave and, hence, how best to interact with them. That skill requires considerable computational powers, and hence a big brain.

Once the Social Brain Hypothesis had been established, it was just a matter of plugging human brain size into the equation for the monkeys and apes. Doing so yielded a predicted value of 148.[7] The original test of this was against the size of small-scale hunter-gatherer communities, since it is in this type of society that our species has lived for several million years. These communities turned out to have an average size of almost exactly 150. Subsequently, this number turned up in a wide variety of other contemporary and historical contexts, including personal social networks comprising all your family and meaningful friends (Figure 2.1). It also turns out to be the typical size of the base unit in all modern armies (the company).

can manage at any one time. We can ask people to list all the friends and extended family with whom they have meaningful relationships, or else map who they phone, text or email. We can look at the number of friends they interact with on Facebook or other social media. Another approach is to work from the opposite direction by charting the typical sizes of natural groups through the ages, from hunter-gatherer societies to historical villages, church congregation sizes or even the size of science collaboration networks. On whatever basis we choose to make our calculations, we invariably end up with groups that comprise between 100 and 200 people (see p. 20). Averaging this out across nearly thirty datasets, an overall average of 155 emerges (Figure 2.1), which, for the sake of convenience, usually gets rounded down to 150. This is now known as the Dunbar Number.

In terms of our personal social networks, the Dunbar Number defines the maximum number of people for whom we feel a sense of obligation based on a relationship that involves seeing the person on a reasonably regular basis (say, at least once a year) and has a history (we have known the person for some time).[8] It is the set of people we would go out of our way to help if they asked for it without necessarily expecting any payback. Beyond this circle of 150 people, we are a great deal more circumspect in our willingness to act altruistically. We expect to be paid back in kind sooner or (at least not too much) later. Often, that is something agreed at the outset: I will help you if you agree to pay me a fee or offer me a favour in return later. In other words, after the 150-boundary things become much more transactional.

That this limit really is imposed by the size of our brains has become clear from more than a dozen neuroimaging studies published in the last decade. These studies used brain-scanning technology to examine the relationship between the number of friends that a person has and the size of key regions of their brain. Irrespective of how the studies measured the number of friends, the results were always the same: the number of friends is correlated with the volume of these brain regions.[9] The most important of these brain regions turn out to be the frontal lobes (that sit immediately behind your forehead), the temporal lobes (the sausage-shaped lobes that run along the side of the brain just inside your ears) and the limbic system (the area deep inside the brain that manages emotional cues). These are linked by massive wiring conduits (known as white matter because the neurons are sheathed in fatty white coats to improve their conductivity, much as electric cables are sheathed in plastic tubes). What is important about these brain areas is that they turn out to be the key regions involved in managing our social world. Damage these areas, and we lose our ability to manage our relationships effectively.

Perhaps the most celebrated evidence for this comes from studies of the life of the nineteenth-century American construction foreman Phineas Gage. In 1848, while employed as a supervisor on the construction of the Rutland and Burlington railroad in Vermont, USA, Gage had the misfortune to have a dynamic charge he was setting blow off and drive the three-foot-long tamping iron he was using through the left side of his face into his brain. Remarkably, he recovered from the physical injury but, as the tamping iron passed through his brain, it destroyed the key areas necessary for managing social relationships. Overnight he went from being a very highly regarded supervisor, good with people, much loved by those who worked under him, into someone who was never able to hold a steady job again, had limited ability to manage relationships, and was prone to risk-taking and gambling. It is a salutary lesson both in terms of how important our brain is for managing our social world, and how easily it can all fall apart.

The Problem of Scalar Stress

The importance of the 150-person limit is that, so long as a community remains below this size, most things can be managed on a democratic, person-to-person basis. Above the 150 level, 'scalar stresses' kick in that increasingly destabilise the group. It becomes more difficult to negotiate arrangements, information doesn't flow well round the community, processes don't work quite the way they were intended, silos build up that don't communicate with each other, people start to be suspicious and less trusting of each other. Some kind of more formal management system becomes necessary to control relationships and transactions.[10]

One solution to the scalar stress problem is, of course, never to allow a group or organisation to exceed the magic 150. This is the solution adopted by the Hutterites (originally from eastern Europe) and the Amish (who have Swiss German and Alsatian roots). These two fundamentalist Anabaptist Christian sects, based mainly in the Dakotas and Pennsylvania respectively, live on communally run farms. Their old-fashioned ways, nineteenth-century clothes, archaic speech and rejection of modern technology (the Amish won't even allow motor vehicles, never mind radios) invariably attract bemusement among outsiders. In fact, they offer us a very relevant lesson about scale. They are quite explicit that by keeping their separate democratic communities limited to 150 people, they are able to deal both with business decisions and social problems through face-to-face dialogue, without need of laws, regulations, hierarchies or police forces. Everyone knows everyone else, and so has a sense of personal obligation to the rest of the community. To preserve that sense of communality, they divide a community when it threatens to become too large, establishing a daughter farm somewhere nearby. Over the past 100 years the average size of a Hutterite community at the point of fission has been 167.[11] This overpitch in the point of fission seems to be the result of a trade-off between, on the one hand, trying to avoid the community spending too long above the 150 threshold and, on the other, a need for a community to be large enough when it undergoes fission for its daughter communities to approximate 50 and 150 respectively, because communities of around 100 are less stable and have to undergo fission again sooner than communities of 50 or 150.[12] It seems that something just doesn't quite work at intermediate values, leading to increased fractiousness in community relations and a premature second fission.

Rather similar findings have been reported for more conventional Christian denominations. Extensive research over the last two decades indicates that once the size of a church congregation exceeds the 150 limit, problems start to set in: members begin to feel less engaged, contribute less per capita to the church's funds, and feel that the church isn't meeting their needs.[13] For their part, the minister who presides over the community finds it difficult to get to know all its members, and struggles to give each one the attention they require. The solution is either to split the congregation and establish a daughter church somewhere else or to involve more ministers and give each their own sub-flock, so creating an informal management structure. Either way, there seems to be an unspoken rule that a single minister or priest can only cope effectively with a congregation that numbers 150 or fewer, and that communities of this size are less likely to be adversely affected by fractious relationships than larger ones.

One reason for this may be that, as the physicist Bruce West and his colleagues have shown, a community size of 150 seems to reach a critical tipping point.[14] As network size increases towards that number, information flow round the system improves steadily. Once the network size exceeds 150, however, information flow falls off dramatically (Figure 2.2). Something flips when communities exceed 150. They can no longer meet up so regularly. They have a natural tendency to sub-divide into silos whose members only talk among themselves. At a stroke, they cease to be well integrated and well organised and become subject to rivalries and inefficiencies. In other words, 150 represents an optimum: it's a trade-off between two different functions that pull against each other. The first has to do simply with the total number of people you have time to inter-act with, directly or indirectly; the second has to do with the effectiveness or quality of the relationships. In the mathematical study

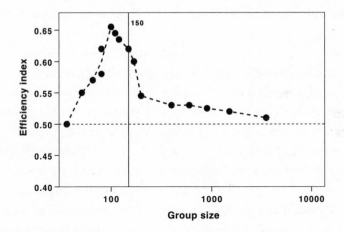

Optimal Group Size

Figure 2.2. Efficiency of information flow round social networks of different size. Efficiency can vary between 0 and 1, with a value of 0.5 (the horizontal dotted line) representing random information flow: values above 0.5 indicate increasing efficiency, those below 0.5 increasing inefficiency. Efficiency rises steadily with group size, but crashes once the size exceeds 150 (the solid vertical line). Source: West et al. (2020)[15]

of dynamic systems, such points are known as *attractors* – points to which the system will naturally gravitate if left to its own devices because they are unusually stable.

In his book *Imaginization*[16] on business organisation, Gareth Morgan (Professor Emeritus of Organisation Studies at the Toronto Schulich School of Business) uses a metaphor of the spider plant, that stalwart of houseplants, to illustrate the way in which this process of splitting allows healthy growth while maintaining connected structure. He argues that the way new, smaller plants branch away from the parent spider plant to form a decentralised organisation of parent–daughter units is a model for healthy human organisations. For the spider plant, the sense of unity is created by the stems that connect parent and daughter plants; for human organisations, that sense of unity is maintained by a series of minimum specifications (so-called 'min specs') or principles, as well as the shared purpose that ties the whole organisation together. This, he argues, is a corporate structure that could take a company beyond 'the weird stuff' into multiple stages of growth.

The Layered Structure of the Dunbar Number

One hundred and fifty is not the sole element of the Dunbar Number. In fact, it is just one of a series of circles or layers in personal social networks, albeit perhaps the key one. These layers form a set of concentric circles around you (Figure 2.3) that follow a common and very specific pattern: when counted cumulatively (such that each circle includes the individuals in the circle immediately inside it), each layer is three times the size of the one immediately below it. For simplicity, the layer sizes are given in rounded form as 1.5, 5, 15, 50, 150, 500, 1500 and 5000. The Indian mathematician Santanu Acharjee named this pattern the Dunbar Graph ('graph' used here in the mathematical sense of a pattern relating to a set of objects in a network), and we will refer to it as such.

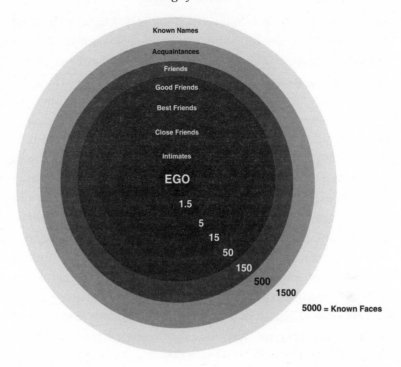

Known Names

Acquaintances

Friends

Good Friends

Best Friends

Close Friends

Intimates

EGO

1.5

5

15

50

150

500

1500

5000 = Known Faces

The Dunbar Graph

Figure 2.3. The Dunbar Graph, showing the typical sizes of layers in personal social networks. EGO indicates the person whose network is being described. The layers are determined by the frequencies with which the individuals in a personal network contact each other. It also reflects their sense of psychological closeness. Redrawn from Dunbar (2020)[17]

Each layer of Figure 2.3 corresponds to a set frequency of contact or emotional closeness to the individuals within it[18] (these two indices turn out to be closely correlated). They can be identified with relationships of a particular quality – intimates (it's 1.5 because some people have one and others have two), close friends (5, also known as the support clique), best friends (15, also known as the sympathy group), good friends (50, your principal social circle), just friends (150), acquaintances (500), faces you can put names to (1,500) and individuals you recognise as having seen before but can't necessarily put a name to (5,000). In the context of small-scale hunter-gatherer societies, these layers turn out to be roughly the equivalent to cohabiting couples (1.5), households including children (5), family clusters (15), bands (overnight camp groups, 50), local communities (or clans, 150), mega-bands (clusters of local communities, 500) and tribes (1500).

These patterns are present everywhere.[19] We even find them in the online gaming world. In this latter arena, of course, the individual groupings, at least in the lower levels of the hierarchy, are often very transient. Even so, players create temporary, constantly shifting alliances of five or fifteen people to deal with particular of-the-moment tasks and challenges. In this, they resemble the temporary work groups one finds in a business. In general, these alliances are typically made up of people drawn from the same community – the people you already know. In large part, that's because you have linked up with them in the past and so know how trustworthy they are and what skill sets they have to offer. As with friendships, the smaller, more intimate layers seem to be more stable.

Another instance of the Dunbar Graph at work is provided by an analysis of some 8 million trades between 22,000 investors on the Chinese Shenzhen 100 stock exchange.[20] Here the networks involved formed a layered structure with layer sizes averaging 2, 7, 20, 54 and 141 – remarkably close to the 1.5, 5, 15, 50 and 150 of Figure 2.3. Even in the frenetic environment of the trading floor, it seems, our behaviour is governed by hardwired social structures. This shouldn't come as a particular surprise. Trading is as much about trust as anything and, when the risks are as high as they can be on trading floors, this deep need to know whom we can trust seems to restrict the numbers of people with whom we are willing to trade.

In an explicitly business context, the Dunbar Graph is apparent in the size of Communities of Practice (CoPs), informal associations of individuals (usually, but not always, from different organisations) who meet on a regular basis to discuss matters of common interest and to develop recommendations for good practice within their field.[21] The study that revealed this provides some very relevant insights into management requirements. It seems that there is a phase transition at a CoP size of around forty members. Up to that number, a very informal approach can be taken to organisational arrangements: members take turns to organise meetings, and topics are effectively decided by democratic vote. At the forty mark, formality creeps in, complete with a committee and all the formalities of a chair, a secretary and a meeting organiser.

The switch between informal management systems and hierarchically structured ones is well illustrated by the Algonquian-speaking Native Americans of the American and Canadian Midwest (notably the Blackfoot [*Siksika*], Cree [*Paskwâwiyiniwak*] and Cheyenne [*Tsêhéstáno*] nations) in the nineteenth century.[22] For most of the year, they lived as hunter-gatherers in small nomadic bands of thirty to fifty in size, each roaming its own territory. The bands usually had a leader, or chief, but most decisions were taken democratically. Then, every spring, all the bands converged for the annual buffalo hunt and Sun Dance ritual, when they lived in an extended camp of 1,000 or more. With so many people living cheek by jowl, frictions and squabbles were inevitable. To mitigate these stresses, the individual band chiefs formed a village council, elected a Big Chief from among themselves, organised male clubs or secret societies where the more troublesome younger males could let off steam (and be tactfully managed), and appointed a group of senior warriors to act as the village police to enforce good behaviour. Special rituals were enacted to resolve internal disputes. For example, the warring parties might be made to sit down together in a teepee to undergo a 'sacred pipestem' ritual in which everyone shared a 'peace pipe' that served to calm tempers. Among the Cheyenne, leadership functions were divided between two kinds of chiefs: hereditary 'peace chiefs' (medicine men) were responsible for strategic decisions and resolving disputes, while 'war chiefs' (who won their status by displays of bravery on the battlefield) were responsible for organising and leading both war bands (to protect the tribe) and hunting parties.

The hierarchical structure of modern armies provides a more contemporary example. Military organisation is governed by the same 'Rule of Three' where each layer is three times the size of the one within it.[23] With some variation in the names for the larger groupings across countries, these consist of sections (typically 12–15 in size), platoons (typically 30–50), companies (120–180), battalions (around 500), regiments (around 1,500), brigades (around 5,000), divisions (around 15,000), and corps (around 50,000). Notice how closely these groupings map to the layers in Figure 2.3, and how they keep the ratio of three going far beyond the 1,500-grouping size that characterises normal human social networks. It should, perhaps, come as no surprise to find that there is sometimes an innermost layer of four to five, often referred to as a specialist fire team. This grouping of four to five is the standard operational unit in special forces such as the British SAS (Special Air Service) and SBS (Special Boat Service) and their American equivalents (the Green Berets and the Navy Seals). The members of a special forces' unit have to be very tightly bonded so that they will stand by each other even in the most difficult of operational conditions, often isolated behind enemy lines. To produce this level of bonding, special efforts are made during training to ensure that each team lives, breathes, eats and plays as a unit all the time so that the members know each other intimately. And this can only be done with very, very small groups.

Retired general Tyrone Urch reflects on the fact that these structures have remained surprisingly consistent since Roman times, especially the size of the smallest unit – the 'fire team' of four people. In the Roman army, this smallest team was called a 'contuberian': it was the maximum number of soldiers that could sleep in a tent while on operations. This unit is still the cornerstone of the British army. 'It's not normally their country that soldiers die for in combat, but it's . . . the members of that small team,' says Urch.

The numbers in the Dunbar Graph are not just defined by our evolutionary biology. They emerge out of a combination of the efficiencies of information flow (Figure 2.2) and how we best optimise our investment in relationships of different quality to maximise the benefits they offer us.[24] It seems that, in social networks, the 15, 50, 150 and 500 layers define points at which information flow is optimised; either side of each number, the efficiency of information flow drops off very rapidly. The value of 150 is dominant in that it produces a much bigger effect than the other layers, but the lesser limits at 15, 50 and 500 create stable points to which the system can converge. One implication here is that when an organisation increases in size from one circle to the next, it needs to do so rapidly. Any organisation that grows slowly between any of the circles will encounter counterproductive drops in efficiency as it does so. This is borne out by the Hutterite example we mentioned in the preceding section: if a community's size following fission was around 100, it was likely to undergo a secondary fission sooner than ones of 50 or 150.

Characterising the Dunbar Graph

For our purposes, there are four significant numbers associated with the Dunbar Graph: the layers at 5, 15, 50 and 150. Although each number varies somewhat between individuals, in part as a function of their personality, these numbers are remarkably consistent across populations and cultures.

The Five . . .

- This represents the number of close relationships that a person can have. This number is very stable over time and represents a mix of intimate friends and intimate family. This group is often called the 'support clique' because it consists of all the people who would not hesitate to drop everything to give support or help to you if you needed it.
- This number plays a crucial role in buffering us against the stresses of living in groups, as well as countering mental and physical ill-health.
- It is also important in the context of a work team that is focused on delivering an outcome. When a team or group contains between four and six members, it requires no formal leadership and can self-direct. Teams of this size

can take action more speedily and effectively than larger
ones.

- Teams of this size also find it easier to reach decisions.
Voting in very small groups is more likely to reflect
individuals' actual opinions. As group size increases, there
will be an increasing tendency for individuals' decisions to
be influenced by others' opinions or emerging trends so as
not to be seen as being 'out of line'. It is worth noting that a
team of odd numbers will always find it easier to arrive at a
decision if that decision relies on a democratic vote.

- There is a very strict limit on the size of conversations at
four people, after which they flip into lectures dominated by
one or two very forceful individuals.[25] A conversation of four
or five allows for equal contribution and airtime, which are
important in the context of listening to every voice.

The Fifteen . . .

- This represents the layer of people who can be considered
best friends – the people you socialise with most regularly,
and with whom you exchange such favours as mutual
childcare. It is often defined as the number of people whose
death tomorrow would really upset you. Christian Buys and
Kenneth Larson called this grouping the sympathy group for
this reason.[26] Within this layer lies the four to six people in
the support clique.

- Sixty per cent of our total social effort is devoted to this
group of fifteen people.[27]

- Relationships involving fifteen people have a shorter natural
shelf life – they require some form of regular connection to
be maintained and this is always best done face-to-face. In
the absence of face-to-face connection, such relationships
will naturally decay in a matter of months (Figure 2.4).
In this context it is worth bearing in mind the findings of
Microsoft Work Trend Index Annual Report in the wake of

the Covid-19 pandemic, which reported that 'anonymised collaboration trends between billions of Outlook emails and Microsoft Teams meetings reveal a clear trend: the shift to remote working shrunk our networks. At the onset of the pandemic, our analysis shows that interactions with our close networks at work increased, while interactions with our distant networks diminished. This suggests that, as we shifted into lockdowns, we clung to our immediate teams for support and let our broader network fall to the wayside.'[28]

The Fifty . . .

- In modern life, fifty contacts represent your main social circle, the people you would invite to a social gathering like a big garden BBQ or major birthday event.
- In hunter-gatherer societies with no formal leadership structure, fifty represents the largest number of individuals that can live together at a campsite for any length of time without disputes escalating out of control.
- Among hunter-gatherers, these groupings can be quite fluid over time, in that families that fall out with their neighbours can choose to move elsewhere and join another camp group (though usually one from the same local community).
- Groups up to fifty in size can work effectively without need for any leadership structure: in hunter-gatherer societies, for example, there are rarely any specialist roles. But when groups exceed this size, they need some kind of management structure to give them coherence – and prevent the leader's time budget becoming overstretched to the point where they lose control of the organisation.
- In the business world, research on Communities of Practice (CoPs) suggests that fifty is the maximum at which it is possible to run a group on simple democratic lines without a formal management system in place.[29]

The 150 . . . The Dunbar Number

- In hunter-gatherer societies, this constitutes the local community – a distributed group that shares a common hunting territory even though its members do not all live together in the same place.
- For this number of individuals to live (or work) together in proximity (as happened after the adoption of agriculture and the establishment of permanent villages), it is necessary to adopt behavioural mechanisms that mitigate the stresses that arise from living in close physical proximity to a large number of other people. These usually involve such activities as laughter, singing, dancing, feasting and storytelling.[30]
- One hundred and fifty represents the number of people we can engage with socially through personal relationships – the group of lifelong friends and extended family who will happily turn up for one of those once-in-a-lifetime events like a wedding celebration. It marks the limit on the number of people we are willing to act altruistically towards on the basis of personal knowledge and out of a sense of obligation.
- In personal social networks, the 150 will usually be split roughly evenly between extended family members (including in-laws) and true friends – although those who come from large families usually have fewer friends.[31]
- In the contemporary world, this grouping provides us with the 'eyes and ears' on what is happening in our local world – the so-called 'weak ties'[32] that keep us informed as to where the best supermarket deals are, what new music or films have come to town, etc.
- The mid-point between fifty and 150 appears to be an unstable group size. As we've seen earlier, research on Hutterite communities in the US suggests that daughter communities were most stable (as indexed by how quickly they needed to fission again) if they approximated 50 and 150

in size.[33] There seems to be something intrinsically unstable about communities of around 100 members.

Growing Large by Staying Small

In our work with organisations, we came across many leaders – and employees – who felt stranded and disconnected, sometimes even overwhelmed, by the sheer scale of operations in which they were involved. It was a recurrent theme. Some businesses, of course, have successfully pre-empted this problem by inventing their own version of the Dunbar model. Frank Stronach, the founder of Magna, the hugely successful Canadian car components company, started off in the 1950s working out of his garage with just a few colleagues. The view he developed was that if an organisation gets to a certain level, it can't continue to grow under the same roof, but must split into separate entities. So, in Magna's case, the 'garage' became half a dozen different garages and then multiples of garages. Now Magna has plants all over the world. Stronach's counterintuitive discovery was that the best way to grow large was to stay small, and that, as founder, his main job was to find good leaders for all of these offshoots. These leaders would then build the business in fractals, bit by bit.

Stronach's approach was of a piece with that adopted by another company we mentioned earlier: Bill and Vieve Gore founded the company that is best known for Gore-Tex™ garments and medical devices. Gore, was, among other things, a chemist, well used to 'doing the numbers'. He deliberately designed the shape of his new firm in reaction to his experiences of working in a very large, bureaucratic corporate. Large organisations, he felt, had a tendency to restrict the energies and ideas of their people: information didn't flow to the right places, people were not always willing to do favours for each other, and silos built up that reduced trust between units. Smaller taskforces he had worked with, by contrast, exhibited a real sense of urgency and purpose. They broke rules in an exhilarating and inspiring way. And they offered a level of intimacy and accountability that was absent from larger enterprises. Gore duly put his mathematical skills to work to calculate the optimum number for an enterprise and came up with a figure around the 150 mark. In a local newspaper interview in 1982, he observed: 'When an organisation exceeds some limit, typically 150, people start thinking in terms of "they" rather than "we".' 'In-groups' and 'out-groups' form around this natural 'breakpoint' and trust starts to dissipate.[34]

The Gore '150' is not a rigid number, but it still acts as a corporate guiding principle. Debra France, retired global leader of learning and development at Gore & Associates, the contemporary incarnation of Bill Gore's original company, puts it like this: 'We have evolved over time. A commitment to smaller working groups requires investment in more, smaller buildings over time. While our plants were originally set up as small units of 150, they're now more like 250 – but probably with three shifts a day, so in reality the human unit is still small. Contrast this with huge corporate headquarters that pack so many people into a single building with hopes that proximity will lead to more cooperation and collaboration. When we start to get near 300, we get quite nervous.' She remembers visiting one of their medical plants (all their centres are still called plants, regardless of whether or not they are used for manufacturing). The head of the plant is in some ways like the mayor – accountable for everything from the appearance of the reception area, to what refreshments are available, to meetings, communication and HR, although decisions about the environment are taken in a communal manner. This particular leader called a meeting that Debra attended. 'He had a real heart for the company. He asked, "Have we got too big – do we all know each other?"' Everyone acknowledged that size had become an issue. So they decided, democratically, to build another small plant in the backyard. The people moving to the new plant designed their own form of celebrations, started their own volleyball team, set up the social components of the plant – all the rituals needed to ensure a vibrant culture and sense of community for the new entity.

The breakpoints that Debra France alludes to have been echoed by others. Chris Cox, who was Chief Product Officer at Facebook back in 2005 when the company had fewer than 100 employees, put it like this at the Aspen Ideas Festival in 2019: 'I've talked to so many start-up CEOs who say that after they pass this number [150 employees] weird stuff starts to happen.' Patty McCord, former Chief Talent Officer at Netflix, attributes this 'weird stuff' to a phenomenon she calls the 'stand-on-a-chair' number:[35] if you stand on a chair and shout and people still can't hear you, then you need to rethink how you're organised. At the limits of this 'stand-on-a-chair' number, more formal systems and structures typically need to be put in place – often the very structures that have caused entrepreneurs to leave larger, bureaucratic companies and start up on their own. This point can sometimes mark a moment of fracture that changes the whole ambience of a company. The transition needs to be handled very carefully.

It's an awareness of the dangers of cultural change beyond a certain size that has been a hallmark of global giant Mars, Incorporated since its inception. Jay Jakub, Chief Advocacy Officer at the Economics of Mutuality Foundation and a former Senior Director at the Mars, Incorporated corporate think tank Catalyst, describes how hard Mars has worked to balance its huge global presence with the sense of being the small family business that it started out as. 'Mars is egalitarian at heart – there are no secretaries or executive perks for even the most senior leaders,' he explains. The leadership team sits with everyone else and uses the same facilities. There is a high premium placed on face-to-face contact. Originally the Mars family settled on the number fifty as the appropriate size for the HQ. Indeed, one member of the Mars family would regularly come into the office to count all of the punch cards (even the CEO had to punch a time-card at the start of the workday until 2008) and raise the alarm if there were more than fifty of them. Because Mars grew so much, so quickly, Jakub says, 'it capped the number of associates allowed to be based at the global HQ at 100 – following the Mars acquisition of Wrigley's – and I doubt there would ever be more than that many including visitors in the HQ at any one time.'

His view mirrors Kim Howard's. She worked in organisation

development at global investment management company Ninety-One in South Africa, and argues for a similar strategy of growth through the conscious maintenance of small units, and for a philosophy that regards a business as being a collection of fractals bound together by a shared purpose, ethos and culture: 'The CEO is keen to grow the business but not to grow the teams – his experience is that mini-businesses seem to work better.'

One final example of how the numbers of the Dunbar Graph have been used in business is provided by the Flight Centre Travel Group. When its CEO Graham 'Skroo' Turner started the company in 1982, there was a relentless focus on growth. The initial assumption was that by growing the size of teams, they could grow profits in their travel centres. After a while, they started to notice that beyond a team size of six or seven, extra staff in fact did not increase profits – only costs. The average 'good' manager could not leverage these extra employees to increase productivity. This realisation led to Skroo becoming interested in evolutionary psychology and, in due course, to structuring the company in a familial, tribal manner with shared principles combined with the freedom for the small groups to determine their own culture and ways of working. As their website puts it: 'The backbone of Flight Centre's organisational structure is the Stone Age concept of Family, Village, Tribe. Our structure is simple, lean, flat and transparent, with accessible leaders.' Flight Centre has strong guiding principles – 'ownership' and 'empowerment' being two of the foundational elements – and deliberately few layers (four or, at a push, five):

Family (three to seven members)
Villages (three to five families)
Tribe (up to twenty-five families)
Nations/Brands (eight to fifteen tribes)

Beyond that are the more conventional Region/State/Country groupings and, of course, the Board and senior leadership team. This structure has created huge loyalty and connectivity through the forty years or so of the company's history, despite the ups and downs of the travel industry, not least due to the pandemic.

Time and Social Capital

The layers in personal social networks (Figure 2.3) are determined by the frequencies with which members of the network contact each other. These turn out to have very specific values.[36] For someone to be in your five-layer, or 'support clique', for example, you need to contact them at least once a week; to be in your fifteen-layer, or sympathy group, at least once a month; in your 150-layer, at least once a year. These are not averages, but minima. Drop below these frequencies, and the person in question will, in a matter of a few months, slip over into the next layer. Figure 2.4, which shows how frequently a large sample of women from the UK and Belgium contacted the individual members of each layer of their social networks, illustrates the point: the women surveyed here tended to focus most of their time and attention on a very small number of people. In general terms, it seems that our inner core of five people receives 40 per cent of our total social effort, and that another 20 per cent is devoted to the additional ten people who make up our fifteen-layer. In other words, the fifteen people in our sympathy group share 60 per cent of our total social capital, time, effort, attention *and* emotional commitment.[37]

The amount of time devoted to each layer seems to correspond to a particular level of psychological closeness. That closeness is what allows us to appreciate how someone else thinks, how they are likely to react in a given situation, how to elicit their support, how best to handle them when there's a difficult decision to be made, and how to approach them with bad news. It also determines our willingness to act altruistically towards someone by helping them out when they ask. One estimate is that it takes around 200 hours of face-to-face interaction over a period as short as three or four months to turn a stranger into a good friend (say, someone in the fifteen-circle).[38]

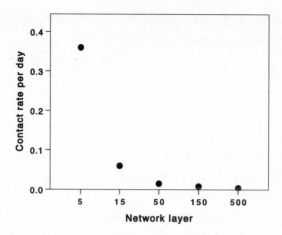

Person to Person Contact Frequency

Figure 2.4. Average frequencies per day with which people contacted the individual members of each of the layers of their social networks. Around 60 per cent of our social time is directed to just fifteen people. The data are from 250 women's social networks, sampled in the UK and Belgium. Redrawn from Sutcliffe et al. (2012)[39]

Because there are only so many hours in the day, this amounts to serious effort. Needless to say, we don't make that effort very often – not least because it takes time away from our other relationships. By comparison, the investment needed to keep someone in the outermost 150-layer is very modest – on average a mere thirty seconds a day each – and greater tolerance is shown over any failure to keep in close touch. As a result, more people can be held in this layer without imposing too much stress on the system. That's what allows us to meet someone, build an initial low-key relationship with them, and then keep them in a holding pattern until we really need them. Up to a point, the next circle out – the 500-layer – works in a similar way, but at an even lower time cost: a pool of acquaintances on hold until you need to turn one into a friend, rather like planes stacked up in a holding pattern around an airport waiting for a landing slot.

One key lesson here is that failure to continue investing at the requisite rate for the particular circle within which an individual sits results in a rapid weakening of the relationship. This causes the friendship to slide slowly but surely down through the layers until, eventually, the person will drop out of the friendship circles altogether and join the layer of acquaintances. This weakening of relationship quality is noticeable within as little as three to six months. A classic study of the decay in friendships among a group of Chicago bankers (Figure 2.5) illustrates how quickly this can happen. Importantly, casual friendships developed among work colleagues decay faster than 'home friends', and these in turn decay faster than family relationships, indicating how bond strength (reflecting how long the friendship has existed) can slow down the rate of decay. Notice that bond strength only slows down the rate of decay: nothing preserves a relationship forever in the absence of at least occasional contact.

Piers Ibbotson, an Associate Professor at the Warwick Business School and former theatre director, reflects on the problem of the trade-off between the investment of time required for the inner circles and the need to extend boundaries and relationships in the outer circles. 'At one level the mathematics of six degrees of separation is extraordinarily powerful,' he observes. 'I could quite easily – for instance, perhaps in even less than six steps – have direct contact with the Pope, say.' However, this connection would require Piers to invest so much time and social capital outside his immediate social bonds and bubble that, as he wryly observes, 'my partner would probably leave me!' We are profoundly bound by our immediate sphere of close relationships. Indeed, we generally don't trust those (the social climbers, professional networkers, super-salespeople) who regularly do step outside these circles. Nonetheless it is the job of leadership to create the conditions where we do just that, if our organisations are to develop and improve.

Horses for (Some) Courses

One obvious question is whether the layers, and their psychological constraints, limit the relevance of some group sizes for particular

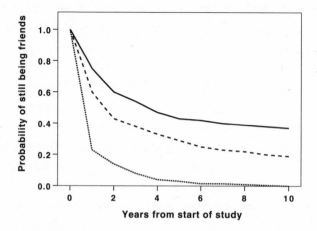

The Fragility of Friendships

Figure 2.5. In a famous study, the sociologist Ronald Burt followed the changes in the relationships of a group of Chicago bankers over a number of years. Friendships decay (dashed line) faster than family relationships (solid line), but not as quickly as business 'friendships' (dotted line). Redrawn from Burt (2000)[40]

tasks. If task completion requires very close understanding between the members of the task group, then fives will work, and fifteens may not. Alternatively, if the task demands are less focused and something closer to brainstorming is required, then fifteen is a better number since the larger number will provide a greater range of different view-points and draw on more external sources. Committees comprising more than fifteen people are unlikely to work unless they are simply there in a rubber-stamping capacity. The real work will always be done in smaller sub-committees – which is, of course, why we have sub-committees and why they are typically around four to five in size.

The graph in Figure 2.6 illustrates this fundamental truth via a mapping of the fluctuations in inflation rates against the size of the central bank monetary policy committee in seventy-one coun-tries in 2005. The sampled committees had a mean size of about seven members, but it is clear that fluctuations in inflation rates were minimised when the committee size consists of three to four members. In other words, the data suggest that smaller committees made better strategic decisions. Economists and psychologists who have explored and modelled the workings of committees conclude that they involve a trade-off between two key variables: the speed at which a committee reaches a decision (quicker in smaller committees) and the breadth of information available among the members (better in larger committees). The consensus is that five is probably the upper limit for an effective monetary policy committee.[41]

There's a practical issue to be considered here, too. Given the problematic logistics inherent in coordinating people's diaries, it follows that the more often a committee has to meet, the smaller it needs to be. A large committee might be able to get together only once every six months. A small committee, by its very nature, is more agile. And because it can meet more frequently, its members are better placed to build close relationships with one another than those who attend committees that, because of their size, meet only occasionally.

Large teams suffer from several unavoidable structural disadvantages. One is the simple fact that the number of communication exchanges that have to take place to ensure everyone is up to speed increases exponentially with the size of the team. With a team of four, there are six pairwise connections; with a team of ten, there are forty-five, a proportional increase of 300 per cent. The result is an inevitable increase in inefficiency, in part because there is more opportunity for 'social loafing' or coasting, while letting the rest of the group make the effort required. The term 'social loafing' was popularised by the social psychologist Bibb Latané[42] and refers to individuals who are part of the team (or committee in this case) but don't actually pull their weight. (Economists would refer to them as 'freeriders', or 'free-loaders'.) An analysis of thirty-nine project teams from the European automotive industry yielded a mean size of 9.4 (range 3–16), which was judged by both the members and the consultants as being too big by at least one person.[43] That's one salary that could have been used on another project. An analysis of fifty-eight software development teams found that the five most successful teams averaged 4.4 members (range 3–6) in size, while the five least successful ones averaged

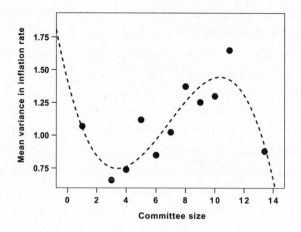

Committee Size and the Efficiency of Monetary Policy Decisions

Figure 2.6. Average variance in annual inflation rate between 2000 and 2005 (indexed as standard deviation of mean) plotted against the size of the monetary policy committee for seventy-one countries ranging in size from Tonga to Russia. Data points are the average values for a given committee size (with two to fourteen countries per point) and reflect the committees' ability to minimise unstable fluctuations in the future inflation rate. Redrawn from Erhart, Lehment & Vasquez-Paz (2007)[44]

7.8 members (range 7–9): teams of three achieved only 63 per cent of the output of the best team, while teams of nine achieved a mere 28 per cent.[45] The numbers speak for themselves.

The Benefits of Staying Small

If small groups allow for speedy decision-making, they're also well suited to creative work and to achieving tight deadlines. 'Clients are often made nervous by the small size of our teams,' say award-winning inventors and designers Clara Gaggero Westaway and Adrian Westaway; 'but if we are doing an intense design project, we find it inefficient to work with more than five people.' 'Oddly,' Clara adds, 'clients seem to get comfort from seeing large numbers of people on a project.' But, as she points out, it's a false comfort. When a large team is involved, much time is wasted on briefing and keeping other members of the group up to speed. By contrast, 'with four or five we can work alongside each other most efficiently. We know intuitively and literally what the others are doing. We don't have to take time out for communications and explanations. We know each other's strengths, and weaknesses, trust each other's judgement and rely on what each brings to the work – we're all on a level with one another. It's a hugely productive group size.'

This thought is echoed by complexity scientist Dave Snowden, the founder of the Cynefin Company, an action research and development hub for applied complexity science. He also recognises that, in a crisis, having more than five in a decision-making group is not effective. In fact, for any decision that involves questions to do with contested issues, five is the ideal number. Five is also a perfect number for making decisions at pace: there is always someone who can cast the deciding vote, so avoiding stalemate or a stand-off.

If small groups speed good decision-making, they also enhance the willingness of individuals to speak up and feed into that process. It's with that precept in mind that performance coach Owen Eastwood – who has worked with the England men's football team and Royal Ballet School as well as with the Command Group of NATO, and corporate leadership teams – adopts the policy of breaking the group down into ever smaller units in order to nurture individual confidence before he then reconstructs the full group again. He points out how difficult it can be to challenge the status quo if you're one of many, a problem compounded by the extent to which different cultural traditions influence the individual's willingness to participate: 'If you move away from Western societies to those like Polynesia or East Asia, which are more collectivist and hierarchical communities,' he says, 'it can be difficult to question a father, a boss or a chief, particularly if you're a woman.' However, if you start with small, safe groups of three to five, you can instil in each member of each group the confidence to express themselves.

Once that confidence is established, each will feel able to speak up among fifteen people, and from there progress to a group that is fifty strong and then 150 strong.

There is, of course, a danger inherent in small groups: because only a handful of people are involved, the pool of talent necessary for innovation is restricted and the chances of coming across fresh perspectives and new talent that much less. But there are ways to counter this tendency. Leadership expert and adult developmentalist Jennifer Garvey Berger describes how, in her own small organisation, numbering about fifty people, she is constantly aware of the need to take action to stop established groups falling into a rut. 'We know we are at a threshold,' she says. 'We now have to pay attention to what we need to make happen, knowing that it would have happened naturally if we were just fifteen.' Her solution is to create artificial new, horizontal structures that cut across existing groups. 'We call them "Growth Groups",' she explains; 'we continually and deliberately make and break these to form and re-form different horizontal clusters. We don't want organisational ossification – we are constantly trying to add a horizontal element that reaches across the natural groupings, designing in opportunities for different people to connect – and keep connecting.' In other words, she works both with and against the natural groupings of the Dunbar Graph. She makes space for natural connections; at the same time she deliberately disrupts the tendency of the groups so formed to foster a sense of dynamism and creativity over time. Her approach takes the best of what a small group can achieve, and guards against its potential drawbacks.

Stepping outside our immediate circles is often necessary in order to help us make better decisions, to keep learning and avoid being trapped in a circle of groupthink. That's precisely what networking events allow us to do – but notice that these still depend on personal one-to-one contacts. That round on the golf course or quiet meeting over a coffee or a beer may seem superfluous, but it creates the kind of serendipitous contact that often pays dividends – sometimes several years down the line. Not every meeting turns out to have a fairy-tale ending. But if you're not there on the day, you won't be in a position to exploit the opportunity it presents on that unforeseen future occasion when it suddenly promises to offer the perfect solution to a problem.

Summary

- Natural human groups and communities are limited to around 150 individuals, as are personal social networks. This number defines the maximum number of meaningful relationships we can maintain at any given time.
- Such groups typically have a characteristic ripple structure, forming a series of grouping levels at 5, 15, 50 and 150, with the sequence continuing beyond this at 500, 1,500 and 5,000. There seems to be something naturally stable about these 'rule of three' numbers.
- This characteristic ripple structure is partly a consequence of the size of the human brain (and its capacity to manage relationships) and partly a consequence of the way we choose to allocate our available social time so as to maximise the return on our relationships.
- The quality of our relationships (and hence our willingness to trust and be helpful to others) depends on how much time we spend with particular individuals, with high-trust relationships demanding significant investment of time and energy.
- Different tasks demand different sizes of group. Decisions are most quickly and effectively made by groups comprising three to five members. Groups of ten to fifteen may be better suited for brainstorming because they have access to a wider range of sources and ideas. Groups of fifty demand the imposition of structure and more directive leadership. Groups above 150 in size require significant levels of logistics, process and structure.

- Once a group exceeds 150 members, fault lines appear. 'We' becomes 'us' and 'them'. Silos very quickly emerge.
- There is a biological basis for the organisational challenges (silos, internal rivalries, dysfunctional group dynamics etc) that emerge in every organisation. All human groups throughout history have struggled with these same dynamics.

3.

A Sense of Belonging

'*Like orphans to whom are pointed out two faces in a crowd
and told, That is your father, your mother.*'

William Faulkner[1]

If you walk into the offices of Airbnb in San Francisco, you feel as
though you're walking into a home – a home away from home. The
partition walls may be made of glass, but each room is built as a kitchen, a bedroom or a sitting room. It's like walking into a life-size
doll's house. Airbnb declares: 'We must create a world where people
can belong anywhere, we must take real steps to build a workplace
where everyone feels welcome, and all voices are heard.' They refer,
after all, to their employees as 'Airfam'. Theirs is a particular vision
of belonging – one that has no need of history, one that apparently
can be experienced anywhere, instantly, by anyone. But one, nonetheless, that keys into our universal need to belong and, at work as
well as at home, to feel some sense of family that stretches beyond
our own. It is a concept reminiscent of McDonald's original marketing insight: if every outlet is the same, and offers the same menu,
customers will feel at home, won't feel nervous about coming in for
fear of not knowing what to do or where to order their food . . . and
will keep coming back.

The flip side of Airbnb's effort to create a home away from home
is the ubiquitous hot-desk office where the opposite seems to be true.
Ideas of efficiency coupled with the cost of office space have led, in
many places, to the creation of a no-frills, transactional environment

where social time is seen as wasted time. Many modern urban offices – with their security gates, reverberating atriums, ranks of desks and black leather/chrome décor – look like airports. Office workers can feel like the Tom Hanks character in Steven Spielberg's 2004 movie *The Terminal*: trapped in an environment from which there is no escape but to which they do not feel they belong.

The experience of working from home during the pandemic made many employees re-evaluate their sense of connectedness to their workplaces, to question whether they wanted to return to offices that lack a sense of belonging or of family, and that fail to acknowledge people's universal desire to feel part of something, to leave an imprint. The findings of the 2021 World Happiness Report reinforce the importance of this missing element in people's work lives.[2] The most important factor in making people feel happy in their work, it concluded, was a sense of belonging. It's that simple.

Why we feel this need, how those feelings are enabled and, importantly, what benefits a sense of belonging can bring is the subject of this chapter.

The Pull of Family

The small-scale communities of our evolutionary past were composed mostly, if not entirely, of family members – some related by marriage, some by birth. Outside this unit of 100–200, people were seen as Other: 'they'. The Dunbar Number of 150 is sometimes referred to as the tipping point from being part of the 'us' – the basis of a natural division – into a 'them vs us'. Kinship forms the core of small-scale societies such as hunter-gatherers: being able to specify exactly how someone is related to you shapes how you interact with them, whom you can joke with, whom you can (or cannot) marry.

Even in the modern world, this deep-seated need to know who we are at a personal and familial level is still with us. Family ties play a central role in our biology. They are what bind people together. A combination of shared genetic material and so much time spent in each other's company creates a willingness to help family above all others when they are in need or distress. This is known as the 'kinship premium' – the apparently selfless behaviour that is most often observed within kinship groups. The current fascination with tracking family histories via such websites as Ancestry.com shows this urge at work. So, too, does the Māori word *whakapapa*, which describes the fact that each of us is part of an unbreakable chain of people, going back to our ancestors and going forward to our grand-children and great-grandchildren yet unborn, and beyond them to every descendant who will ever live. Performance coach Owen East-wood describes how every new player who joins the New Zealand All Blacks rugby team is taken up to the boardroom of the club before they play their first game to be patiently shown the photos of all the past players, one by one – from the members of the very first All Blacks team of 1907 right up to the present. They are the club's ancestors, if you will. The new player is welcomed into the family and to its history by this ritual.

How do we create a sense of belonging? There are two important components. In everyday life, one factor is simply biological related-ness: it defines family and is extended by analogy to cover in-laws (to whose family, after all, our offspring also belong). The other factor is what is known as homophily – the 'birds of a feather flock together' effect. Between them, these two factors explain most of our natural social preferences as to whom we spend our time with.

The Sense of Kinship

Biological kinship, or family, provides an all-encompassing principle on which social relationships are organised in all human societies, as well as the societies of many of our closest relatives among the Old World monkeys and apes. We are more willing to act prosocially, or altruistically, towards kin than non-kin, and towards close kin than less close kin (see p. 53). Kin are commonly the object of moral par-tiality on our part – our tendency to expect everyone to adhere to society's moral code and pay a penalty when they do not, except for close kin who we are often willing to protect even against the full force of the law.

Our sense of kinship is so strong that we even draw our close friends into this family circle, minimising the biological difference by sometimes referring to close family members as our 'best friends' and our best friends as 'closer than family'. The now slightly old-fashioned use of the English term of address 'Aunty' to describe a parental close female friend goes further, explicitly merging friend into family. The fact of the matter, of course, is that our best friends may spend almost as much time with our immediate family as our cousins do, sometimes more. That time spent together builds close bonds – perhaps not quite as all-encompassing as family bonds, but certainly of a similar kind. It has been estimated that a best friend is about as psychologically close as a first cousin – for women, perhaps even closer than that (see Figure 3.1). In small-scale societies, strangers arriving in a community have first to be accorded family status – in some cases, by the village headman adopting them as a son or daughter. This 'fictive kinship', as it is known, places them in the community and allows everyone else to know how they should behave towards them.

A kind of fictive kinship is also at work in some of the most successful organisations. Creating the illusion of family can create a very strong tie even when it doesn't involve family and close friends. Retired general Tyrone Urch reflects on how many young recruits come to the army 'gasping for family', many having been denied that containing structure thus far in their young lives. The close-knit interdependence of so-called 'tent groups' where people eat, sleep, march, suffer and relax together replicates that family bond. They become a true band who share the business of living and surviving: one may carry the food, one the tent, one the ammunition. Unless they all stick together, the very basics of survival are threatened. An army works effectively when people literally fight for the survival of their tent group 'band'. Selflessness in this case ultimately benefits oneself.

Family Matters

If we ask individuals to incur a cost for the benefit of others, their willingness to do so is directly related to their genetic relatedness to the beneficiary. In the experiment whose results are summarised in Figure 3.1, individuals were paid for how long they could hold a painful physical position, with their earnings being given in successive tests directly to either themselves (Self), three named relatives of different degree, their best friend of the same gender, or a children's charity. It's a sad fact that people invariably worked hardest for themselves,

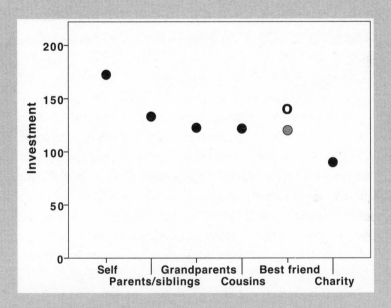

Relationship Strength and Altruism

Figure 3.1. In five experiments, people held a painful position for as long as they could in order to benefit a named individual with a cash prize determined by the length of time they were able to hold the position. The black symbols are the mean values for men and women combined; for best friends, the white symbol indicates women, the grey symbol men. The data are averaged across three studies in the UK and two studies of Zulu populations in South Africa. Redrawn from Madsen et al. (2007)[3]

and then progressively less hard in proportion to the degree of genetic relatedness – with the children's charity doing least well.

There was a striking gender difference in one respect, however: women treated their best friend almost as well as they treated themselves, and better than they treated a parent or sibling. In contrast, the men were much less generous than the women, treating their best friend slightly worse than a cousin – the least closely related family member.

Close bonding between women, as suggested in Figure 3.1, is reflected in an observation that Margaret Heffernan makes in her book on women and leadership. In every single interview that she set up with a female leader, she was surprised to find that the woman brought along members of her team.[4] The interviewee's conception of leadership – and it was the same across the board – was of a collective, a 'we' rather than an 'I'.

This sense of family can even develop across deep political divisions in the most febrile of times if there is a more meaningful and greater cause at stake. David Storey, now a partner at EY, one of the largest professional services networks in the world, describes his own experience of building a familial identity among warring political parties, security services and civil society formations in South Africa during the low intensity war leading up to the 1994 democratic elections: 'As the apartheid system began to dismantle, political violence became increasingly endemic resulting in the ANC, led by Nelson Mandela, terminating negotiations on the future of the country. This led to the 1991 National Peace Accord (NPA) aimed at preventing violence and managing peace-keeping efforts to create the space for transitional negotiations to restart. The NPA was driven by a network of multi-party regional and local structures designed to regularly meet to share information and negotiate, and to monitor their behaviour in implementing them. While leaders sat across tables from each other in facilitated forums to hash out local agreements, the real peace-keeping power of the NPA arose from its on-the-ground monitoring activities held together by a series of symbolic acts that not only bound people to shared principles and helped the mechanisms of communication stay open, but also gave combatants an opportunity to humanise each other. I coordinated monitoring efforts to uphold the NPA in the then Witwatersrand region. The monitors operated in groups of three or four, always combining a civil society representative with a volunteer from both the ANC and the IFP, the two primary warring political parties at that time. Over the next few years over 5,000 would volunteer as monitors and develop their own skills, experiences and stories. We had to think quickly about something that could work as a bonding mechanism – something that would be easily recognisable and that would communicate that the person with the item came in peace. We came together and designed hi-viz T-shirts, flags, and car decals with the Peace Accord logo – a dove – which of course is one of the most recognisable symbols for peace. Simple T-shirts ended up communicating so much, but the most important was the message that we go where other people don't and can't because we come in peace. The dove on the T-shirt didn't just protect the wearer, it enabled him or her to transition – at least for the time they were wearing it – from their party affiliations to team members with a common purpose and shared responsibility to protect each other. The act of literally trusting the "other" with their lives as they criss-crossed respective "no-go zones" bonded the teams and allowed people to connect to a bigger idea. When people donned the T-shirt they saw each other differently; they focused on the bigger prize of peace; they worked together as a team. During that time, we trained people in the basics of negotiation skills, we trained people in active listening, we trained people in the basic building blocks. And the T-shirt was always the connecting point.'

Even in the physically less adventurous atmosphere of the office, these same feelings can be activated. New Zealand Regional Public Service Commissioner Ezra Schuster thinks of the public service as being *farno* – or family – to him. If someone new joined from outside, the existing team would perform a *mihi whakatau* – a Māori ritual form of welcome ceremony overseen by an 'elder' in the office. The key values of *mihi whakatau* are: *manaakitanga* – the process of showing respect and care for others – and *whakawhanaungatanga* – of establishing relationships. They did this even when they were meeting virtually for the first time under lockdown. The ritual connects the newcomer to the ancestry of the office and the team to the identity of the newcomer. Here, the invitation is not to be an equally contributing member in a corporate family, but rather to focus on the assimilation of the new recruit into the existing organisational culture. Family implies consideration of all the dimensions of the new employee – their past, their identity, what they stand for, their values.

Few organisations treat induction in this reciprocal way. Most corporate induction processes are first and foremost focused on the organisation rather than the recruit. In fact, so common is the idea of induction (the word itself with its one-way etymology from the Latin *inducere* – 'to lead into' – is hardly invitational) that entire consulting arms are devoted to ensuring effective orientation and induction programmes for new recruits. Perhaps recruits watch a 'vision and values' video or are given a presentation about the numbers, possibly even a word or two about the founder, but rarely is there a reciprocal attempt to connect the identity and background of the new recruit with the identity of the company – or to see the value of such an exercise not just to the newcomer but also, ultimately, to the performance of the organisation.

When the emphasis is on corporate assimilation rather than belonging, it is hardly surprising to find a typical management journal lamenting that 'it's ironic that companies often spend significant resources on external strategy advice while ignoring one of the most fruitful sources of strategic insights: their own employees. Unfortunately, employees whose ideas about strategy aren't listened to may quit – and take their ideas with them.'[5]

The Birds-of-a-Feather Effect

Biological relatedness notwithstanding, friendships, and even family relationships, are strongly influenced above all by one overriding factor – homophily, the tendency for our friends to resemble us in many different ways.[6] Like it or not, this is such a dominating feature of natural human relationships that we cannot simply ignore it. If we do, it will inevitably come back to haunt us. It is what drives echo chambers on social media, silo effects in organisations, and narrow thinking.

Homophily comes in two forms: endogenous (elements that are part of your make-up that you can't do much about) and exogenous (traits that you acquire or learn as you traverse life's convoluted pathway). The first consists of a disparate group of variables that define you as an individual: gender, age, ethnicity, personality. The second identifies the cultural community you belong to: it consists of what has become known as the Seven Pillars of Friendship,[7] a set of cultural traits that you acquire during your formative years that, to some extent, define you for life. Between them, these identify, first and foremost, the community you belong to.

Among the endogenous effects, gender is by far the strongest: our friends, and even the family members we feel closest to, are highly gender-specific: 70 per cent of women's personal social networks consist of women, and 70 per cent of men's consist of men, with this figure remaining remarkably stable across the age range from five to eighty-five.[8] Friendship networks also tend to be strongly age-biased: from early childhood onwards, our friends tend to be the same age as us, even though the individuals involved may change considerably over time. Friendship networks also tend to be ethnically and culturally biased – one reason why immigrants tend to end up living in clusters in cities. In respect of personality, extroverts prefer being friends with extroverts, and introverts, though somewhat less choosy, prefer introverts – if only for the reason that wanting to be out socialising every night doesn't work especially well if the other person would prefer to stay in with a pizza to watch a film.

In contrast to the endogenous factors, the exogenous homophily effects are wholly cultural in origin – things we learn from the community in which we are socially immersed. They form the Seven Pillars of Friendship. The Seven Pillars are what you tell me about yourself, the things you like and dislike, your life experiences – in short, who you are (see p. 59). They are like a barcode that identifies the cultural community to which you belong. I can gauge your age, gender and ethnicity with reasonable (though by no means perfect!) accuracy at a glance, and I can probably have a very decent guess at your personality after watching your general demeanour and how you behave for just a few moments. I can do all that from the other side of the room. But your position on the Seven Pillars depends on language, and I have to engage you in conversation for some considerable time before I can establish where you stand on all of them.

Once I've had a chance to establish where you are placed on each of the Seven Pillars, our friendship immediately has a foundation. How close a relationship we will have, should we decide to pursue one, is determined strongly by how many of the Seven Pillars we have in common (Figure 3.2). If we share six or seven, we are likely to end up in a close friendship; if we share only one or two, then, after the initial flurry of interest, we will see each other less often and our relationship will slide gradually down through the layers of the Dunbar Graph (Figure 2.3) to settle out at a mutually convenient position lower down in our respective social lists.

Because the Seven Pillars are cultural and learned, they can, and do, change to some extent over time as we are exposed to new ideas, people and places. This is least true of our dialect, which we learn very early in life: we never quite speak a second language that we learn later in life in the way a native speaker does. We never quite have the accent right, or we sometimes use a word in the wrong place. Dialects in all languages are incredibly fine-grained. The moment you open your mouth to speak, I know where you are from. Someone with a good knowledge of English dialects, for example, can

The Seven Pillars of Friendship

Although the concept of friendship 'homophily' (the fact that friends tend to resemble each other) had been known about for at least a decade, the concept of the Seven Pillars of Friendship emerged from a project on 'pervasive adaptation'. This particular project was concerned with the technology that would allow mobile phone masts to be replaced by using other people's phones as way stations to connect up two callers. The question that arose was: how would you decide when to trust a stranger's phone having access to the data on your phone?

The Seven Pillars provided a solution. If everyone coded into their phone a set of personal preferences rather like a supermarket barcode, your phone could then check the incoming phone's barcode and decide if it liked what it found enough to trust it with access to your phone.

To determine which traits correlated with relationship closeness, people were asked to rate their friends and relatives for similarity on a wide range of traits. On the basis of the ratings, the traits were reduced to seven core dimensions (or pillars):

- Language (or, better still, dialect)
- Growing up in the same location
- Educational and career experiences (notoriously, medical people gravitate together socially, and lawyers do the same)
- Hobbies and interests
- Worldview (an amalgam of moral, religious and political views)
- Sense of humour
- Musical tastes

Figure 3.2 shows how trust increases with the shared number of pillars. The results of this particular study were subsequently used to develop the Safebook 'secret handshake' software for use in online security.[9]

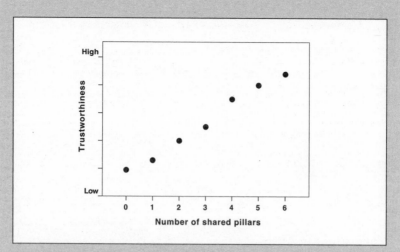

Trust and Connection

Figure 3.2. How trustworthy a named individual (a sibling, cousin, friend etc) was deemed to be in an individual's own social network is plotted as a function of how many of the Seven Pillars of Friendship they shared in common. Redrawn from Curry & Dunbar (2013)[10]

place a native English speaker to within 25 miles of where they were born from just the first few sentences they say. Something as simple as how you pronounce the vowel 'a' is enough to tell me whether you come from the north (short ǎ) or the south (long ā) of England. But even if I am not an expert linguist, I know immediately whether you come from the same town as I do. Even by the age of five, children can identify someone's speech as not being their local dialect.[11] We can, however, change where we have lived, our careers, our hobbies, moral and political views, sense of humour and musical tastes to accommodate new ideas we are exposed to as we move from one social community to another. It is this that allows us to blend in with a new community, although that can take some time to take effect.

These homophily effects are not necessarily conscious or unconscious biases. They relate much more directly to common interests, common attitudes and a shared cultural viewpoint – the things that make it easier to engage socially and maintain relationships over time. Conversations are less stilted and flow better when you have many things in common and share a similar conversational style. (We'll have more to say on this in Chapter Five.) We cannot do much about the endogenous effects: they are simply how we are. We can do something about the exogenous effects in the workplace by seeking to create a more engaging culture. But, either way, we cannot afford to ignore them, because these effects will unavoidably come to structure relationships within organisations just as they inevitably do in everyday social life. That these homophily effects have much more to do with easing the processes of social interaction is evidenced by the fact that the endogenous factors (including ethnicity) are quickly overtaken by the exogenous effects: if you and I share the same Seven Pillars, I am much less interested in whether we are the same gender, ethnicity, age or personality (Figure 3.3).

What the Seven Pillars seem to identify is the wider community to which we belong. Two factors are involved here. First, common interests inevitably make conversations flow better. Second, if we share the same Seven Pillars it means we are both part of a very specific, rather small community: we share a common worldview, we hold similar attitudes towards right and wrong, truth and honesty, we have the same obligations to each other and to the other members of our community. I know how you think, how you view the world, what behaviours and attitudes you find acceptable or not – in short, how much I can trust you. When we come from the same cultural community, I don't need to explain to you the subtle nuances in the meaning of a word – or, for that matter, why a joke is funny. We know how members of our community see the world.

In traditional, small-scale communities of the kind in which we have spent almost our entire history as a species (see p. 12), the local community is, in effect, extended family. Family is not only the bedrock of our social support, but it also functions as an informal police force that regulates how we interact with each other, maintaining order and good behaviour in the interests of everyone. If I upset one of my cousins, someone is likely to say something about it – not least our mutual grandmother, who is likely to take a more neutral view of the squabbles of her various grandchildren. In other words, over and above the fact that family hold obligations towards each other simply by virtue of the fact that they are related, the densely networked community that an extended family forms makes it more difficult to hide from communal displeasure when we offend against community mores – and at the same time we are for the same reasons less willing to ignore others' remonstrations.

This feature of human behaviour has two important implications for organisations. First, it means there will always be a tendency for like-minded people to gravitate together, creating natural silo fault lines when set against the limits on the number of people with whom we can maintain relationships. Second, no matter what people may say to the contrary, how well two people get on will always be informed by their degree of homophily, and that degree will always influence, for better or for worse, how well they work together.

Although, in the context of friendships, the Seven Pillars seem to be interchangeable (any one is as good as any other), when it comes to assessing strangers for their potential as a friend (and hence their trustworthiness), it seems that we place much more emphasis on the 'worldview' pillar (shared moral/political/religious views) and, rather surprisingly, shared musical tastes (Figure 3.3). Similarity of musical tastes seems to play an especially powerful role in creating friendships. Notice that ethnicity plays only a very limited role, if at all, in this respect: it seems that, at close quarters, shared ethnicity is not considered an especially reliable indicator of trustworthiness or friendship potential. It is shared culture that seems to be more important. Ethnicity only provides a first pass guess as to whether a stranger would make a good friend, and that is only because it is a (very) rough guide to culture. As soon as you get to know someone at closer quarters, it is their cultural Seven Pillars that override everything else.

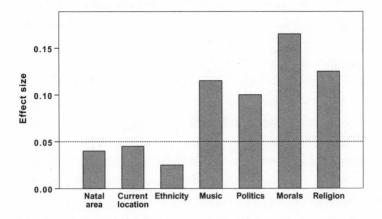

The Making of a Friendship

Figure 3.3. When people rated complete strangers on their Seven Pillars profiles, the dimensions that most strongly predicted whether they thought they would make a good friend were their worldview (moral, political and religious views) and, surprisingly, their musical tastes. The horizontal dashed line indicates random performance. Source: Launay & Dunbar (2017)[12]

Turning Organisations into Family

From the corner grocery store to large multinationals, family can be, and has been, a very effective basis for building businesses. Indeed, many large successful companies began life as family businesses, and many have remained so – at least in their management or ownership structures. The Mars corporation is one well-known example; BMW and Walmart are others.

A sense of 'family', rather than actual kinship, can be important even at the micro-scale in large organisations. Yet, in too many organisations, people are promoted as individuals, thus wrenching them away from the hard-won trust and relationships that they have built up in their teams, often to the detriment of working relationships if not friendships within the organisation. We might therefore consider more often the concept of team promotion or redeployment instead. This approach maintains the shared experi-ence that a familial unit gathers as it works on projects together, which, in turn, saves vast amounts of time that otherwise has to be devoted to the establishment of new support networks and the development of trust, mutual understanding and rapport between people who have only just met. The team experience, when it thrives, creates common ground for all kinds of different individ-uals and perspectives.

Nothing comes for free in biology or real life, however, so there are, inevitably, downsides to working with family members and with people we treat as family that we need to guard against. For better or for worse, we are unavoidably prone to moral partiality when it comes to those closest to us: we are willing to forgive family mem-bers and close friends for moral lapses that we would never allow in a stranger. We are less likely to take family to task when they cheat the system or fail to live up to their promises, even though they weaken both governance and performance through their actions. In organi-sations actually run by blood relatives, those at the top can become inflexible, clinging on too long to power and hampering the next generation from adapting to the changing times and coming into their own. There is also the risk that extreme homophily limits the capacity for creative, agile and diverse thinking.

Many of the family businesses that have thrived over several gen-erations, such as Unilever, Mars, Heineken, BMW and Mercedes, have understood the need to bring 'outsiders' into their governance structures and to develop robust succession policies. It is therefore important to understand the beneficial aspects of kinship – a greater sense of trust, ease of communication, shared experience – while at the same time creating conditions where all the members of an organisation, whether immediate family or not, can benefit. None-theless, the pull of family, even when fictional, is so powerful that creating a sense of family is one way in which businesses can culti-vate a productive sense of belonging and incorporate new ways of thinking at the same time.

Friendships at Work

For thirty years, Gallup has included the question 'Do you have a best friend at work?' in its engagement surveys. Gallup asks this question because, in its experience, the answer it gets is so clearly linked to performance. Of those women who answer 'yes' to the question, 63 per cent are likely to feel 'engaged' at work, compared to only 23 per cent of those who answer 'no'.[13] Those employers who wish to have a diverse – as well as a productive and safe – workforce would do well to pay close attention to the social aspect of work and not dismiss it as hard-to-measure, nice-to-have serendipity.

Strong workplace relationships matter for many reasons. The Microsoft Work Trend Index highlights the benefits of solid work-place networks, namely productivity and innovation. 'On produc-tivity, people who said they feel more productive also reported stronger workplace relationships than those who don't. They also feel included on a typical workday. On the contrary, those who said their interactions with colleagues have decreased this year were less likely to be thriving at things that lead to innovation, like thinking strategically, collaborating or brainstorming with others, and pro-posing innovative ideas.'[14]

Recognising the importance of friendship at work, leadership expert and adult developmentalist Jennifer Garvey Berger instituted 'Growth Groups' across her coaching and leadership development organisation to try to create an elasticity of horizontal relation-ships over time and space. 'Friendship is not happenstance – it is an intentional part of the design,' she says. So, she established a series of organisational practices that expressly 'have no point'. In other words, her teams are intentional about creating uninten-tional conversations, 'to make space for people to see and hear each other'. They set up different sorts of channels for different sorts of conversations. They even have an 'I feel like shit' channel. She is constantly looking at how the relationships in the organisation

Why Friends Are Good for Your Health

By far the biggest medical surprise of the past decade or so has been the extraordinary number of studies showing that the single best predictor of your psychological and physical health and wellbeing is simply the number and quality of close friendships you have. By comparison, all the traditional factors that your doctor usually worries about on your behalf make only modest contributions.

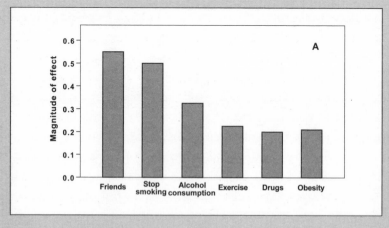

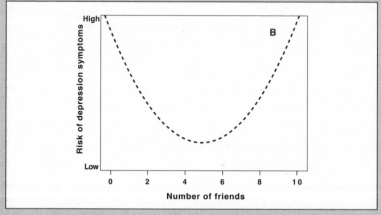

Friendship with Benefits

Figure 3.4. (a): Relative effect of different factors on probability of surviving for twelve months after a heart attack, based on 148 epidemiological studies (total sample of 310,000 people). Redrawn from Holt-Lunstad et al. (2010)[15] (b): Risk of developing symptoms of depression in the next two years as a function of the number of close friends one has, based on a survey of 38,000 over-fifties in thirteen European countries. Redrawn from Santini et al. (2021)[16]

Figure 3.4 (a) illustrates the results of one such study that collated data from 148 different studies on the influence that a variety of factors had on your chances of surviving for a year after your first heart attack. Although the usual suspects like diet, obesity, amount of exercise taken, the amount of alcohol consumed and the quality of the local air you breathe all made a contribution, by far the best predictor was the number and quality of close friendships. Only giving up smoking came close to having the same magnitude of effect.

Another large transnational study found that the chances of someone developing symptoms of depression within a two-year period was least for those who had five close friends (Figure 3.4, b). In contrast, having more than five friends was increasingly detrimental, probably because social effort was divided among too many people and resulted in friendships that were insufficiently strong.

naturally segment and then tries to create structures that run horizontally across those segments in order both to enable and to extend the possibilities for friendship and relationships to grow. This approach, she believes, strengthens the trust and commitment in her organisation.

When innovator Melanie Howard was doing research for a project called 'Night Club'[17] for the consultancy The Liminal Space, she spent time with two groups of male workers in the UK, both of which worked nights. One group operated in a food retailer's warehouse, stacking and packing; the other group worked for a rail network, repairing broken line and signals. Although working conditions for both were apparently fairly poor, she found that the mental health of the railway workers was much more robust than that of the warehouse workers. The railway men did three night-shifts in a row, during which time they worked together as a team in difficult conditions, ate together, joked together and supported each other. They worked in a companionable way. The warehouse work-ers were communicated with through earphones, so they had little opportunity to communicate among themselves. They had separate breaks and worked individually. There was no sense of community, because they never sat down together as a group for a coffee or tea. In effect, theirs was the solitary life of a hermit despite being sur-rounded by other people. Their mental health and sleep patterns were worse, and the interviews revealed that their work meant little more to them than wages per hour. In contrast, the rail workers expressed pride in playing their collective part in keeping travellers safe.

Given that we spend over half our week at work, it is not sur-prising that the workplace should provide a source of friendships. In the 1960s, the renowned American sociologist James Coleman showed that the likelihood that someone socialised outside work with friends from work was determined by how large the organisa-tion was.[18] People were most likely to have friends at work in small companies or factories with 90–150 employees, but in companies larger than this they tended to socialise with friends from outside the workplace. Lynne Pettinger, a sociologist at the University of War-wick, found in her research that younger women working in retail often formed friendships at work, not least because their place of work gave them access to people they might otherwise never have met. These outside friendship networks were also important in con-necting people to job opportunities and as a result there were loose ties in and outside of work. While older workers might not have socialised outside of work due to family commitments, workplace friendships were often quite intimate and provided opportunities for 'shared confidences about their own, and their partners' and their children's lives'.[19]

Samantha's own lived experience working for SABMiller for more than seventeen years is a testament to the power of friendship at work. SABMiller consciously replicated a social environment in workplaces across the world by making the 'office pub' a central meeting point. This encouraged colleagues to meet up for one of the SABMiller products after work (this included both alcoholic and non-alcoholic options – so suggests that it was more about the *opportunity* to socialise, rather than the alcohol encouraging the socialisation). This provided a metaphorical village square where all colleagues were welcome to gather. Several years after the acquisition of SABMiller by AB InBev, friendships made at work live on. The SABMiller Facebook Group remains active, local meet-ups continue to take place and the SABMiller network (often including suppliers) is alive and well.

Given the benefits of friendships, engineering a companionship/friendship work environment has much to recommend it. It's something we considered as we prepared for a face-to-face cultural gathering for an insurance company in the wake of long months of working apart during the Covid-19 pandemic. Aware that we needed to bring groups back together but also ensure the creative energy that comes from disparate voices, we drew on the Seven Pillars methodology to prepare a questionnaire that allowed us to group people in conversational fours with colleagues who shared the most friendship pillars so they could easily discover common ground. It seems that those who had only interacted virtually during lockdown – or at the most extreme had been recruited virtually and actually never met any of their colleagues in person – found this exercise especially helpful. The fact that their first encounter (and some were nervous about coming out from behind their screens) was with people who shared their pillars – people who shared interests, or worldview or even a sense of humour – seemed to ease the process of integration. It made re-entry into analogue life less scary.

Later on in the exercise, we used the answers from the questionnaire in the opposite way to create small groups of 'distant cousins' – those who didn't share any pillars of friendship. We grouped, for example, embroiderers with fell runners, artists with coders, optimists with doom-scrollers, in order to challenge them to try to build common ground together, beginning with a foundation of mutual difference rather than sameness. By deliberately disrupting their homophilic tendencies, we encouraged people to experience the vibrancy and value that comes from seeing the world through different lenses. We designed special packs of cards with questions around personal and corporate values as well as ideas about the future. In their small, structured groups they used the process of posing and answering these questions to find out about each other and to develop common ground.

David Harrison and colleagues describe the power of differing perspectives thus: 'Maximising differences in knowledge, skills and abilities, while minimising differences in job-related beliefs, attitudes and values might create especially effective teams.'[20] It is the job of leaders to convene and structure these diverse conversations so as to disrupt the formation of the silos and cabals that otherwise coalesce so naturally. Equally, as we found, when there is stress or fear there is advantage to be found in bringing together those who share pillars of friendship, even – and perhaps especially – at work.

Turning Organisations into Tribes

As we have already described, the tribes we belong to form the outermost layer beyond our friendship groups. In small-scale societies, the tribe identifies a group of 1,000–2,000 people (essentially the 1,500-layer in Figure 2.3) who speak the same language and share a worldview and set of rituals associated with community bonding. The community of 100–200 (the Dunbar Number) is the source of your everyday support, whereas the tribe exists to provide you with

How Do I Know You Belong to My Tribe?

Tribes make use of several markers of belonging:

- Identity. Markers or symbols are used to indicate belonging to a particular tribe. For example, in the UK, members of the National Trust receive a badge to put on their cars. While this is ostensibly to enable free parking at the thousands of National Trust car parks across the United Kingdom, the badge also signals that you belong to a bigger tribe of people – a tribe whose members appreciate the preservation of beautiful historic buildings and spaces, who enjoy a sense of history, who appreciate the work of the Trust.
- Language. The word 'tribe' refers to people who speak the same language. Knowing the language of the tribe provides insider status – whether it is the language of an online gaming group or the acronyms specific to an organisation, shared language is core to a sense of belonging.
- Foundation stories. Identity stories and foundational rituals are the platform on which a shared sense of belonging to a tribe is created.
- Out-groups. Because tribes are rich in symbols, language, sense of origin and shared experiences, it is easy to see out-groups as 'other'. A sense of 'us v them' reinforces the sense of belonging: however bad things get, we hang together in the face of attack by our neighbours. The downside, of course, is that out-groups can easily be vilified and disparaged, or, in the worst examples, dehumanised – something to guard against.
- Shared sense of obligation. Members of a tribe have a sense of obligation towards each other. Once I know you are my tribe, I treat you as family and will try to help you out.

a fallback for those unpredictable rare occasions when things get really tough, such as during famine or raids by strangers from far away. In such societies, the territory 'owned' by a tribe usually covers a large enough area (typically over 1,000 square miles) for there to be at least one community that is not so badly affected, and so able to take the others in as temporary guests.

Even in small-scale societies, individual tribes are sufficiently large that individual members may never meet all the others. To get round this problem, we conveniently mark everyone with cues that signal tribe membership: dialect, hair style, form of clothing, tattoos, even the patterns of decoration on clothing, weapons or cooking pots (see p. 71). Many companies and organisations seek to emulate this sense of belonging through their badged products, workspace style (think for example, of Starbuck's classic outlet design and menu, which are deliberately the same everywhere in the world), code words and acronyms, and brand loyalty. In a corporate setting, this is why, over time, organisations develop their own 'lingo'. It is key to their identity.

Once, when engaged for an assignment to a global consulting firm, Tracey was told she had freedom to advise on any number of parameters, but one element was sacrosanct: stay away from our language. The firm's language defined them. It was non-negotiable. Home-grown terms such as the 'waterline decisions' of Gore or Amazon's 'pizza teams' (a team should never be bigger than the number that can share a single pizza) form the 'dialect' of the tribe. One global retail company that Tracey worked with used to call their meetings with management 'interrogations'. Employees had become strangely used to the word and it had lost its aggressive connotations in the corporate context. A company Samantha worked with always allocated 'the A' at the end of each meeting – it stood for accountability. Newcomers would have to ask what this mystery 'A' was – it became a way of inducting them into the company.

Even if the language is at times brutal or thin – business tends to love abstract nouns and acronyms – it is a precious repository of identity. Getting the language wrong instantly betrays outsider status. A private language imparts both a sense of mystery – of knowing the secrets of the universe or of success – and, at the same time, creates a sense of belonging. It also presents a barrier for new joiners who often have to navigate through a thicket of 'in-words' and phrases (without a dictionary or phrasebook) before they can earn their place as a 'true' member of the tribe.

Language is not the only tool at the organisation's disposal. As with all tribes, foundation myths and stories are important aids to help us to know who we are – and who is who. It is out of this deep ancestry that family membership and a settled sense of identity derives. The late, Black American writer James Baldwin recounts a story of a visit to the British Museum in the 1960s.[21] A man of West Indian origin working there asked where he came from. 'Harlem,' Baldwin replied. 'No,' the man insisted, 'I mean – where was your mother from?' 'Maryland,' Baldwin replied. 'Your father, then?' 'New Orleans.' Pushed to go further back to account for his origins, Baldwin had to say he didn't know where he was from. The man was dismayed that Baldwin had no sense of his origins, of the foundations of his ancestry in Africa. Baldwin tells this story to make just that point. 'It takes a lot to wrest identity out of nothing,' he remarked.

The traditional identity stories and foundational rituals that cultural coach Owen Eastwood observes and cultivates in his work are the platform for shared identity in the sports teams he coaches. The fact that sports teams even have 'cultural coaches' emphasises the importance of a sense of belonging for great performance. Stories and rituals also have a powerful place in corporate contexts: they don't simply reflect identity, they also construct it by bringing together past, present and future, and focusing them through a particular lens. At its height, the global brewer SABMiller united around pioneering stories from the past of brave founder members establishing breweries in some of the most far-flung places in the world, of derring-do, of bringing communities along with them, of shared passion for their product. These stories – told and retold – formed the cement of the company's culture and patterned out the work-force's idea of themselves. Thanks to the current media emphasis on personal identity, we all too easily forget the importance of a sense of belonging and a shared history. When Owen Eastwood asked a Samoan All Black about his personal sense of purpose, the rugby player replied that those words had no meaning for him. They were just words. For him, the team – the tribe – was everything.

The other tribal tool that organisations can draw on is the process of initiation into the tribe. In society as a whole, the deliberate process of inclusion and welcome is an important part of growing and refreshing a shared identity. The ritual of matriculation for example, is such an initiation. Matriculation is practised at universities across the world as a ceremony that marks a student's formal admission to the university. At Oxford University, it is accompanied by a set of formal and informal rituals. Informally, it is a day of drinking and perhaps taking a swim in the river Cherwell – arguably a fool-hardy if important initiation rite given the weather in mid-October. Formally, there are official ceremonies in gowns and academic hats before the vice-chancellor in which words of admission in Latin are solemnly pronounced over the assembled throng.

So often in corporate life, however, this initiation process is rushed – or even cut out altogether. A senior leader we spoke to at a large tech company reflected on her re-entry into work after maternity leave and how bleak and difficult it was at a human level. Her former desk was now occupied by someone else. She literally had no place. She knew that things would – and must – carry on without her, but was disconcerted to find that no thought had been given to welcoming her back into the community – never mind remembering to put her back on the meeting invitation list. As the prevalence of people working on short-term or zero-hours contracts or even as external consultants increases, this question of the importance of shared identity and the creation of a sense of belonging becomes harder to answer.

Managing the Tribe

Traditional management structures are hierarchical and top-down. Decisions are made at the top, and instructions and policies are passed down through the layers to the workers at the bottom. At root, a hierarchy is simply the easiest way to coordinate large numbers of people once you are beyond the number at which you can rely on personal relationships. But if you have someone in charge, you need enforcers (middle managers and supervisors) to ensure that the commander's decisions, handed down from on high, are acted on. And the bigger and more sprawling the organisation, the more layers of enforcers' enforcers, and enforcers for the enforcers' enforcers, you need. They all cost money, and each layer puts more distance, and less intimacy, between the leadership and those at the edge or the bottom. Rigid hierarchy produces a fragile structure with natural fault lines and shatter points that can collapse when the slightest stress is placed on them.

There is, so far as we know, only one context in which this model has worked effectively: the military. Since the advent of modern military organisation (around 300 years ago), military planners have evolved mechanisms for coordinating very large numbers of (sometimes very unruly) strangers. The core to the structure of modern armies is the company of around 150 individuals. Creating a bonded unit, where individuals feel sufficient loyalty to each other to stick together no matter how tough the going gets, involves replacing family and friends with the company. This unit was not called a 'company' for nothing. As the Army often puts it, the company *is* family. In part, this close relationship is achieved by sequestering the soldiers in barracks and cutting them off from their home environment, so that the primary source of leisure-time friendship is restricted to other members of their company. It is then reinforced by many of the training regimes to which new recruits are subjected together as a group: parade ground drill not only instils discipline but its rhythmic qualities, combined with synchrony, press all the endorphin buttons that dancing and the rituals of religion do in civilian life (more on this in Chapter Four).

But this sense of family only works at company scale. At battalion, regiment and brigade levels, a hierarchical management structure is needed to ensure coordination in action. This always involves strict discipline and formal rules ('always obey a senior officer, no matter what', 'always salute a senior officer'). When people's lives are at risk on the battlefield, it is essential that everyone plays their allotted part to the full. If that trust is lost or discipline breaks down, the outcome can be catastrophic and many lives may be lost unnecessarily. But the military is a very special case, and does not translate easily into civilian contexts. Instead, something more subtle is needed, and that subtlety shares a great deal with the sense of family that exists at company level. It is the sense of commitment and obligation that comes from being part of the tribe. You might even say that it is a form of bottom-up rather than top-down management.

When a more inclusive, egalitarian model of organisation is required in which commitment is bottom-up – commitment to the community that stems from the individual – the Gore management model with its relatively flat lattice structure comes to mind. Debra France describes this structure at Gore as 'low hierarchy': 'the central idea is that everyone should be able to have direct access to anyone else. We have very few layers for an organisation of 11,000 people. Early Gore documents talk about sponsors, and for more than sixty years we have also talked about leaders not managers. The clear distinction is in the words. Sponsors for example are a very specific (voluntary) role to help another associate succeed at Gore. They are in addition to leaders. Every individual associate has a leader *and* a sponsor. The leader is an organisationally (and individually) recognised person who takes on certain tasks to help the team succeed. Every associate *also has a sponsor* who is a form of "learning buddy" – someone committed to their success, helping them make commitments that require their unique set of skills and fulfilling their unique interests. The sponsor advocates for them, gives them ongoing feedback, and serves several other developmental roles.' How does this lattice hierarchy work in practice? Debra gives a small practical example. 'I was in the room with our CEO when she received an email from someone out in the business with an idea about developing leaders. She asked me to come and look over her shoulder as she responded so I could contribute my ideas as a leadership expert. She copied me into the email, thereby in a moment creating an onward momentum for that idea and a connection between the three of us, regardless of hierarchy.'

The creation of more agile and timely ways to access knowledge – from wherever it emanates – and the reduction of hierarchical decision-making bottlenecks will be a key feature of resilient organisations. The safe, settled comfort of the Dunbar layers is important for leaders to understand if they are to design better ways to capitalise on the power of relationship – and to be able to disrupt them if they become inward-looking or overly self-reinforcing.

Summary

- We are all naturally governed by the pull of the family: family ties will always trump other relationships. These pressures and pulls inform our human motivation.
- Humans crave a sense of kinship or belonging. This sense of belonging creates the psychological safety net needed as a backdrop for risk-taking and innovation. It is also the foundation for long-term thriving and wellbeing.
- We can artificially replicate the most productive elements of kinship at work if we design for shared traditions, language, ritual and stories – the things that we naturally use to create a sense of tribal belonging.
- Friendship revolves around 'Seven Pillars'. The more pillars we share, the stronger the bond and the more willing we are to be generous with each other. Friendship at work

contributes to improved mental health and discretionary performance.

- We tend to be homophilic: we are drawn to those who are like us. Homophily, though, is a double-edged sword. While friendships at work may offer comfort and easier working relations, innovation and the best decisions require diverse perspectives. Good leaders need to recognise our natural tendencies both to encourage friendship at work and also, at times, to force people out of their silos.
- The convening and facilitation of groups of different people with different perspectives as well as the welcoming in of new people from the outside is one of the key jobs of leadership.

4.

Bonding

*'Be careful, cries the mother to her child tumbling
Forward, pulling ropes tied to his waist.'*

Wang Ping[1]

The central message of Chapter Two was that communities of around 150 are more stable, and retain a greater degree of coherence and integrity, than larger communities. One reason why this is so is that we are much more willing to be altruistic towards, and offer support to, people we know well. Our willingness stems from the bonds that, in small face-to-face communities, are built up over time between friends and family members, that are forged both by the nature of our interactions and their frequency, and that are reinforced by a lattice of intermediaries, all of whom will be keen to keep the peace in order to maintain the security of our shared identity. In a face-to-face context, it is surprisingly difficult to refuse to be generous to people whom we have known personally for many years. This effect is as strong in the world of work as it is in our private social lives. Knowing someone as an individual makes it more difficult to refuse the requests that they make.

These effects come about because the activities that forge these bonds, and create the sense of emotional closeness that underpins them, trigger the release of a cascade of neurohormones in the brain, creating a feeling of wellbeing that simultaneously makes us feel less stressed and more trusting. We don't generally pay much attention to them: they occur below the event horizon of consciousness. In organisations, they may even be dismissed as trivial and unimportant. But the neurohormones are there nonetheless, and it is important to understand how they contribute to the formation of the social capital of organisations. The fact is that bonding processes help individuals feel part of a larger social group, encouraging commitment to the organisation as well as prosocial behaviour.

Time for team bonding is often overlooked in a time-pressured modern world. Teams may be convened in haste in response to some pressing need, then repeatedly tinkered with as members get moved from one project to another as their skills are needed elsewhere, or individuals leave. With today's inevitable focus on cost efficiencies, on doing more with less, taking time to create an initial environment in which team trust can be built is often forgotten. If someone joins a project halfway through, the chances are that they will be hurriedly welcomed and then told to get straight on with the job. In some organisations, notably government departments, the system decrees that people cannot be promoted without first switching between different roles. All these tendencies are understandable, and in the case of role-switching there are clear benefits to be gained from ensuring that individuals gain direct experience of different parts of the organisation. But there are costs involved, too. Constant reorganisation, even at the team level, can be very dispiriting. It can be dispiriting, too, particularly if individuals are taken away from tasks that they have taken months to get their teeth into or find that the project they have devoted so much time and energy to has been simply cancelled.

The problem is that organisations tend to focus too much on the individual and not sufficiently on the group. Personal development is regarded as key. Group development attracts much less attention. Such a worldview can lead to unintended consequences. It's not uncommon, for example, for an individual in a high-performing team to be identified as a future leader, and so be promoted to a role where, deprived of the knowledge and support of their group, they find themselves struggling. Incorrectly handled, personal development militates against bonding activities. It causes people to concentrate on their separateness rather than their connectedness; it works against the grain of the discretionary effort, cultural capital and sheer shared commitment that can come from a bonded team.

This chapter explores the natural dynamics of our small-scale social world. Understanding just how these social bonds are built up and, through these, how communities are created will help us to understand how and why they contribute to the formation of the social capital of organisations.

A Lesson in Bonding

The education sector may seem a counterintuitive place to look for an example of how to bring a group together, but the clearly measurable outcomes of exam results make schools a good laboratory for testing such hypotheses. In her twenties, Tracey worked as an English teacher in an academically selective girls' school in London. Results league tables had recently been introduced by the government, which resulted in a more intense sense of competition between schools, and greater scrutiny from parents. The students' examination grades were outstanding in this school, but each year there was always a small tail snaking down the alphabet of marks in the public exams taken in the most senior year. The English department was summoned into the head teacher's office and urged to find a way to eliminate their 'grade tail'.

Casting their minds back over the previous few years, the teachers realised that these historical near-perfect results always came when a year group had somehow gelled – when a degree of trust and camaraderie had emerged naturally, when classroom groups had successfully bonded over shared ideas. They demonstrated a generosity of spirit. They became collaborative rather than competitive and they succeeded as a consequence. Could such conditions be created artificially, the teachers wondered – and across all of the teaching groups?

With that goal in mind, they embarked on an experiment. For the first half of the long autumn term, rather than engage in academic study all the pupils were encouraged to become involved in activities closer to play. The set texts were deliberately set aside – something that would be impossible now with current sixth form schedules. Instead classes painted posters of metaphors, cut up recipes and made them into poems, wrote anonymous first paragraphs of essays, shuffled them round and critiqued them collectively. Scenes from great Shakespearian tragedies were acted as if they were comedies and vice versa, poetry was team-taught from widely differing perspectives. The students were invited to present what they were reading for pleasure to their peers. They were encouraged to apply insights from the other subjects they were studying to their appreciation of literature. The teachers joined in, too, even having to go through the hair-raising business of submitting their own written work anonymously to have it critiqued by the students. In effect, the teachers tried to create the conditions where these highly intelligent young women were not daunted by one another or too scared to make mistakes, to enable an environment where the students could discover the strengths (and weaknesses) of the group, be prepared to pitch in and help each other – and to have fun.

The experiment did not run without a hitch. At about the halfway point, parents began to enquire doubtfully why their daughters were having so much fun. The head became nervous that the English faculty did not seem to be knuckling down in the way other departments were. The students, too, were aware that this didn't 'feel like A-level'. They were also bewildered that their English teachers didn't seem to agree about every text. Frankly, there was nervousness in the teacher cohort, as well. Conducting such an experiment for half a term in an environment where failure was frowned upon was risky. The stakes were very high. Still, the teachers persisted with their experiment and, gradually, started to notice a sea change among their students. Now those who were ahead started to respect the questions asked by those who were still catching up. The historians in the class brought context, the scientists brought method, the musicians rhythm. Hierarchy and deference – including towards the teachers – was set aside. The classes of eleven to fifteen students had laughed together, listened to each other's stories, ventured out together to plays and museums, overcome fears, encouraged each other, looked foolish, failed together, been admired together, valued each other.

By the time, many weeks later, that the first mighty page of the set text, Milton's *Paradise Lost*, was opened, the class had become a tribe. Milton didn't suddenly seem a doddle, but those studying the work had acquired a collective confidence that they could tackle it. The group had become more than the sum of its parts. Eighteen months later came the moment of reckoning when the students got their results. There was no tail of grades. All the students had performed above and beyond expectations right across the cohort. This was a hard, measurable outcome to an experiment that had begun softly and that had involved making time and space for play-fulness and for everyone to get to know each other through shared experience.

So, what was actually going on beneath the surface? The exercise started with play – a context in which some of the constraining status anxieties that might exist in a group could be addressed. Time was created for eating together and sharing stories and reminiscences, and laughter. Classroom time was redesigned to shift the focus from the individual to the group through shared experiences – and it was these experiences that then provoked an emotional response that in turn gave rise to a prolonged sense of connection. Micro-risks were designed (the critiquing of one another's anonymised writing, for example), but the sense of interconnectedness, the shared experience of risk-taking, took the fear of failing and built a mini-community centred on trust. When you feel trusted, pushing the boundaries seems so much easier.

The bonds that facilitate healthy and productive social interaction are deeply ingrained within us. They also exist in other apes and monkeys. And it's to the social world of monkeys that we turn first to show how social ties and connectedness function at the most fundamental of levels.

The Intensely Social World of Monkeys

By the standards of the animal kingdom, monkeys and apes live in unusually complex societies. Like us, they create bonded relationships that involve a desire to be with particular members of their group, to engage in social contact, and even play, with them as often as they can. Those individual friendships are, in turn, linked together in formations that spread like an expanding wave through the other members of the group, creating networks that are held together by a form of social glue that has been the secret of their evolutionary success as a zoological family. These relationships resemble in every way those that, in humans, we would not hesitate to refer to as friendships. Outside simple monogamous pair bonds (and these exist with only a single reproductive purpose in mind), such intense relationships are virtually unknown in other mammals and birds. They are what allow monkeys and apes to buffer themselves against the stresses and vagaries of everyday life living in close proximity to others, providing a measure of resilience against the worst that the world can throw at them.

Monkeys and apes build up, and service, their friendships through reciprocal grooming. Indeed, some of the more social species may spend as much as a fifth of their day engaged in the intimacies of this ritual. Grooming involves leafing through another individual's fur, removing bits of vegetation and dead skin and anything that gets matted into the fur (but not fleas, as the urban myth assumes – wild monkeys don't actually have fleas, only humans do). All that fur-cleaning is no doubt very beneficial, but the really important aspect of it is in fact the stroking action. This triggers the release of chemicals in the brain known as endorphins (see p. 85).

For monkeys and apes, the intimacy of grooming – and the endorphin flood it releases – creates friendships. How close a friendship is, and how willing the animals are to come to each other's aid when one of them is threatened, depends directly on how much time the

Endorphins – The Brain's Own Opiates

Endorphins are a family of specialised neurochemicals in the brain that are part of the brain's pain management system. They are chemically closely related to morphine, hence their name: 'end[ogenous m]orphin[e]', meaning 'the body's own morphine'.

As with all opiates, endorphins dampen down our sense of pain, and create a feeling of relaxation, calmness, happiness, euphoria and trust. Grooming is so relaxing that monkeys being groomed will often fall asleep. On a weight-for-weight basis, endorphins are thirty times more powerful as painkillers than morphine.[2] A slight chemical difference, however, means that we don't get addicted to endorphins in the way we get addicted to morphine and other opiates.

Humans also indulge in primate-style grooming, though we probably don't think about it in those terms. Although we don't have fur to leaf through (aside from the tuft that's left on the top of the head), we continue to use a variety of forms of physical touch (stroking, hugging, caressing, a pat on the arm or shoulder) to express the emotional closeness of our relationships, sometimes even as a gesture of comfort to a stranger in distress. Brain-scanning studies have shown that, in humans, stroking and caressing trigger the endorphin system in exactly the same way as grooming does in monkeys.

You'll be familiar with this every time you visit your hairdresser. With all that washing, stroking and combing of the hair it's not surprising that you come away feeling relaxed and buoyed up, ready to face the world with renewed confidence. It is not the new hairstyle that matters so much as what your hairdresser did while creating it. Physical touch is, and continues to be, a natural part of our social communication, at least with those with whom we have close emotional ties. We are not always aware of it, in part because our communication is so completely dominated by language. But, in fact, it forms a natural and essential part of our social world.

If you are a regular jogger, you'll be familiar with endorphins in another context. It's what gives you that 'second wind', otherwise known as the 'jogger's high', that kicks in ten minutes or so into a run. Suddenly, without any warning, the cares of the world drop from your shoulders, and you feel as though you could run forever. The endorphins released into the brain elevate the pain threshold, dampening the muscular stresses of running.

In addition, endorphins seem to have a dramatic effect on the immune system, activating in particular the production of 'natural killer' (or NK) cells that target viruses and some cancer cells,[3] and thereby improving our physical health as well as our psychological wellbeing – one reason, perhaps, why regular joggers tend to be healthier than their more sedentary peers.

When our ancestors reached the point where group sizes of 150 became desirable, it proved necessary to find new and more efficient ways to trigger the endorphin system in order to bond these larger groups. Since the intimacy of social grooming makes it a strictly one-to-one affair in primates (and humans), the only way they could increase the efficiency of bonding was to find ways to trigger the endorphin system without having to touch the other person. Doing

two animals spend grooming each other – and hence on the amount of endorphins circulating in their brains. If they groom less, there will be less circulating endorphin, and the next time danger threatens they won't be quite so willing to go to each other's aid. It's a simple time-dependent effect.

And herein lies the drawback of the system. Because a minimum time is needed to create a friendship of a given strength (see Figure 2.4) and there is a limit on how much time an individual can afford to devote to social grooming each day, there is an upper limit on the number of individuals that can be bonded in this way – and, hence, on the size of group that monkeys can maintain as a stable unit. That limit stands at about fifty individuals, a number that therefore turns

so would allow several people to be 'groomed' virtually at the same time, thus allowing larger groups to be bonded. They solved the problem by discovering that laughter, singing, dancing, feasting (eating and drinking socially) and emotional storytelling are all very effective triggers of the endorphin system, and hence elevate the sense of bonding (Figure 4.1). Today, these constitute the core of the social toolkit that we use to engineer group bonding.

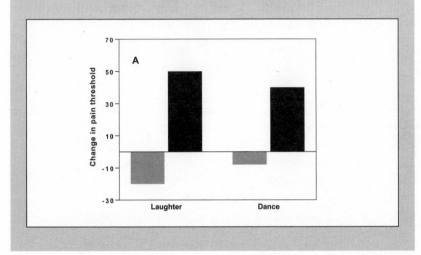

out to be the natural limit on the size of monkey and ape groups. (Larger groups have been observed, but they lack the coherence of smaller ones and are therefore always unstable.) It's a simple matter of time constraints of the kind we are all familiar with.

Endorphins are, of course, only one of a suite of hormones and neurotransmitters that are involved in managing our behaviour (see p. 89). These play a variety of important roles, not all of which are directly related to social processes. Endorphins work in tandem with dopamine to create a push/pull effect: dopamine creates a sense of exhilaration, while endorphins create a lasting sense of bonding. Much has been made of oxytocin (the so-called 'love hormone') in the media, and it certainly plays an important role in the context of

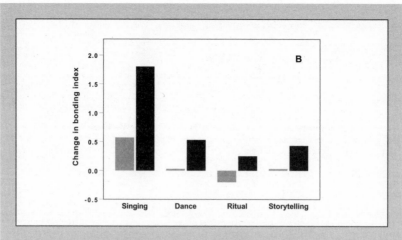

Bonding and the Shared Experience

Figure 4.1. The various kinds of grooming-at-a-distance behaviours that we regularly use in our social lives really do trigger the endorphin system (a) and result in an enhanced sense of bonding in groups of strangers (b). Black bars: specified activity (e.g. watching a comedy video that stimulated laughter or engaging in vigorous dancing); grey bars: control activity (e.g. watching a factual documentary video during which no one laughed or making dance-like arm-movements while seated). Ritual refers to religiously versus non-religiously motivated physical actions (e.g. yoga exercises); storytelling compares an emotionally wrenching tragedy film (black bar) versus a factual documentary (grey bar). Endorphin uptake was indexed as the change in pain threshold from before to after undertaking the specified activity; change in bonding index is to other members of the experimental group, all of whom were strangers. Source: Dunbar et al. (2021)[4]

mother–infant and romantic relationships. However, its main function seems to be to make *you* more generous and loving towards another person. In essence, you either have the right gene for generosity or you don't. Because we can trigger the release of endorphins in other people, endorphins have the distinct advantage that they allow us to make *other people* more generous and trusting towards us. That's why they play such an important role in bonding friendships as well as communities.

The Social Hormones

Much of our social behaviour depends on the fine balance between different hormones secreted by the brain and associated glands. These often form a cascade where one triggers the release of another. Many of these act as neurotransmitters, facilitating the firing of neural networks in the brain; others predispose individuals to behave in certain ways. There are seven of these hormones that are normally considered important.

Testosterone. Associated mainly with aggressive behaviour and unswerving focus on objectives. Though most often associated with men, in fact women can also have high levels of circulating testosterone, especially once oestrogen levels (that normally counterbalance testosterone) decline after the menopause.

Oxytocin. Sometimes known as the 'love hormone' because it is instrumental in triggering the maternal response in female mammals, and helps to underpin romantic pair bonds. Though it can be triggered by physical contact, its most important characteristic is that you either have it (stronger in women) or not (less so in men). It makes you feel generous towards other people, but doesn't affect how generous they feel towards you. Its effects are relatively short-lived (measured in minutes rather than hours).

Vasopressin. Physiologically similar to oxytocin, it is often thought of as the male equivalent of oxytocin. In fact, its role in regulating social behaviour is probably much less important than first thought.

Endorphins. Part of the brain's pain management system, endorphin activation is triggered by physical contact and a number of other socially important behaviours (see p. 85). It acts as the principal pharmacological platform for creating and maintaining long-term social relationships, as well as predisposing us to be social. It is the principal neurohormone involved in social bonding, mainly because we can trigger its production in people we want to bond with, making them feel well disposed towards us. Its effects last for several hours. A dose of endorphins also sharpens up our cognition.

Dopamine. *Sometimes known as the 'happiness hormone', it is responsible for the sense of exhilaration that we get when a social interaction goes especially well. It also plays an important role in facilitating neural signalling between different units in the brain and in making us more attentive.*

Serotonin. *Mainly modulates mood (low levels are associated with depression) as well as physiological processes like vomiting and vasoconstriction (when blood supply is cut off to the less important parts of the body, such as the intestines, to make more available to the areas that are immediately more essential, such as the muscles to facilitate flight).*

Adrenalin (epinephrine): *Often known as the 'flight/fight' hormone, it prepares the body for action by raising the breathing rate and increasing blood flow to the muscles. Which action is taken depends on the situation, not on the adrenalin itself.*

To these, we might add **cortisol.** *Though strictly speaking a hormone designed to trigger the release of energy from the liver (e.g. during starvation or sudden rapid action like flight or fighting), it is often used as an indirect index of both physical and psychological stress.*

The Magic of Synchrony

There's one more piece of the jigsaw to put in place: most of these social activities involve a significant degree of behavioural synchrony. When we laugh, we do so together in time with each other; when we sing or dance, we do so in tandem with those around us; when we eat or drink, we engineer synchrony through bringing courses out at the same time or by proposing toasts.

When various forms of behaviour are coordinated in this way, they seem to ramp up the endorphin production by 100 per cent for no extra effort.[5]

It was a study carried out on the Oxford University boat crews involved in the annual Boat Race against Cambridge University on the River Thames that first alerted us to the link between synchrony and endorphins.[6] Researchers monitored the crews for a week as they did their hour-long preparatory stints on rowing machines in the gym to build up their strength and rhythm, prior to going out to row together on the river. The following week, they monitored them again, but this time they arranged the rowing machines as a virtual boat so that they rowed together in synchrony. The effect was dramatic. Although the effort the crews put in was the same each week (as measured from the gauges on the rowing machines), their pain thresholds (the proxy for endorphin uptake in the brain) in the second week increased by 100 per cent over the first (Figure 4.2). Rowing in time with each other had had a transformative effect.

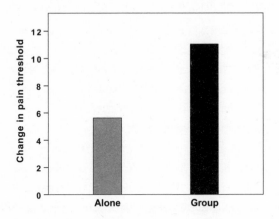

The Rower's High

Figure 4.2. Using the change in pain as an index of endorphin uptake in the brain, the sheer physical effort of rowing elevates pain thresholds (grey bar) but rowing in synchrony as a group doubles the effect without the need for any extra effort (black bar). Source: Cohen et al. (2010)[7]

Quite why this should be is not yet understood, but it's a phenomenon that has now been frequently observed in experiments involving a wide variety of other activities.

You'll be familiar with the power of synchrony if you go jogging regularly with others. When everyone is in step, you may have noticed that the rhythm and the synchrony help boost an elevated mood and the feeling that you could run forever (at least early on!). So mesmerising is this effect that if someone happens to fall out of step, perhaps to avoid an obstacle, they will swiftly slip back into the collective rhythm again.

Shared experiences can create a sense of synchrony, too. Synchrony occurs, for example, among theatre audiences laughing together at a comedy or having their collective heart strings tugged by a tragedy. Tragedies can prove particularly powerful: because we feel psychological pain in exactly the same part of the brain as we feel physical pain, the endorphin response is the same. This was demonstrated by an experiment that involved inviting volunteers to watch either a modern tragedy based on a true-life story or a factual TV documentary.[8] Those who watched the tragedy exhibited elevated pain thresholds after the event; those who watched the factual documentary together did not. More importantly, those whose pain thresholds were elevated felt significantly more bonded to the other people in the audience – even though they had never met before – than those who watched the documentary (Figure 4.1, b: extreme right-hand data marked 'storytelling').

It's a phenomenon with which theatre producers are very familiar: as they often say, people go into a performance as individuals but come out as a community. As audiences make their way back to the foyer after the performance, they feel less socially inhibited, more willing to talk to strangers and exchange comments about the play, and are sometimes prepared to share the kind of confidences that would normally be reserved for more familiar friends. It's the endorphins at work.

So how can we capitalise on the powers of synchrony in our work lives?

Designing Connection

If we think of group bonding in an organisational context at all, it is likely to be in the form of away days, Christmas parties, team bonding exercises or focused talks by professional coaches and inspirational speakers. And because we're not aware of what is actually going on in our subconscious minds when we're taking part, we tend to badly underestimate the astonishingly beneficial impact such shared moments can have. All too easily they can seem like a distraction from the main task at hand. We don't realise that they are actually an essential part of it. Indeed, just about every aspect of the bonding behaviour we see in our social lives plays an essential part in community bonding within an organisation, too.

Shared Experience

Army training offers perhaps the most extreme example of how getting people to interact forges a powerful sense of group. Retired general Tyrone Urch describes how important it is to prepare soldiers for 'whatever we may want them to do' in operational life, and for the tensions, fears, shocks and confusion that this will entail, by bringing them together into tight units. In fact, being trained for 'readiness' is often regarded as more important than being taught mastery of any particular specialism or qualification. Trainees might be taken abroad for example, where the environment is strange and undifferentiated. Here, as they experience what it is like to be lost or scared or under live fire, they come to depend absolutely on their companions. Alternatively, they may undertake adventure training in the form of rock-climbing or caving. Again, dependence on others is forged in environments that involve high levels of stress and adrenalin as they have to rely on a comrade holding a rope or a torch for them. Out of this experience emerge bonds of loyalty that are enhanced by the synchrony of marching together, sharing a tent or feeling tired, scared and wet and hungry together. Such bonds are, in General Urch's words, the country's insurance policy. It's interesting to note that, in the corporate world, teams that have undergone an extreme experience together – such as a merger, a breakthrough, a meltdown, or even just an intense period of pressure – tend to trust each other more after the event and to stay in touch long after the shared experience is over.

Successful interaction does not, of course, have to involve quite such stressful situations. Associate Professor at the Warwick Business School and former theatre director Piers Ibbotson describes how important it is at the beginning of a production to break down any status anxieties that might arise from having, say, an Oscar-winning actor as Hamlet and a recent drama school student playing the part of the gravedigger. 'As a director, you need to build an environment within which they can take risks together, trust each other and surrender their egos to something bigger,' he says. Faced with an ensemble of perhaps fifteen people, who may differ enormously in experience and reputation, he looks for ways in which to enact a kind of psychosocial levelling so they can bond and collaborate successfully. This might involve a significant amount of time spent simply playing games, or undertaking inconsequential activities or finding ways to laugh together. By the end of it all, a group of individual actors have become a troupe.

Piers has also applied these principles in his work at Warwick Business School, where the group size is significantly larger with perhaps as many as 400 students attending a lecture. In such an environment, as Piers observes, 'it's impossible to know or relate to them as individuals'. For some elements of the course it was possible to divide the students into groups of twenty-five. He soon realised, however, that this approach was only partially effective as students were taught the widely used Tuckman 'forming, storming, norming, performing' group model.[9] In the acting world, truly high-performing ensembles don't need to 'storm', because they don't bicker. Indeed, they barely have to speak to each other to course correct, or to revise the way they're playing a scene. 'Bonded ensembles are already in possession of the story; they don't need to negotiate it. It's a kind of social physics,' he says. Instead, he introduced the games, rituals and tools he employed as a theatre director, thereby enabling the students to build trust with each other and to collaborate more effectively together.

Such 'social physics' is also observable among the routines followed by the boys who make up the treble section of an Oxford college choir. In their rehearsals before evening and weekend services, they will certainly practise, but they will also play and laugh together. The end result is a group of children, often as young as eight, who know each other and the score so well that, if one of them makes a mistake, he simply raises his hand to acknowledge the error and the singing carries on. There's no need to stop. No intervention from the choir master is necessary. The higher-order shared purpose takes care of the details below the waterline.

And if playfulness and a business environment seem unlikely bedfellows, it's worth bearing in mind how, from as early as 2006, the Lego company famously designed a process whereby executives could come together to 'play' with Lego pieces as a means to design their future strategy. The fact that this approach has now been emulated across thousands of businesses, over many different sectors, testifies to its effectiveness.[10] It's not just a question of establishing a forum in which strategy or new ideas can be discussed. It's the fact that people bond through synchronous activity and serious play while they are there that is key. 'You can discover more about a person in an hour of play than in a year of conversation,' as Plato famously said, but the process also yields tangible business results. 'The purpose of serious play is to create potential energy. This then becomes kinetic energy when the team members implement it – when they literally put it to work.'[11]

Professor of Strategy Claus Jacobs came through customs many times from his home in Switzerland to Oxford with a suitcase full of Lego with the aim of teaching strategy on the Oxford Senior Leadership Programme. The process of playfully prototyping future solutions, building them in 3D, being able to walk around them and get feedback, making real-time adjustments, literally 'seeing' how the future looks (albeit in coloured bricks) is powerful. One successful South American CEO in the oil business found himself constructing a mini business school out of bricks in one of these sessions, rather than the model of the future of his business. A fellow participant quizzed him: 'Where do you see yourself in this model?' Somewhat surprised by himself, the CEO hesitated and then plonked a Lego mini figure right in the centre. Three years later, he no longer worked in oil and was indeed at the centre of running a business school in his home country. That moment of serious play, he reflected, was pivotal.

Eating Together

One key way in which communities have traditionally bonded is by eating together. It's also been a means by which strangers have been welcomed into a community. Nourishment in itself, of course, provides a feeling of wellbeing. Alcohol, where it is served, reduces the sense of inhibition and stimulates a willingness to engage. But it is the effect that both the act of eating and the consumption of alcohol have on the brain's endorphin system that is the really important factor in promoting bonding between those who eat and drink together.

According to a study conducted in collaboration with the campaigning charity CAMRA (the Campaign for Real Ale), people who were regulars at the same 'local' pub not only knew the staff and clientele well, but also had more close friends, were happier, felt depressed less often, viewed life as being more worthwhile, and engaged with and trusted their wider community more than those who lacked this social centre.[12] The message seems to be that the village pub, café-bar or even restaurant seems to function as a kind of community centre where people meet up in relaxing circumstances, meet old friends and perhaps have the opportunity to make new ones. Very similar results emerged from a later study of social eating carried out in collaboration with The Big Lunch (an offshoot of the famous Eden Project) that encourages people to go out into the street where they live once a year and hold a communal lunch where they can get to know each other.[13] Every year, streets are blocked off to traffic, trestle tables set up and as many as 10 million people (one seventh of the entire UK population) sit down to a communal lunch with neighbours and friends. One study revealed that holding a Big Lunch event at work could increase productivity by 12 per cent.[14] The importance of eating together, of coming together over a meal (or a number of meals), drives the biggest voluntary migration every year. As Lynda Chen, Senior Fellow of the Economics of Mutuality Foundation, puts it: 'Nothing is more important for Chinese families than coming together for Chinese New Year. This moment of reconnection and re-engagement can sustain families until they meet again the following year.'

It's for this reason that the historian Theodore Zeldin, through The Oxford Muse, his foundation set up to stimulate courage and invention in personal and corporate life, designs 'menus of conversation' to be used at shared meals with strangers that are held in venues that range from town squares to churches. The menus contain questions – not details of food – and are designed to bring together pairs of people who have not met before and, in the process, to create greater understanding and community in a congenial setting. Those who take part eat a meal together: endorphins are released, and bonding occurs as though by magic.

In similar vein, The Felix Project, a charity that delivers excess fresh food from supermarkets to other charities or schools – and the NHS during the Covid crisis – to be cooked for those who would otherwise go hungry, sees social as well as nutritional value in what it does. Co-founder Jane Byam Shaw argues that the shared meals it produces are 'food for the soul'. Atul Jaggi, President and Deputy Managing Director of automobile parts manufacturer Gabriel India Limited, describes how the act of sharing food has been a significant way of building tolerance and respect across the various cultures in India. 'Every important festival is celebrated by bringing together the teams over a meal – this gives each person a chance to share the food that is significant to them as well as building connections. We have always done that and it is a core part of culture at work.'

The point here is not just that people are eating and drinking together. They are also chatting, laughing and reminiscing.[15] As they do so, a sense of bonding and camaraderie is built and enhanced. Interestingly, it seems that evening social events are more effective than midday ones in this regard. There is something magical, primitive even, about social events in the semi-dark. Just as we find evening theatre or concert performances more uplifting and engaging than matinee ones, so meals at night seem more engaging than lunchtime ones. On the Oxford Strategic Leadership Programme we always ensure that the final evening ends around a huge bonfire in the woods – even in November. It has an astonishingly primal bonding effect on the group.

The effectiveness of meals can be increased by the way in which they are presented and eaten. On the OSLP programme, for example, we insist on having small, round tables brought in for intimate suppers and we give considerable thought to how long meals should last. We even plan the menu around our ambition to bring people together. The welcome dinner on the first day, for example, is always a curry. Because it involves many small dishes, it requires everyone to ask others to pass them food or to help serve them, which, of course, means that they have to talk to each other. At the same time, the hot spices in curry fire up the endorphin system because they trigger a mild pain response. The following night is always a street food evening, involving food from around the world. As our international visitors recognise scents and flavours from their own countries, they are prompted to share stories about their culture, their national food and drink. On this occasion, there is no formal seating, so people are free to move around and change places as they eat and talk. Table sizes are limited to five to six people to facilitate easy conversation.

If any of the meals takes place in an Oxford college, on the other hand, ideas of ritual and setting are emphasised. Grace is sung in

Latin, the college silver is laid out, and there are beautiful flowers on the table. Such formality and tradition stimulates different types of conversation and it also lodges very firmly in people's memory: they take photographs of the occasion and talk about it when they get home. Care is taken, however, to keep the dinner short. Long, formal evenings, particularly for those who don't drink alcohol, can ultimately drag, kill conversation and so threaten to be counterproductive.

'In our organisation, there is always food,' says Kim Howard, when talking about her time at the South African Ninety-One investment company. 'We are big on birthdays, fun and joy.' For its part, Improbable, a tech start-up in London, provides a high-quality free lunch for around 400 employees each day. Its directors recognise that this provides a social occasion for younger 'techies' who normally spend their time coding at their computers to spend time with some of the older employees who liaise with clients. Without the lunches, there could be a disconnect between the two parts of the business, which could ultimately undermine it. As it is, employees can share perspectives and learn to understand one another's specialisms. After all, the words 'company' and 'companion' come from the late Latin word *companio* meaning 'bread fellow' or mess mate: one who eats with you.

For her part, Samantha has always attributed part of the reason for the success of SABMiller, the South African brewing giant for whom she worked for a number of years, to its emphasis on making time for social activities and for having a central gathering place at the heart of its buildings. The culture of having places in the workplace where people came together to share a lunchtime meal and a drink together after work played a huge part in its corporate success. SABMiller outperformed all of its FTSE peers bar one over the fifteen years before its acquisition by the brewing conglomerate AB InBev. Those working for the company continuously rated it on Glassdoor as one of the best companies to work for. It was also ranked as one of the most empathic companies in the world in 2015.

The Original Bonding Experiment?

During the 1980s, American business thinkers became intrigued by the fact that the employees of the big Japanese companies did group exercises by their desks every morning before the start of the workday. In fact, the Japanese had been doing these morning communal exercises since 1928, with national radio broadcasting a ten-minute music programme each day to accompany them. Company retirees even continued to gather under the cherry trees in city parks to join in with the same radio broadcast from loudspeakers hung among the trees.[16]

There was a widespread view that this communal exercise was at least partly responsible for the deep sense of loyalty to the company that characterised Japanese workers and management alike, and that this in turn might explain the meteoric rise of the post-war Japanese car and electronics industries. In the hope of emulating some of this success, other countries like Thailand and China later followed suit.

However, in the new millennium, the value of this practice began to be questioned in the aftermath of a series of economic shocks sustained by Japanese industry. It became viewed as a ritual that, in creating a strong sense of team, undermined the independent thinking required for the challenges of the new century. By 2020, most large companies had abandoned the practice, though retired workers continue to indulge in their gentle public calisthenics.

But were companies right to abandon such communal exercises? It's possible that in seeking to refocus on the individual, they lost out on the bonding and trust that such activities created among employees. Whether or not industry has read the runes right in this giant social experiment or has been panicked into the wrong kind of change remains to be seen. But it's arguable that the upside of synchronised activities greatly outweighs any possible downside.

On the OSLP programme at Oxford, we offer optional tai chi out on the lawn early in the morning before classes begin.

Exhausted, jet-lagged executives seem to relish the communal solitude, being outside together but not having to talk, and the peaceful shared rhythm of the exercise. In its slow way, the shared experience fast-tracks the bonding of participants who are with us for only a week.

Dancing and Singing Together

For some, the notion of dancing or singing together in an organisational setting might seem literally a step too far. There is no doubting, though, their extraordinary power. Dancing is a highly synchronised activity: even when we dance in freestyle, our movements are set by the rhythm of the music, and so we inadvertently synchronise as we (try to) keep time to the 'beat of the drum'. The rush of endorphins, and the feelings of exhilaration and happiness and bondedness that go with them (see p. 85), create a sense of being part of a group. Dance seems to generate a double hit of endorphins: the physical exercise itself triggers their release, while dancing in synchrony dramatically ramps up their output, leading to a significant additional increase in pain thresholds and an enhanced sense of bonding (as with other physical activities such as rowing, see Figure 4.2), even when complete strangers are involved. Singing has a similar power (Figure 4.3.). In singing, the synchrony effect seems to come through harmony – the well-known magical fifth 'angel's voice' that is so familiar an experience to those who sing in barber's shop quartets.[17] The reason why sea shanties (with their call-and-response style) became such a fixture in the British navy is that sailors were able to pull harder and for longer on the ropes when hoisting the heavy sails on eighteenth- and nineteenth-century sailing ships – thanks to the fact that singing in synchrony elevates pain thresholds.

Samantha and Tracey once found themselves dancing at the end of a leadership programme that they directed for the Ariane de

Rothschild Legacy Fellows at the Gulbenkian Museum in Lisbon. It involved a diverse group of extraordinarily talented people whose work involved encouraging and supporting voices from the edge, whether migrants, refugees, marginalised religious groups, homeless people or disadvantaged children. The museum itself provided a rather grand and hushed setting. At the final learning session, one of the participants put a speaker in the middle of the room with 'Saturday Night Fever' playing. It was a mischievous nod to one of the faculty who had let slip over dinner that she had got 100 per cent in her disco-dancing written final exam as a teenage student in Alabama.

Somehow, although it seemed to tick every social embarrassment box (dancing in a museum when exhausted at four o'clock in the afternoon with other participants who were similarly no longer twenty), it was hard not to dance. The chefs who were finishing up in the museum café, still in their blue nylon caps, came out and danced too with the diverse group of leaders. It was that moment of joy, relief and shared rhythm that bonded us as a group long past the week of shared learning. Almost three years after the four-day programme ended with the group dispersed across the globe, a WhatsApp group is still alive where members share successes and life stories.

A forensic psychologist in the prison services describes the power of singing: 'One of the things that always melted my heart was when prisoners combined this need for synchrony through singing with spontaneity. When I had just started out as a forensic psychologist I had an office right on a wing, quite a big wing with many women prisoners. Often I would be working and would hear the women break into a song – a song that everyone contributed to and that meant that one of the women had completed her prison sentence. This was never an organised thing but arose out of the instinct of the importance of beginnings and endings. Most of the women in prison have never had good beginnings or endings – so this can have a profound effect. This spontaneous singing really moved me as it was heartwarming and uplifting and would have

The Ice-Breaker Effect

Over the last decade or so, the endorphin-activating properties of singing have been studied experimentally in some detail.

One study involved Popchoir, a non-professional London choir that practises in small groups of about twenty people before coming together as a giant choir of around 200 at the end of the year for a public performance. It was found that not only did endorphin take-up in the brain (as indexed by a change in pain thresholds) increase after singing, but so did people's sense of bonding. Interestingly, the effect was much more dramatic in the large choir than in the small ones (Figure 4.3a). In another study of novice singers, it emerged that people felt more bonded to a group of strangers after just an hour of community-style singing than when they spent the hour together engaged in more passive exercise such as hobby classes. This effect persisted over a seven-month period (Figure 4.3b).

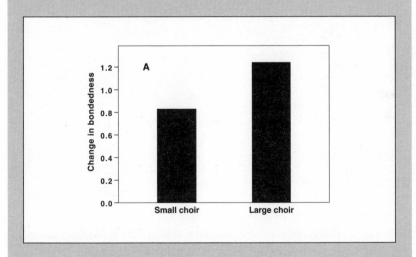

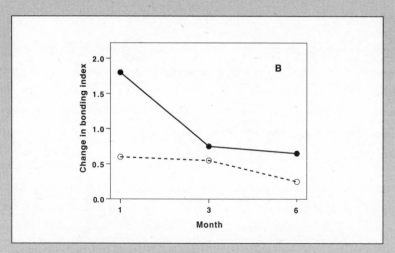

Singing as a Bonding Mechanism

Figure 4.3. (a) Change in rating of bonding to other members of a small (twenty singers) versus a large (200 singers) choir after an hour singing together. Bondedness was rated on a standard one-to-seven scale. Source: Weinstein et al. (2016)[18] (b) Change in bondedness to other group members for novice singing classes (filled symbols) versus hobby classes (dotted line). Source: Pearce et al. (2015)[19]

It seems as though there is something almost magical about singing that has a very dramatic effect, as anyone who sings regularly in a choir will tell you. The endorphin effect that underpins this seems primarily to be associated with the breath control involved in singing which relies on long exhalations and is physically much more taxing than the effort required for ordinary speech.

been very important to the women leaving – a lasting positive memory.'

The power of choirs to foster a sense of identity and individual wellbeing is now widely acknowledged thanks – in the UK, at least – to such ensembles as the Military Wives Choir (associated with Gareth Malone), the Choir with No Name for the homeless (originally founded in London in 2008 by Marie Benton), the choirs for cancer patients run by the Tenovus charity, and the choirs for long-term prisoners run by the charity Beating Time[20] (established by Heather Phillips). Organisations have been slow to take up the idea. But where they have done so, the results have been striking. In Norway, for example, it's been shown that Sound of Wellbeing choirs run for staff at two hospitals yielded better health outcomes and greater levels of commitment and engagement at work among those who took part in comparison with those who did not.[21]

In South Africa, as Samantha discovered in the 1990s when she worked for the country's first democratically elected ANC government, the formation of a choir in one of the departments not only contributed to improved performance but also helped connect old and new civil servants at a very important moment. Samantha and her colleagues had faced a very particular challenge. The new government had decided not to clear out the civil service of those who had worked for the previous administration but to keep those who were prepared to work with the new government, while augmenting their numbers with new ANC-affiliated staff. Perhaps unsurprisingly given the history, two camps emerged. One was composed of mostly white, Afrikaans-speaking public servants who had until recently been responsible for upholding the apartheid laws of the land, and overnight they were required to dismantle the systems they had been working on for forty years. The other consisted of the very people those laws and systems had been designed to oppress. Day-to-day interactions were polite and task-focused. But there was an understandable backdrop of pain and suspicion. It was a febrile time for the country and for the new government.

Then someone suggested that a choir be set up and take part in local competitions. The head of department, a stalwart of the anti-apartheid movement, was enthusiastic. And so it began. Rehearsals were held during lunch breaks and in the early evenings. The choir built up a repertoire of traditional songs, gospel choruses and more modern, upbeat pop songs. A uniform was designed and bought – all wore it – and performances were given to the rest of the department. Soon membership swelled as public servants rushed to join. It was hard not to be moved by the joy and collaborative spirit the choir engendered – or not to be inspired by the sense of connection it established with its audiences. That year, the department won an Investors in People Gold Award for outstanding performance.

It's not only singing that has this effect. Any kind of musical experience will deliver the same endorphin release and accompanying feeling of visceral joy. Conductor Peter Hanke, reflecting on one of his most memorable concerts, talks of music's ability to create 'a sense of collective readiness, a spark of the moment – a sensory and crystalline quality that comes from the experience of human cohesion in the present. It's an unforgettable thing.' David Storey, a partner at EY, one of the largest professional services networks in the world, describes how, when the advent of Covid-19 hit the morale of his team, he challenged everyone to contribute one song to a communal playlist and a paragraph about why that song made them happy. 'People loved the playlist, constantly diving into the songs in subsequent meetings. It really helped us to make the people connection in a tough time.' What's true of music is also true of laughter, emotional storytelling, even religious ritual (which, of course, may well involve singing).

Everyday Bonding

Any activity that triggers endorphins helps bring people together and brings out the best in them. If you and those around you need to make a difficult collective decision, it will prove that much easier if you find time to have lunch or dinner together or even simply go for a walk: as you fall in step with one another, your endorphin systems will be triggered. Such synchronous behaviour will also enable you to make the decision more quickly, more amicably and with greater trust shown all round. Walkshops really can be more effective than workshops. More generally, a workforce that engages in communal activities is likely to be a happier, healthier and more productive one.

In a post-Covid world, where more people will be working from home or in a hybrid pattern, leaders will need to spend more time thinking about how their teams bond and cohere. Their decisions will have major implications for the mental health of employees, for the loyalty they feel both to each other and to the company. Whatever policies are enacted, it is essential to bear in mind that bonded teams feel safer, are more productive, more willing to take risks, are more likely to be prosocial and constructive and, crucially, enjoy their work more. As we saw in Chapter Two, they are also likely to be healthier. And if they are healthier and they enjoy their work more, they will be more productive. It's a virtuous circle.

Summary

- We form social bonds with each other through taking the time to engage in shared activities and experiences that include eating and laughing together, singing and dancing, storytelling, and reminiscing.
- Such behaviour, along with physical touch, activates an evolutionary bonding mechanism (common to all the monkeys and apes) involving the brain's endorphin system, creating a sense of elevated mood, belonging and trust. Beneath the consciousness horizon, this is a primal bonding mechanism that connects us with our inherited biology.
- It is possible to measure the beneficial hormonal effect of these activities just as it is possible to assess when there is a negative hormonal impact such as unhealthy levels of cortisol in the system.
- Behavioural synchrony (moving together, singing to a beat, dancing, marching, jogging or laughing together) magnifies the endorphin effect, creating a super-bonding effect.

- It may seem logical that the seemingly simple joys of singing or dancing, feasting together, or collectively watching a play, are the preserve of home life but it is easy to overlook their potency in the work environment to deepen bonds. Having a shared meal *before* a tricky meeting or a difficult joint decision, rather than afterwards, can create the right environment for a positive outcome.
- Bonding comes with a health warning. It can create a sense of 'us' and 'them' and can lead to acts of exclusion and a culture of inward-looking clannishness. For bonding to benefit the many not the few, these experiences need to be carefully designed and monitored and occasionally disrupted, to break bonds.

5.

The Medium and the Message

'We are the sweet cold water and the jar that pours.'

Rumi[1]

Communication is central to organisations. But its importance and its pitfalls are often overlooked. Instead, we tend to focus on the apparent elegance of the PowerPoint presentation, the chart, the depth of the data, the font size or the accuracy of the numbers. We fail to appreciate precisely how people really communicate and how they respond to the linguistic subtlety of messages. The existence of organisational hierarchies complicates matters even further as communications are 'cascaded' or 'rolled out' from top to bottom, or centre to edge. The problem is that humans are for the most part better talkers than listeners, and this tendency becomes more pronounced the higher the status they enjoy. Most corporate communication energy is devoted to the talk, not the listen.

Yet language is an essential part of our social environment. It constitutes a potent force in binding us together. For example the historian Theodore Zeldin aims to go beyond offering opportunities to tell one's own story or to listen to someone else's. His Muse Menu is designed 'to produce a meeting of minds where facts are not just exchanged but transformed, and new implications drawn from them, not reshuffling the cards, but creating new cards'.

At the group level, language plays a crucial role in enabling the Seven Pillars of Friendship to take effect. We recognise members of our community by the words they use and the jokes they tell, as well as by the way they pronounce particular words. Recognition of someone's dialect as being the same as our own is as near instantaneous a cue of tribe membership as it is possible to get.

The job of implementing change at any level is to make sure that the right message gets through – sometimes despite the noise and the distraction of the medium. This requires a more deliberate focus on form as well as content. Just before Christmas 2021, the CEO of the ironically named Better.com fired 900 people in a short Zoom call.[2] Clearly, this was the wrong medium for the message, not least for the psychological effect it likely had on the staff who weren't fired on this occasion. Avoiding these kinds of pitfalls, finding the right form of words and the right way of saying them, are the secret of success for those who lead organisations of all kinds.

In this chapter, we want to show how a deeper understanding of how we communicate can help forge tighter social bonds in the workplace and elsewhere, and also help us avoid the pitfalls of miscommunication that are likely to have the opposite effect by causing distress, dissension and conflict. Failure to recognise the implications of *how* we say things – rather than what we say – places serious limitations on our ability to function well as a group, both in the workplace and elsewhere.

Words and Meaning

Perhaps the first place to start is with the words themselves. Words are inherently ambiguous communication tools – notoriously so in English. English has an unusually large vocabulary, often having several words (borrowed from different languages) meaning the same thing. This allows fine nuances of meaning to be expressed, depending on exactly which word is used. For example, in describing something as being 'very good', we might say it is 'great' or 'wonderful' (like 'good', both from Old German via Anglo-Saxon), 'brilliant', 'excellent' or 'admirable' (all from Old French), 'superb' (from Latin), or even 'pukka' (from the

Hindi for 'well cooked') and – most confusing of all – as 'not at all bad'. When we go to bed, we might wear pyjamas (a Hindi word), nightwear (combining two Old English words), sleepers (whose root is Old German) or a negligee (from the French). The words 'guarantee' and 'warranty' mean slightly different things (one is a promise based on a metaphorical handshake, the other a written assurance), but they are actually just the north and south French pronunciation of the same word brought into England a thousand years ago by William the Conqueror and his Norman knights (from the north of France) and the southern French mercenaries that they brought with them.

Conversely, any given word can have different meanings in different parts of the world: in a business context, for example, the verb 'table' in American English means 'to postpone indefinitely', while in British English it means 'to discuss during a meeting'. Individual words commonly acquire new meanings over time or vary in their force according to context. You might 'love' carrots or a particular individual, but the implications are not the same in the two cases. Casual language – slang, in particular – is especially open to different interpretations, as meanings are flipped or metaphors stretched to novel contexts. 'Awful' originally meant 'full of awe, or wonder' but now means quite the opposite – 'very bad'. 'Not bad!' in English actually means 'very good' – a source of great confusion to speakers of other languages. These changes occur on a generational time scale, and are a warning that, even within a community that speaks the same language, one generation should not assume that a younger (or older) generation interprets the meaning of a word in the same way as they do.

Although English is exceptional in its absorption of words from other languages, all languages exhibit this kind of flexibility to some extent. In part, that is because many of the words we use rely on metaphor for their meaning. We navigate these nuances on a daily basis, often unthinkingly, because ambiguity is a natural part of our system of communication. We often put this to good use by being deliberately vague with our meaning so as to keep the truth from someone or avoid committing ourselves in order to be polite. But this also means that it can be very easy to miss a small verbal nuance in the course of a quick-fire conversation. The slippery subtlety of the spoken word is well demonstrated by how different it is from the written one: someone writing an email, for example, is rarely able to replicate the cadence and intonations of everyday speech. It can easily lead to misunderstanding.

Words are, on the whole, a precise enough medium for conveying our thoughts when it comes to the physical world, but they are a surprisingly blunt tool for conveying psychological states and intentions. Listeners have to devote a great deal of mental effort to disentangle just what it is that the speaker has in mind. For their part, the speaker has to check constantly whether their message has been received and understood – and, if necessary, try making the same point in a different way. As a result, conversations are two-way processes that are open to constant misinterpretation, with both speaker and listener having to navigate a veritable minefield of ambiguity and uncertainty. We might think that our casual chat around the water cooler is about a colleague's recent holiday on some remote Pacific island or the confusion sown by the latest piece of administrative bureaucracy. But there may be sub-texts there that we don't immediately spot, not to mention cues we miss as to what that colleague is really like, what they believe in, even how honest and reliable they really are.

To help us make our way through this minefield, we rely heavily on the non-verbal cues that accompany the spoken word. We use inflections of the voice to provide emphasis, to express irony or mockery, mark questions or indicate dissatisfaction. We also use our face, our hands, sometimes our whole bodies to help emphasise the point we want to make. In the work Samantha and Tracey do, the body language and observed social dynamics of board meetings are analysed to help teams to be more effective. By turning down the volume on what is said and paying close attention instead to expression and gesture, it is sometimes easier to get to the heart of what is really being communicated and where the power in the room sits. When it comes to power the person sitting at the head of the table is positioned as the leader: the long rectangular table is designed to denote who is at the literal 'head'. In our experience, the seating arrangements *surrounding* the head of the table reveal more about where the real power lies. Small signals can denote positioning in the pecking order. Who is sitting to the right hand of the leader ('the right-hand man'), or who chooses to sit farthest away? Who takes assiduous notes of everything that is said and who does not, and what does that tell you about them? Who serves others by offering to fetch the refreshments and who is waited upon? How much physical space is being taken up and who by? Which contributors make their voices heard early on, who leans forward and who leans back when speaking? Who builds on the comments of others and who speaks in statements? And what about how people talk about their work – do they use the collective we or the individual I? In every exchange, power is ricocheting around the boardroom table and evidenced in the gestures and small movements of individuals in the group. Those who really pay attention will pick up the signals being sent. But it's by no means a given and most people don't even notice.

Minding the Mind

What underlies our ability to use language and infer what someone else actually means is the psychological capacity known as mentalising or mind-reading. In essence, this is the ability to use and comprehend a group of verbs known collectively in the philosophy of language as intentional terms: verbs such as 'like', 'intend', 'believe', 'suppose', 'imagine', 'wonder', 'think', 'want' and 'expect'. All these are verbs that display our capacity to reflect on our own internal thoughts, our mindstate. When we can also use them of someone else – 'I wonder whether you believe . . .' – then we are said to have what is technically and rather awkwardly known as 'theory of mind' (a belief or theory on our part about what someone else is thinking at that particular moment). This sophisticated metacognitive ability – a proficiency to think about thinking – is one of the capabilities that sets humans apart from other animals.

Your ability to reflect on the contents of your mind is known as first order intentionality. Your ability to reflect on what someone else is thinking is second order intentionality (or formal theory of mind). If you correctly understand what they in turn are thinking about what a third person is thinking, that's third order intentionality. The typical upper limit for adult humans is fifth order intentionality (Figure 5.1).[3] We can handle up to five minds at the same time, including, of course, our own. In effect, we *believe* that Peter *wants* Kadisha to *suppose* that Rajendra *thinks* Martha *intends* to do something (where the five mindstates are indicated by the five italicised intentional verbs). This imputing of the intention behind words and

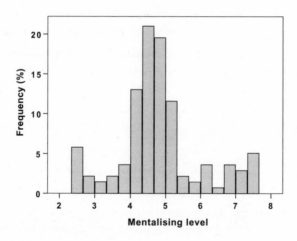

Our Mindreading Capacities

Figure 5.1. People vary in the number of other mindstates they can keep track of at any one time. The values plotted here are the percentage of adults whose upper limits on achievable mentalising level varied between two and eight levels of intentionality. Most people can happily cope simultaneously with five levels of mentalising (their own mindstate and the mindstates of four other people). A few people can only manage second or third level mentalising. Similarly, only around 20 per cent of people can do better than fifth level. Source: Lewis et al. (2011, 2017)[4]

actions is the wellspring of trust ('I understand that when you say you intend to do something, you really mean it' – itself a third order intentional statement). So simple a statement, yet it has already taken up much of our mentalising capacity.

By the time we are adults, we are so practised at mentalising that we take it for granted. However, people do vary a great deal from one another in how many different minds they can keep track of at the same time (Figure 5.1). Most adults vary between about third order intentionality (they can manage two other minds besides their own) and sixth order (they can manage up to five other minds). This difference directly affects how many people we can engage with in a conversation, how many close friends we can have, how complex the language we use is (at least as indexed by how many clauses we can include in a sentence and still make sense of it), how much we enjoy and appreciate fictional literature, and even how complex the jokes are that we enjoy.

The degree to which we can mentalise is also likely to affect our ability to understand complex arguments or think our way through complex design processes, management structures, sales pitches and a dozen other demands of the everyday world. A speaker will often falsely assume that the audience has the same mentalising skills as they themselves do, leaving some of their audience baffled and confused by what they have to say. Sometimes, trust will be withheld simply because the message or mode of delivery is too nuanced, too challenging or too complicated for the listener – or, at the other extreme, perhaps even just too simple.

In very closely bonded groups, mentalising assumes such sophistication that it may not even require a verbal intervention. Orthopaedic surgeon Professor Justin Cobb describes how in a well-run operating theatre the anaesthetist will know, without having to ask, what the surgeon wants; the theatre nurse will pass whatever instrument is required even before it has been requested by the surgeon. Delaying even for a moment to seek clarification in such an environment could have serious consequences that could be life-changing. It's the equivalent of the 'blind pass' in football or rugby, where a player knows exactly where the intended recipient of the pass will be without having to look because they know how that player will read their intentions. This intuited understanding of what needs to be done comes from a combination of not only working together but also learning together – acquiring the social and technical skills needed to make these critical in-the-moment decisions. He goes on to explain that, by using Virtual Reality, the surgeon and scrub tech learn faster together, and, after just four sessions of VR training, end up making fewer errors and are faster than those trained alone.

Obviously, these are very specific, often highly rehearsed, examples of expert mentalising in practice, but they underline the fact that we are surprisingly good at the improvised versions of this – provided the number of people involved is kept small. Once the group expands, however, mentalising becomes first exhausting and then impossible. Yoge Patel, CEO of Blue Bear Systems Research, an innovator in the defence, aerospace and civilian markets, describes how when she started out with her own company she was determined that it should be structured like a family. Once it had grown to about eleven people, however, she found the cognitive effort involved in mentalising about so many other minds was proving very draining. She was stretched beyond her capacity. Ultimately, she realised that if she wanted to continue to expand she would need to introduce new systems, such as another layer of leadership. Her personal mentalising capacities had reached their limit.

Such mentalising challenges are inevitably more pronounced within large and complex groups. Your ability to manage relationships with other members of your team will obviously depend directly on your mentalising skills – the more developed they are, the more easily you will be able to maintain working relationships with a large number of people. But account also has to be taken of individual levels of mentalising skill within the group. Women are typically more adept in this area than men.[5] Within the genders, narcissists, on the other hand, are particularly poor at it. Those with a more mathematical bent will typically have worse mentalising skills than those whose mathematical competences are more limited. The fact that individuals vary in their mentalising abilities inevitably

A Natural History of Conversation

Two thirds of natural conversation time is devoted to social topics; this is as true of English speakers in the UK as it is of Farsi speakers in Iran.[6] We are overwhelmingly drawn to discuss people, what they do and how they behave, in preference to talking about anything else. Conversations about technical issues, or even politics, are hard mental work, and the time we give to them is correspondingly limited. The only real exception to this is that men (and only men) suddenly find work and technically related topics of unusual interest when there are women present – something that seems to be more related to an attempt to advertise personal qualities of cleverness to the opposite gender than anything else (it is not meant to be exclusionary).[7] That aside, our preoccupation with the social means that we invariably find technical discussions that last any length of time hard work.

Another problem with conversations is that there is a very strict upper limit on the number of people who can be involved in a conversation, and that limit is four (Figure 5.2). If more people join, the group will quickly split into separate conversations. This fission happens at speed – often within less than a minute of an extra person joining. A conversation will only remain united when the group increases in size if it turns into a lecture – but that usually happens only when there is a dominant individual present who can hold court while the rest listen dutifully in silence.

There are several reasons why conversations are limited to four people. One is simply the limitations of our mentalising abilities: we can't manage more than four other mindstates at the same time (Figure 5.1). Notice that this limit is slightly lower than the five friends we can manage in the innermost circle of the Dunbar Graph (Figure 2.3). That's because managing a conversation is much harder work – it's an 'in the moment' issue. Since we rarely have to manage all our five best friends simultaneously, the additional cognitive freedom allows us to cope with the extra person.

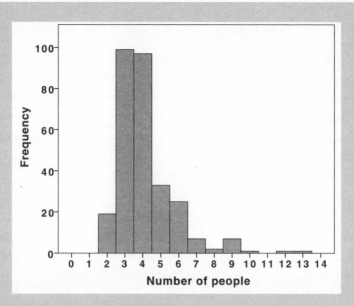

Natural Limits on Conversations

Figure 5.2. The sizes of natural conversation groups, based on a UK sample. Source: Dunbar (2017)[8]

A second reason for the limit on conversation size is that an individual's share of speaking time decreases rapidly as the number of people in the conversation increases. If you keep being prevented from having your say, you inevitably lose interest and will begin to look for a smaller conversation where you can have your say. A third reason stems from the fact that we feel uncomfortable about sitting or standing too close to others, and so we space ourselves out at rather characteristic distances – a pattern of behaviour that long predates Covid-19. Once there are more than four people in the conversation, it becomes difficult to hear clearly what everyone is saying across the circle.

The effects of spacing are a particular issue for women: their naturally lighter voices carry less far, making it more difficult for them to be heard when group size is large. As a result, women tend to drop out of the conversation sooner than men, retreating to the sidelines to become observers rather than contributors.[9] This effect is exacerbated in environments where there is background noise – for example, at a party or in an acoustically poor, echoey room. Our natural instinct in such circumstances is to stand closer together, and then to try to speak more loudly. But this soon becomes exhausting. After a while, it descends into a monologue with the listeners smiling and nodding enthusiastically in the vague hope that their response is appropriate – because they cannot hear what the speaker is actually saying. Eventually, people simply drop out of the conversation until there are only two people left.

creates problems. The temptation might be to bring together like-minded people because they will tend to gel more effectively and have a greater natural understanding of each other's intentions and thoughts. At one level, that will have undoubted benefits. But it risks creating an environment for unproductive groupthink.

Cultural differences also pose mentalising challenges. Just because someone is smiling, it doesn't necessarily mean they are happy about what you are saying. Someone who is nodding is not necessarily agreeing with you, however much you may hope that they do. Effective mentalising is essential when there is the need for nuanced, interpretive attention and in a globalised world where businesses become more complex and have to engage with multiple stakeholders and competing concepts, the mentalising capabilities of their leaders are key differentiators. Often unmeasured and unappreciated, mentalising is a crucial capability for leaders and managers charged with taking their organisations into the future.

Conversations Within Limits

Because conversations require those taking part to function effectively with each other in order to maintain their flow, there is inevitably an upper limit on how many people can be involved (Figure 5.2). If several people try to talk at the same time, mayhem ensues – partly because it becomes hard to concentrate simultaneously on more than one speaker and partly because the separate streams of speech actually interfere with each other. This is why large committees need a chair who can impose discipline such that everyone gets space to say what they want. In the chair's absence, a meeting will quickly break up into several small sub-conversations. Try watching what happens at your next meeting. The result is invariably a dramatic increase in background noise levels, because everyone is trying to be heard at the same time. Large committees can only function so long as we are willing to abide by the rule that only one person speaks at a time, and everyone else agrees to listen in silence. In effect, it requires listeners to cede the floor to one speaker and turn the conversation into a lecture.

It's intriguing to note, in this respect, that Shakespeare intuitively understood the fact that mentalising imposes a limit on a conversation: he never has more than four speaking parts in a scene at any one time (three if the characters are discussing the state of mind of someone off stage) (see p. 121).[10] It seems that he instinctively understood the mentalising capacities of his audience. Given that we can naturally only keep track of five mindstates at a time, and allowing for the audience member's own mindstate, he was anxious to ensure that his audience wasn't cognitively overloaded by the number of minds in the action on stage. A masterclass in the study of human psychology.

Conversations in the form of committees or meetings face an additional problem. The larger the group, the more difficult it is to reach a consensus, in part because there are too many conflicting opinions and in part because it just takes proportionately longer for everyone to get their say. Small committees reach decisions faster and seem to make better decisions (Figure 2.6). Large committees are always in danger of becoming rubber-stamping exercises – endorsing the views of the most forceful members with the loudest voices.

Mentalising in Shakespeare's Hamlet

In the opening scene of *Hamlet*, three men witness the bewildering and alarming appearance of the ghost of Prince Hamlet's father. In deciding how to react they have to enter each other's mental worlds, an act that involves knowing how each normally thinks and behaves, intuiting roles and imputing thought even to the ghost itself ('It would be spoke to').

Barnardo infers what the others are thinking – 'Looks it not like the king?' knowing that they all know what the king looked like. They do not have the time to 'report back' or get into a huddle to debrief. They have to move towards understanding as one, without leadership or facilitation.

Such an act of mentalising or stepping into the brain-world of others takes up a lot of mental computing power. The fact that an audience is present adds an extra layer of intentionality. For these reasons Shakespeare always ensured that there were never more than four characters engaged in a conversation at any one time (here, the silent ghost constitutes the fourth character).

> Enter Ghost
> MARCELLUS: Peace, break thee off; look, where it comes again!
> BERNARDO: In the same figure, like the king that's dead.
> MARCELLUS: Thou art a scholar; speak to it, Horatio.
> BERNARDO: Looks it not like the king? mark it, Horatio.
> HORATIO: Most like: it harrows me with fear and wonder.
> BERNARDO: It would be spoke to.
> MARCELLUS: Question it, Horatio.

Shakespeare was particularly sensitive to ensuring that he did not overload the cognitive abilities of his audience, and if they are discussing the mindstate of someone who is offstage, he will reduce the number of people in the conversation to three.[11] That way, the audience is always within their mentalising limit of five.

With adroit management, larger groups can be places for an effective exchange of views, but they are rarely forums for creative discussion or debate. It is for this reason that the real business of the day frequently takes place outside the committee room. Indeed, it is often said that a good chair is someone who has consulted widely and come to a 'collective' decision before the committee even convenes. This fragmentation of the decision-making process as the management group increases in size can pose problems for governance, transparency and accountability unless very carefully designed and managed. Acts of convening, chairing and structured facilitation are crucially important in this respect. So is choosing the appropriate size for the committee. These are often underestimated leadership skills.

The Art of Listening

If group size presents a potential stumbling block in terms of providing a platform for everyone involved to speak, it also poses a major challenge to their capacity to listen. Humans are not good listeners. Because our listening brains move faster than our mouths, we very easily become distracted while waiting for someone else to finish saying what they have to say (think, for example, of the times that you have read the PowerPoint slide behind the speaker's head long before they've finished talking about it – and then allowed your mind to wander while you wait for the speaker to catch up). If we're planning to respond, we stop listening and become focused instead on rehearsing what we want to say. If we feel the conversation is not moving sufficiently swiftly, we may even impatiently jump in to move it along. All these reactions can be conversation killers: they are off-putting for the speaker and they serve to interrupt the natural 'flow' of the conversation. Remote working has, arguably, made things worse. Writing in *The Economist* in late 2021, Sacha Nauta gloomily mused that there was 'little evidence of the hoped-for Zoomocracy where all voices would be heard equally'.[12]

An additional complicating factor is that men and women typically have very different conversational styles. The issue here is not technical competence or managerial ability but social *style*. These patterns were first noted more than thirty years ago by sociolinguists.[13] Women's conversations include a great deal of affirmative 'backchannel' comments ('Uh-huh', 'Oh, yes', 'Oh, wow!', 'Really?', 'Interesting!'). They also often involve listeners repeating the entire concluding phrase as the speaker finishes her utterance ('chorusing'). Men don't generally behave this way, and find such interjections intrusive, even rude (even when men do it). As a result, women's conversations tend to come across as more affirmative and affiliative; men's conversations often strike women as being rather combative – in contexts where men think their chat is merely innocent banter.

These gender differences can easily become distractions to the flow of a conversation, causing one half of those present to focus on style and ignore the substance of the discussion. One consequence is that mixed-gender conversations can sometimes flow less well than either gender would like. In larger conversations, women will often peel off to join a more congenial conversation with other women. In smaller conversations, such as simple dyads, women are more likely to adapt to their male companion's conversational style than vice versa,[14] partly due to women's better mentalising skills,[15] but the effort of shifting gear in this way can become exhausting. These differences in style have their roots in striking gender differences in the dynamics of friendships (see p. 124). Like most things in life, they have costs and benefits, and we need to understand them better so as to exploit the advantages they offer. To ignore them, however, is to risk that they come back to haunt us later.

These gender differences in social style may help explain some of the difficulties that women face in the work environment, not least

The Gendering of Social Style

Rhetoric notwithstanding, there are striking differences in the way the two genders' social worlds are organised, both in terms of their structure and their dynamics. As we noted in Chapter Two, social networks are highly gendered: most of our friends and preferred family members are the same gender as us. Women consistently have more friends than men do in the five- and fifteen-layers of their networks (associated with their greater mentalising abilities and better social skills).[16] More importantly, women invariably have a (usually female) 'Best Friend Forever' in addition to a romantic partner, whereas men have one or the other but almost never both.[17] Even so, the nature of these best friendships are very different in the two genders. Women's close friendships are often deeply platonic, involve the exchange of intimacies and shared confidences and have a physical intimacy that is largely lacking in men's friendships.

These differences reflect the fact that in general women's friendships are more personalised and focused on the qualities of the individual, whereas men's friendships are more casual and clublike (membership of the club can be more important than who you are as an individual).[18] This contrast is reflected in the way relationships are maintained. Women's relationships are largely mediated by conversation; men's tend to be activity-based, with conversation playing only a very muted role in social bonding (often merely an excuse for triggering laughter) (Figure 5.3).[19] Perhaps because of this, women's friendships are more emotionally intense than men's, as a result of which they are more prone to fracture, whereas men's are more likely simply to decay through absence of contact.[20] Men are much less likely to make an effort to maintain even close relationships if they can no longer meet up in person, whereas women will make great efforts to maintain contact by phone or social media.

To a large extent, these differences seem to reflect contrasts in the way social cognition is organised in women and men. In women, three major components (the wider structure of social relationships, romantic relationships and the cognitive processes that manage relationships) are closely integrated, whereas in men they operate in a more independent fashion. As a result, women are more effective at balancing the short- and long-term consequences of their relationships in the context of their wider social network (think first and act afterwards), whereas men are more likely to act impulsively (act first and think afterwards).[21]

The important point is to be clear that one style is not better or worse than the other style. They are simply different ways of achieving the same social objective of building networks of relationships. More importantly, these differences are more deep-seated than many people assume: we find these same differences in our monkey and ape cousins. In humans, the differences are commonly attributed to early social conditioning, but in reality early social conditioning simply reinforces pre-existing differences rather than determining the differences. We do a serious disservice to reality if we try to force either gender to adopt the social style of the other. Rather, we have to learn to adapt to them and engineer our social contexts to take better account of them.

because they suffer from the paradox of needing to come across as both authoritative and warm. Nor does it help that they are so often subjected to a type of physical scrutiny (think of the media's obsession with what a particular woman is wearing) that men seldom have to endure. Occupational psychologist and gender equality expert Sharon Peake describes how such factors affect women's leadership style: 'Another area that is often fraught for women concerns leadership style. Early social conditioning dissuades girls from being assertive or domineering. Subtle cues over a woman's lifetime reinforce behaviours that are collaborative, caring and win-win in nature. These behaviours are not associated with the more typical masculine leadership seen in many senior roles. Research indicates

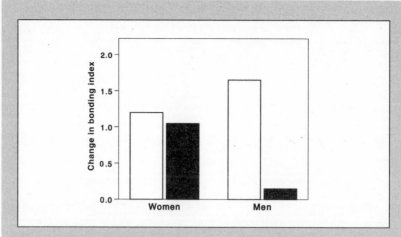

How We Maintain Friendships

Figure 5.3. Men and women differ in the effectiveness of activity-based interactions (white bars) and conversation-based interactions (black bars) in maintaining the emotional quality of a friendship over time. Conversation plays a more important role in women's relationships, whereas men's are much more activity-based. Source: Roberts & Dunbar (2015)[22]

that when dealing with conflict at work, women often use coping strategies that are focused on collaborating with others, rather than directly engaging in the conflict. However, these strategies may inadvertently negatively impact on career progression causing women to remain "behind the scenes".'[23] The desire to avoid conflict may be partially explained by the fact that the ability to be decisive and make tough decisions is sometimes seen to be at odds with a more feminine approach to leadership. It is a double bind for women, as research shows that men's likeability is positively correlated with success, whereas for women it is hard to be seen as both competent and likeable at the same time.[24] In short, women suffer a 'likeability penalty' in roles traditionally associated with men.

In the interests of balance, it is perhaps as well to remember that gender discrimination is not always one way. A man's salary, for example, exhibits a strong correlation with how tall he is – a factor that doesn't affect women's salaries at all.[25] Men's chances of promotion in many walks of life are greater if they are above average stature for the community.[26] Being tall (though not *excessively* tall) has a dramatic effect on many aspects of men's success in life – including their likelihood of marrying and even of having children.[27] In some cases, these apparent biases may actually reflect selection for correlated traits that are genuinely important. One UK study, for example, found that, while there was a physical attractiveness premium worth 5–10 per cent of salary for both genders, the male stature effect identified in the data was not entirely due to discrimination or subconscious bias but was actually indirect selection for cognitive abilities.[28] The correlation between two variables like stature and cognitive ability may not be hard and fast, but it may be good enough for selection on these secondary traits to have worked in the past and so become part of our conventional biases. The lesson here is that while we surely want to minimise unconscious biases, we should beware of adopting a naïvely superficial approach.

That said, creating an environment where people will listen to others with equal attention requires conscious effort. One way, as leadership expert Jennifer Garvey Berger has pointed out, is to ensure that people feel that they are appreciated by whoever is leading the group or meeting. A good committee chair is someone who invites everyone to speak, listens patiently to what they have to say, and then draws their comments together to create a consensus so as to arrive at a decision. They don't simply impose their own view on everyone else. When it comes to balancing male and female voices, it may be worth taking a leaf out of the US Supreme Court's book. A 2017 study found that female judges were disproportionately likely to be interrupted by their male colleagues, and that as a result female justices were altering the traditional style of their discourse in order to reduce the extent to which they were dominated by men.[29] Subsequently, the rules were changed to ensure that everyone had a set time to put forward their argument, followed by a chance (in order of seniority) to put questions. Justice Sonia Sotomayor reported that these changes had 'enormous impact' not only for the female justices but also in stimulating senior judges who had previously remained silent to ask questions. It's not enough to have diversity in the workplace; it is also important to design rules and procedures that create an atmosphere where diverse voices can say what they want to say and are confident that they will be heard.

On the Oxford Strategic Leadership Programme, we create the right environment for facilitated conversations by restricting tutor groups to five or so members. To ensure that all voices are heard, we introduced a 'gossip' format, whereby each individual is given up to ten minutes to describe their main strategic challenge to the others in their group. When they have finished speaking, they are then asked to sit at the side of the room and listen to what others have to say in response, without being allowed to interrupt. This gives each individual the chance to say what they want to say (as in the Supreme Court example), and the other listeners in the group have the opportunity to talk freely among themselves about what they have heard as though the 'owner' of the challenge was not there. As they reflect on what they've heard, they enter into the mind of the individual, put themselves in their shoes, imagine what they would do in their place. They talk together about similar situations they have faced – all without the risk of the individual concerned, now at the side of the room, being able to interrupt with a 'but no . . .' or 'that won't work' or 'I could never try that' style of intervention that would normally crop up in a conversation. Such an approach allows ideas to develop and 'what ifs?' to be pursued much further than they might otherwise be. Unfiltered feedback from others who have really listened can be immensely valuable.

It's Not What You Say, It's How You Say It

In the 1970s, the linguist Albert Mehrabian[30] achieved some notoriety by suggesting that only about 7 per cent of the meaning of any spoken sentence is conveyed by the words; 38 per cent, he argued, comes from voice cues (how something is said), and 55 per cent from facial expressions and other gestures. The true percentages may not be as precise as he claimed, but he was surely correct in observing that we infer a great deal about the meaning of someone's utterance from the non-verbal signals that are wrapped around the words themselves – the tone of voice, the pitch and volume, the smiles or grimaces, the hand gestures, the way the speaker looks at you (or doesn't, as the case may be) (see p. 130). Conductor Peter Hanke can interpret elements of someone's leadership style from just one gesture when they are trying their hand at conducting on the OSLP course. Leaders are amazed that, without any briefing, he can tell whether they are micromanagers, control freaks, laissez-faire or details-orientated back at their desks – all through reading the movement of a hand. The medium is always the message.

We use non-verbal signals to great effect without even noticing. If I want you to like me, I will, during our conversation, naturally – and mostly unconsciously – start to mimic your habits of speech, your use of slang, intonation and phrasing, even your posture. If you cross your legs, I'll cross mine. If you laugh or smile, I'll laugh or smile. In linguistic circles, this is known as Convergence Theory, and it happens all the time without our even being aware of it.

However, as people make their way up the hierarchy of an organisation, this two-way aspect of mirroring can fall away. Using an 'episodic recall task', Adam Galinsky and his colleagues reported that 'a state of high social power reduces the tendency to take the perspective of others'.[31] Sukhvinder Obhi and Carl Michael Galang (neuroscientists at McMaster University in Ontario) make the point that 'social power can have profound effects on cognition and behaviour'.[32] The reason for this is that senior staff are often surrounded by more junior people who imitate them and don't have sufficient confidence or standing to challenge what they say. As a result, over time, bosses become less and less practised at the 'standing in the shoes of the other' mirroring behaviour that got (some of) them to the top. They literally become less capable of feeling how others feel.

Silent Talk

How do you tell the difference between 'That's **won**derful!' when the speaker thinks something is genuinely fantastic and the rather flat 'That's . . .wonder . . . ful' when they really mean the opposite, or a sarcastic 'That's won . . . **der**ful' when they were actually bored by what you said. The answer, of course, is through listening to the phrasing and the tone of voice: in this particular instance, the voice goes up on the 'won-' in the first case, stays flat in the second, and may well stress an unexpected syllable in the third.

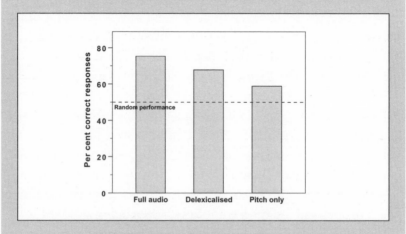

Judging Relationships from Tone of Voice

Figure 5.4. Percentage of instances in which subjects correctly identified whether the relationship between two speakers in a brief scrap of natural overheard conversation was positive or negative. Subjects listened to the same clips in the original full audio version or in versions where either the words had been digitally obscured (delexicalised) or converted into pure tones (pitch only). Had they been responding at random, they would have been correct only 50 per cent of the time (indicated by the dashed line). Source: Dunbar et al. (2022)[33]

A recent study of native English and Spanish speakers nicely demonstrates the vital importance of tone and inflection in conveying meaning.[34] Volunteers were asked to listen to brief recorded natural dialogues and then to assess the quality of the relationship between the speakers. When they heard the audio clip without seeing any visual cues, they correctly identified the relationship as being positive or negative 75 per cent of the time (Figure 5.4). When the words had been digitally obscured so that all they could really hear was tone and inflection ('delexicalised condition'), their accuracy rates dropped by only 5 per cent. They were still 60 per cent correct (significantly above chance still!) when the audio track was converted to pure tones so that all they heard were the shifts up and down in the pitch of the voice, with no other auditory cues such as emphasis and variations in loudness to provide guidance.

Tone, pacing, expression and emphasis are all vital to the communication of meaning, hence one reason why the written minutes of a meeting may differ from each individual's recollection of what was said. It is worth reflecting on this, given how much time we spend polishing the content of the speeches we give and how little time we spend on rehearsing the delivery.

To achieve the rebalancing necessary, various approaches are required. To begin with, it's essential to avoid a flat tone or an expressionless demeanour – if you are hard to 'read', that also means you are probably hard to trust. Hand gestures will help emphasise a point – though too many can prove distracting. Appropriate facial expressions will underscore or tone down the message we wish to convey, as will changes in the tone and pitch of the voice. Even the way we stand or walk speaks volumes. Former German Chancellor Angela Merkel was accomplished at navigating this minefield. The trademark diamond gesture that she made with her hands in front of her body came to be seen as signalling calm dependability; at the same time, her trouser suits largely exempted her from the tedious analysis of brand, spend and trend to which many women politicians and business leaders get subjected.

The importance of these kinds of signals was highlighted by our colleague, improvisation teacher and facilitator, Rob Poynton. He once worked for almost an hour with a business leader, focusing on the different ways in which she entered a room in order to help her to understand what tone she communicated each time. She had been unaware that her facial expression, her body language, the speed at which she entered the room, even how she closed the door, conveyed so much. He asked the tutor group (with her intrigued consent) to comment on what effect she was having on them each time she entered. She was amazed that she could so strongly communicate impatience or self-absorption (for example) simply by the way she walked into a room. She had absolutely no idea that she could be 'read' so easily. Rob didn't teach her to act or to put on a false face, but just to be more conscious and mindful of what she was 'saying' before she even opened her mouth – and to understand better what others were experiencing when she appeared.

Another CEO from Pakistan that we spoke to invited his teenage daughter to spend a day with him at work on 'Take Your Daughter to Work Day'. Once they had walked through the building to his office, he invited her to reflect on what she had seen. He expected her to talk about the building or the scale of operations but instead she said, 'You seemed so arrogant, Dad, when you came into work, so unfriendly.' He was shocked at her response, as he had honestly felt he was greeting everyone as he walked through the building in an approachable and easy-going way. He never came into work without thinking of her response again.

The Power of Storytelling

As we remarked in Chapter Three, stories, especially foundation stories, are the underpinning of successful communities – and organisations are no exception. How a story is presented, however, is as important as the story itself. Foundation stories are like a totem pole at the centre of the village – a focal point around which everyone can gather, an icon that summarises our beliefs and commitments. Having the right story plays a crucial role in how well bonded the organisation is. No foundation story, no community.'

All too often, introductory talks are presented as lectures, replete with PowerPoint slides of production and sales statistics. But a lecture or a briefing is a one-way form of communication. Storytelling, by contrast, is inclusive. It requires the listener to interpret what they're being told: it allows them to add in something of themselves, particularly if the story has an emotional hook. A good story is remade in the ear of the recipient and renewed in the mouth of the subsequent teller. At the same time, it is a powerful way to get a message across, because narrative is how we humans make sense of things and how we relate to one another. The world of PowerPoint, strategy documents and organisation charts lacks this power. As Associate Professor Piers Ibbotson observes, 'Narrative and metaphor are different to this 2D world. They take things into 3D. Metaphors and similes require interpretation: they assume the relation of things to one another – "he's as sharp as a knife", "running as fast as the wind". They hook the teller and the listener together in a participatory act, just as they link ideas.'

Performance coach and author of *Belonging: The Ancient Code of Togetherness*, Owen Eastwood uses stories to help build or reinforce identity. In order to bring the full richness of the British Olympic team together, for example, he shared stories of previous competitors who had diverse backgrounds and life experiences. One story was of Charlotte Cooper, the first woman – who happened to be deaf – to win two Olympic gold medals in tennis in 1900. Another was of Harry Edward, the first Black British Olympian in 1920. As Owen puts it, 'To form a strong team, everyone needs a sense of belonging, to be able to see mental pictures of what we are trying to do together, to be part of a shared story that has a foundation, to see that they have "ancestors" that they can relate to.'

For his part, Dave Snowden, founder of the Cynefin Company, uses stories in a different way, to help people think about the future. 'There is a danger in relying on numbers disconnected from people and context – big data can lead you to think that correlation is causation,' he argues. 'A reliance on big behavioural datasets can instantiate prejudice, it can cluster it.' Many organisations crunch individual insights into research findings. But at the Cynefin Company verbatim interviews are turned into micro-narratives. 'We get people to describe the present and then look for adjacent possibles by asking them to interpret their own stories – what is probable, possible, plausible?' It's something that children do naturally (interestingly, both Snowden and Kim Howard at South Africa's First Rand Group have worked with children as ethnographers). Kim Howard describes her reasoning in the following way: 'Before puberty the brain has most plasticity – you don't see racial prejudice at that age, for example. Children tend to record most closely what they actually hear.' They learn a sequence of events (and so can, for example, reconstruct exactly what sequence of buttons they pressed on the TV remote control), whereas adults convert what they see and do into general principles (and then later try to reconstruct what happened from these principles – which is why witnesses in court so often disagree about what actually happened[35]). Recovering a child's view of the world, therefore, can be very beneficial. What an older person can productively bring to bear is experience and a memory of what has happened in the past, hence the reason why, in hunter-gatherer societies, the older members become the village 'elders': they are respected for a wisdom and insight that draws on experience and memory of the past.

Summary

- Conversations are the foundation of effective decision-making, but too often we pay too little attention to how best to conduct them.
- Language is all around us and structures our world. It is a vital tool for establishing and maintaining social bonds. It is, however, inherently ambiguous, and we need to understand

how we might be misunderstood – or how we might misunderstand others. The message received rather than the message given should be the focus.

- We need to be aware that our limited mentalising powers impose strict constraints on the size of successful conversation groups. If the group is too big, we quickly become unable to cope with the complexity and nuance of the conversation or with people's motivations and thoughts.
- There are important gender differences in conversational style that cannot easily be circumvented and can create misunderstandings.
- Much of what we say is conveyed in non-verbal signals (tone, expression, emphasis etc) rather than by the words themselves. It is essential to pay as close attention to how a message is delivered as it is to the words.
- When it comes to connecting with an audience, stories can prove a very powerful tool. They allow for emotional connection, and create synchrony between teller and listener.
- Listening is an underrated, and underpractised, leadership skill.

6.

The Size of Trust

''Tis a kind of good deed to say well,
And yet words are no deeds.'

William Shakespeare and John Fletcher[1]

In one of his TED talks, Airbnb founder Joe Gebbia conducts an experiment with a live audience.[2] 'Take out your phone,' he tells them. 'Unlock it now and hand it to the person sitting on your left, whether you know them or not.' There is a moment of nervous laughter in the audience, a kind of contained panic. What do I do? Do I just give my neighbour my phone? Or do I wait for them to do something first? Gebbia uses that moment of uncertainty and panic to explore what trust means – and what it feels like.

Trust is based on the simple premise that what is promised is what will be delivered. If that transaction is not enacted in full, and we cease to believe what other people tell us, personal relationships are undermined, groups disintegrate, and society as a whole runs the risk of losing the glue that holds it together.

Trust maps very closely to the Dunbar Graph (Figure 2.3). It operates most naturally within a tribe of around 1,500 people. These individuals hold certain values, certain ways of thinking about the world, in common. They share a similar sense of obligation. Knowing that someone is a member of the tribe is generally sufficient evidence to trust them as individuals – if not on a lay-down-your-life-on-my-behalf basis, at least up to the point of helping them out or giving them shelter when they need it. As we saw in Chapter Three, knowing who a member of the tribe is, and hence that we can trust them, relies on cues of tribe membership: shared values, views, history, and so on.

The Amsterdam diamond market – by far the oldest and most important in the world – is the perfect example of a community sustained by trust. Here, dealers hand over millions of dollars' worth of diamonds to prospective buyers on the basis of a handshake. But then, this market is very, very small and *very* select, comprising mere dozens rather than thousands of individuals. Buyers and dealers all know each other personally and have done so for most of their professional lives. A buyer would no more fail to pay (or return the diamonds if they didn't want them) than stop breathing. It's an old-fashioned world in which a dealer's word really is their bond – and has to be, because anyone who breaks the rules will no longer be welcome.

Most large groups – and certainly many organisations – fail to build these bonds. This failure has been aggravated in a post-pandemic world where the form of work itself has changed. In the pre-pandemic world, bonding was a product of daily face-to-face contact and being present when working on projects and in teams. This 'accidental' bonding in turn led to trust being built, if rather haphazardly. In a world of remote working, by contrast, where colleagues are often physically isolated from one another, such bonding does not take place and, as a result, trust is unlikely to build up.

Groups and organisations where the personal element is downplayed often suffer what amounts to a crisis of faith. Sometimes this happens spontaneously – simply because, once a community reaches a certain size, people no longer know all the other members of the community and consequently lose a sense of obligation towards them. It's the difference between the small village where no one feels the need to lock their doors and the anonymous sink estate in a large city where everyone lives in fear of being mugged or burgled. Sometimes loss of faith is a direct consequence of well-meaning but misconceived organisational attempts to create efficiency, usually involving a focus on process rather than people. In contrast, organisations that are designed to encourage bonding end up reaping all the benefits of building trust, namely the enhancement of employee cooperation, knowledge-sharing and problem-solving. And more trusting employees are more committed to their organisation and end up staying longer.[3]

Take, for example, the problems of trust within the UK's health system. Once upon a time, the local family doctor was, quite literally, the family doctor. She or he had probably seen generations of local families, if not exactly from cradle to grave, certainly through most of the decades of their lives. These doctors understood people's foibles and their particular health issues. In other words, they knew their patients as individuals. And if they didn't, the senior partner in the next-door consulting room almost certainly did. Their treatment decisions reflected that knowledge. The relationship between doctor and patient was close, and mutual trust flowed accordingly.

In recent decades, GP practices in Britain have been subject to a series of mergers, rationalisations, new policies and processes, many imposed from on high, all designed to make the GP service more efficient by allowing staff time to be used flexibly. The principle now seems to be: it doesn't really matter which doctor you see since the doctor's job is simply to act as a semi-automated gateway between your disease and the relevant cure (in the pharmacy or the hospital, as appropriate). Paul Gilbert in his book *The Compassionate Mind* describes this shift: 'General practitioners express the sadness at the erosion of "family" (i.e. relationship) medicine in favour of rapid body mechanic medicine where any doctor will do. The time to really listen and develop relationships with their patients is being pared away.'[4] The practical consequence has been a significant erosion of trust on the part of the patients. The sense that a doctor doesn't know you as an individual, the disconcerting fact that they may have to spend the first five minutes of the ten allocated for your appointment skimming through your medical history on a computer screen (a process that itself can undermine your faith in their expertise), only serves to diminish your trust in them.

For those focused on efficiency, this turn of events may seem, at worst, regrettable but necessary. However, research suggests that such loss of trust has a direct and adverse effect on people's health. According to a 2018 study of data from nine countries, led by Sir Denis Pereira Gray and published in the *British Medical Journal*, continuity of care ensures, among other things, that patients are more likely to follow their doctor's advice and adopt the therapies recommended to them.[5] The trust such continuity engenders is also beneficial at a psychological level: as Professor Chris Salisbury of Bristol University explains: 'When people are ill, it is very worrying; having someone whom you can trust that you can talk to about it is really important.' The *British Medical Journal* study concluded that such relationships actually save lives.

In this chapter, we want to focus on why trust is so often lost, and how to regain and build it.

The Dark Triad and the Breakdown of Trust

It seems almost a cliché to say that trust is hard-won, and only too easily lost. But it happens to be true. As Owen Eastwood observes, 'Trust is a calculation we make to predict the reliability of other people. It's never permanent, never fixed and can be destroyed in a moment.' If a young player who has made a mistake sees their coach despairingly put his head in his hands, they may feel they can never trust him again to be supportive. More generally, a careless action, a gesture of frustration or ill-chosen word can undo hard-won trust in a moment.

We can all bring about a loss of trust through a carelessly expressed thought or action, but certain individuals can make a profession out of such behaviour. These fall into three personality types known as the Dark Triad that are particularly prone to undermining trust: narcissism, Machiavellianism and psychopathy. They overlap to an extent, in part because they all involve people who act only in their own interests, sometimes maliciously. People who score high on these traits are more likely to cause distress to others, more likely to be problematic in an organisational setting, and also more likely to commit crime. All can be deeply disruptive.

Narcissism is perhaps the least harmful of the three traits. It is characterised by grandiosity, egotism, self-pride and a lack of empathy. Narcissists are so wrapped up in themselves that they live in a permanent bubble. So long as they stay there, they don't create much trouble. But their self-belief can result in their rising to the top, not least because we tend to find self-confidence charismatic. Charismatic people attract willing followers. Quite why they should attract followers so readily is not really clear, but, in religious contexts at least, they tend to be convinced that they have discovered some novel universal truth, and their confidence then seems to inspire others to believe in them.[6]

The Machiavellian personality is very different. As the name implies, someone who is Machiavellian is scheming and manipulative – the traits recommended by the Renaissance Italian political philosopher Niccolò Machiavelli as ideal for the aspiring prince. Such people tend to be characterised by a certain amorality and a lack of interest in the consequences of their actions. They can often be cynical, unprincipled and cold. So far as they are concerned, the end justifies the means. Theirs is a strategy largely based on selfish, short-term interests and an attitude characterised by 'let the future worry about itself'. Machiavellians are likely to behave in a considered and deliberate way, with a strategy carefully planned to achieve their objective.

Psychopathy represents the extreme of anti-social behaviour. Psychopaths are characterised by impulsivity, callousness and remorselessness, traits that often start to form very early in their lives (psychopaths will often have had run-ins with the law as children). They are not afraid to use violence when it suits them, in part because they themselves are not afraid of getting hurt. They are typically poor at inhibiting their behaviour, instead pursuing their self-interest – if necessary at the expense of everybody else. And because they are good at empathising without sympathising, they know exactly how their actions will frighten or terrorise others. They tend, therefore, to be bullies.

The Dark Triad is likely to be associated with toxic leadership, but it can manifest itself at any level of an organisation. We are all familiar with those who use soft manipulation to achieve their ends (narcissists), or are both flexible and scheming (Machiavellians) or use hardball tactics (psychopaths). In his book *Personality and the Fate of Organizations*,[7] Robert Hogan observes that all three personality types are ruthlessly focused on self-advancement, but not necessarily on getting along with their colleagues. They have the power to get things done. Some will possess sufficient charm at least to rub along with others. Sometimes their ruthlessness is mistaken for efficiency. But while the more harmful will eventually fall from grace because of the conflicts they cause, the damage they inflict in the meantime can be lasting, particularly in large organisations where they can make their way up the hierarchy without their baleful impact being fully noticed or understood – or perhaps encouraged because they are seen as successful 'go-getters'. An organisation can survive the presence of members who display narcissism, Machiavellianism or psychopathy provided that there are not too many of them. But, if the social contract between people is undermined or challenged too much by these traits, the organisation will collapse and cooperation will die.

There is a general sense in which our tendency to trust those who seem convincing can lead us into trouble. Skilled operators can exploit this to their advantage, obscuring their true message by dressing it up in elaborate language or meaningless psychobabble. Professor of Psychology Cecilia Heyes explains why people can be taken in by leaders who lie: 'They tell very simple stories . . . most of us are drawn to simplicity. Most people like things to be straightforward and easy. When things are easy to digest or absorb, then most people assume that what they are hearing must be true.' It is the reason why charismatic individuals and faith healers attract followings: we believe them because they are very convincing and appear to have esoteric knowledge beyond our grasp.[8] By the same token, give a product an aura of mystery or sprinkle a few terms that sound scientific around it, and people will be convinced and buy it.

Three Easy Steps for Destroying Trust

Whether it be romantic relationships, friendships or organisations, a breakdown in trust is invariably the major cause of relationships ending. It can take a long time to earn trust, but trust can be destroyed overnight by a single thoughtless act. In general, however, the breakdown in trust tends to be cumulative over a period of time until finally one person cracks and terminates the relationship.

In part, that's because trust forms the bedrock of social life: we have to assume that others are trustworthy, otherwise neither social life nor business enterprise would be possible. After all, as Rachel Botsman, Trust Fellow at Oxford's Saïd Business School, puts it, trust is 'a confident relationship with the unknown'. Once trust breaks down, however, it is often terminal: the closer and more trusting the relationship, the more difficult the loss of trust is to repair.

As a rule, the breakdown of trust involves one of three factors:

- Loss of any sense of obligation between individuals or between individuals and organisations. When there is no sense of obligation or connection, there is no compelling reason for people to behave in a trustworthy way. This is especially likely to be the case in overly large organisations where relational ties are non-existent and there is no sense of belonging or shared purpose.
- Freeriders. Communities can cope with a few people who don't pull their weight, but no community can cope with large numbers who abuse the system. There is a natural tendency for the community to fragment into smaller groups within which the members do trust each other.
- Rule-breaking and disregard for societal norms. Individuals or organisations that don't adhere to accepted social norms and codes can be seen as untrustworthy and can erode trust in the institutions and norms themselves.

Another category of untrustworthy person merits discussion here: the freerider or freeloader – the person who is happy to enjoy the benefits of being in a social group or organisation (including, in the latter case, the pay cheque), but can't be bothered to pay their share of the costs or fulfil their side of the contract. Since the freerider is not a fixed personality type in the same way that, say, a Machiavellian is, they can sometimes be deterred from bad behaviour by relatively simple psychology. Back in 2006, for example, researchers at Newcastle University found that even a hint that freeriding might be noticed by others was sufficient to prevent it.[9] Their experiment involved pinning up a life-size photograph of a pair of staring eyes above the honesty box by the coffee machine and alternating it every other week with a photograph of flowers. What they were astonished to find was that people were nearly three times more likely to pay for their drinks when they subliminally felt they were being watched than when they weren't. It's for this reason that many police forces now place posters of eyes above the cycle racks outside city centre premises in order to reduce the rate of thefts.

But within large, more anonymous organisations, freeriding can become the disruptive norm and take over the institutional culture (Figure 6.1). Once this happens, people draw in their horns and retreat to the place where they feel safe to the point where networks become fragmented (Figure 6.2). Internal silos spring up ('It's Department X, yet again. They're always taking long lunch breaks while we work ourselves into the ground to get everything done on time'). Requests for help are turned down ('You sort out your own inefficiencies'). Cooperation across departments fragments ('We've got quite enough to do without having to play catch-up for you lot!'). It's precisely the kind of dysfunctionality that Bill Gore sought to avoid when he was setting up his new company.

Computer modelling suggests that it doesn't take many freeriders in a system to cause a cooperative community to collapse (Figure 6.2). We don't really know how many people naturally behave as freeriders, but we can gain some idea by looking at data on the frequency of habitual liars, a form of behaviour that underlies one kind

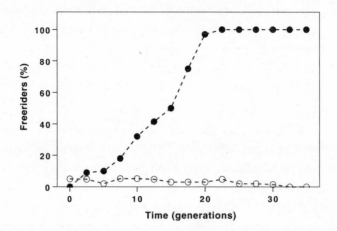

The Tendency to Freeride

Figure 6.1. The results of a computer simulation designed to explore the evolution of communities of cooperators who are invaded at generation 0 by a very small number of freeriders who cheat the socially agreed community rules. When the population consists of naïve cooperators who are easily exploited and have no mechanisms for detecting and managing freeriders (filled symbols), the freeriders very quickly take over because cooperators are disadvantaged and quickly bred out of the population: after just twenty generations, the population consists only of freeriders. However, when cooperators have strategies that allow them to detect and neutralise freeriders (unfilled symbols), freeriders find it difficult to get a foothold and remain at very low frequency. Source: Nettle & Dunbar (1997)[10]

of freerider in our everyday social world. Surveys in the US suggest that a quarter of all lies are told by just 1 per cent of the population.[11] You might think that is comfortingly low and probably manageable. However, as Figure 6.1 reminds us, that 1 per cent can, if left uncontrolled, very quickly take over the population.

This tendency for networks to contract when trust is lost can be found at institutional level as well as the personal level. Whenever financial shocks hit the banking sector, default cascades sweep through the banking network, causing institutions to lose trust in lending to all but their historically most reliable trading partners.[12] Trading decisions become more conservative and lending networks

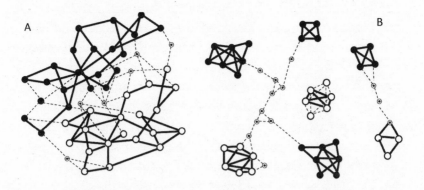

Contracting Networks

Figure 6.2. The effect of habitual liars on network structure, based on a computer simulation of an artificial community. Circles represent individuals, and social contacts between them are represented by the lines. (a) Network structure of a community when all members act honestly. Although there are clearly two sub-communities (the white and black circles), they are well connected via undecided individuals (small circles with central dots) who act as bridges that allow information to flow easily between the two communities. (b) When there are habitual, self-serving liars present, the community fragments into smaller clusters whose interconnections are much reduced. Redrawn from Iñiguez et al. (2014)[13]

contract in ways very reminiscent of social networks collapsing when trust fails.[14]

Managing Trust

A common strategy to tackle issues of trust and honesty is to produce top-down rules and regulations. Its desirability and effectiveness, however, is questionable. Seeking to bring the 1–2 per cent of people who don't behave honestly to heel means imposing restrictions on the remaining 98 per cent. Since the rule breakers will probably ignore the rules anyway, it effectively imposes a double penalty on the well behaved since they will be expected to obey constraints that weren't intended for them and that may be irksome.

Treating people as though they lack the honesty / common sense / competence to behave with integrity – or are incapable of solving a problem when it comes across their desk – is an unsatisfactory approach that smacks of some of the outmoded approaches to management that dominated the 1960s in particular. In the 1950s, Douglas McGregor, then a professor at MIT's Sloan School of Management, argued that 'managerial behavior is a direct reflection of the manager's assumptions about human nature'. He coined the term 'Theory X / Theory Y' to reflect what he saw as two main managerial styles.[15] The 'Theory X' way of looking at the world assumes that people are entirely motivated by self-interest, that they need rewards and punishments to induce them to conform to management's expectations, and that to manage this all actions should be traceable to the individual responsible. Implicitly built into this model is a blame culture that discourages initiative and creativity because it suggests that a mistake can cost a person their job. Theory Y, by contrast, assumes that people are, for the most part, motivated, responsible and fundamentally purposeful, and that confident, instinctive decision-making can come from lived experience. At best, the Theory X approach results in an organisation bumping along in middle gear. At worst, it encourages a kind of 'jobsworth' mindset that can seriously impede innovation. The Theory Y approach allows the 98 per cent the flexibility to find their own local solutions to particular problems and challenges, but it leaves an organisation open to abuses by the 2 per cent who are freeriders. Gore is a company that exhibits Theory Y in practice.

Debra France, retired global leader of learning and development at Gore, reflects: 'We believe that each individual is naturally motivated; they work for salary *and* significance. Most people come to work to contribute something valuable if you don't make it difficult for them to do so. When we are at our best, we create our organizational practices to support them to do what they naturally strive to do. There are some people who are driven by other motivations that are not to do their best and to contribute and collaborate with others. We don't design our organizational practices to constrain the

2 percent of the people who are selfish. We design them for the vast majority who show up to contribute something valuable and to collaborate enthusiastically and sincerely.'

Much of what we do as humans is, in fact, naturally designed to try to minimise the destructive impact of freeriders (Figure 6.1). This includes a particular sensitivity to individuals who break the rules or exploit our trust.[16] The outcry against Volkswagen in 2015 during the scandal over faked emissions results was as heated as it was precisely because the company was seen not to have been playing the game. It was cheating its competitors, its customers – who were being misled – and the regulators by asserting that its vehicle emissions met US standards when in fact they had been fitted with a 'defeat device' that cheated the system. It's worth noting that this situation came about because – in CEO Hans Dieter Pötsch's own words – there had been a history of corporate tolerance of rule-breaking. Pötsch saw the main task of the company in the wake of the scandal as being to 'rebuild trust'.[17]

One weapon we can use to defeat potentially destructive rule breakers in everyday social contexts is gossip. It's something the !Kung San hunter-gatherers of southern Africa – who are among the most egalitarian people in the world – use with particular effect. So important is a sense of equality to the smooth functioning of their society that they are highly critical of any who put themselves on a pedestal or who fail to share the spoils of a successful hunt in the way custom requires. Much of this criticism, certainly in the case of milder infringements, takes the form of joking, gossip, pantomime or put-downs. Though more serious cases might escalate into threats to withdraw cooperation, more overt criticism and even ostracism, by far the best means of dealing with breaches of the accepted code of practice is humour. Organisations where laughter is rarely heard, where gentle teasing is frowned upon or there is no time for gossip around the water cooler, lack those important self-regulating communal practices where people are brought down to size.

Such social strategies work best, of course, when the community is small and people know each other personally: in such contexts, people are always more willing to accept criticism than they would be from strangers, or even members of another group. When someone outside our social circle criticises us, we respond with anger and defensiveness – a reminder that, however desirable direct criticism can be to head off future trouble, it risks an adverse response if it comes from strangers. In fact, when the late Marcial Losada and Emily Heaphy, then both at the University of Michigan Business School, explored the practices of sixty strategic business teams, they found that the ratio of criticism to praise was 1:5 in the highest-performing teams, 1:2 in the middle rankers and 3:1 in the lowest-performing teams.[18] Since, according to Gallup, one of the biggest reasons for employees to leave jobs is lack of appreciation and recognition, this research has important implications for the framing of formal feed-back in teams – hence the tension-reducing informal role that teasing and gossip play in regulating behaviour in social systems. Again, scale plays a part – behaviour that may be experienced as gentle teasing in a small group where there is already a degree of trust may seem like bullying or worse in larger-scale, more anonymous settings.

Such human-scale interventions to counterbalance freeriders are infinitely preferable to the top-down Theory X approach. It's also worth noting that because Theory X, by its very nature, is distrust-ing of individuals, it can have a counterproductive effect regardless of the honesty or otherwise of the people it seeks to control. The recent history of the UK's National Health Service comes to mind in this context. The past few years have witnessed a convergence of pressures on it: increased demand due to a rapidly growing popula-tion, spiralling costs due to the fact that the population is an ageing one and therefore requires more care, budgetary restrictions, and a rise in malpractice cases brought against it (itself a reflection of declining trust). The central management's response to these press-ures has invariably been to develop a Theory X culture of meas-urement, targets and competition. Staff are not trusted to regulate themselves, to make their own medical judgements or decide how wards and beds are managed. Instead they are bound by rules, clini-cal pathways and bureaucracy.

No doubt, those responsible for these changes would argue that they have made the NHS more efficient. But the negative effect has been profound.[19] The much-loved local hospital, self-contained and able to determine how it ran itself, has now become a mere cog in an enormous bureaucratic machine. Management has become increasingly remote, hidden away in the administrative block of the hospital and in various higher-echelon committees and boards elsewhere. Medical staff have had their clinical judgement removed from them by an insistence that they must follow care pathways and clinical protocols dreamed up in far-away offices by people who don't have to work at the coalface of day-to-day patient care. As a result, even senior clinical staff have felt a growing sense of alienation and dissatisfaction, not to say frustration at not being able to adapt care pathways to suit the particular, unique conditions of individual patients. Many staff from cleaners to consultants feel they no longer work for a high-trust organisation in which individual pride in 'their' hospital gave purpose to work. Instead, they perceive themselves as working in a low-trust organisation, full of inefficiencies, ill-thought-out contracts and poorly articulated labour relations.

Trust has been undermined – and not just among staff. This bureaucratic approach to healthcare also damages the intimacy that used to exist between medic and patient that would, in the normal run of events, create a flow of endorphins that both make people feel happier and more engaged with life *and* increase the speed of recovery by ramping up the body's immune system. It's a sobering example of how a change made in the interests of efficiency, cost-saving and management under conditions of ever-exploding scale can have counterproductive consequences for the key outcomes that are at the heart of the organisation's very purpose. This is the Law of Unintended Consequences writ large in what is surely the most personally relevant and important context possible.

It doesn't have to be like this. There are high-trust systems in the health sector that work in entirely different ways. The CEO and author Margaret Heffernan[20] describes how Jos de Blok, the founder and CEO of the Dutch homecare nursing company Buurtzorg, noticed that, within the Dutch homecare system, the day-to-day paperwork the nurses needed to do was predictable and routine and that technology could be employed to streamline much of it. But he was also aware that since every patient is different, their human needs can't be predicted. He therefore carried out an experiment where nurses were able to decide how to deal with their patients within a strong support system. For example nurses kept and shared their records of visits, what happened, what decisions were made – in order that anyone in the team might pick up if that nurse were away or ill. This is also what allowed the system to be audited and, subsequently, automated. And nurses also worked in teams of ten. When it came to decisions about when to see patients, for how long and how often and deciding on the appropriate treatment, all nurses were told to use their judgement. But being in a team meant that they had colleagues with whom to confer, discuss, share knowledge and experience. What he found was that when care operated in this way – a combination of support and trust – patients got better in half the time and costs fell by a third – a huge gain very easily won.

Earning Trust

If there are strategies we can call on to bring those who threaten to undermine trust back into line, there are also ones we can use to build it before things get to that state.

Consistency

When it comes to creating and reinforcing trust, consistency is an underrated trait. It can seem boring. But just as good parents behave consistently to their children, so good leaders behave in a consistent, reliable way towards those who follow them. It's a far more effect-ive approach than occasional bursts of brilliance alternating with fireworks. Conductor and musician Peter Hanke, in his training of young conductors, describes how essential a trait this is for people who seek to lead groups of musicians. Consistency from the conductor gives the musicians a reliable framework within which they can express their individual talents. Owen Eastwood argues: 'Consistency from a leader creates the space within which others can show their promise – it derives from sensitivity, connection, trustworthiness, and is, crucially, understandable to everyone.'

Openness and Humility

'Sometimes, as leaders, it is really hard to be vulnerable – most leaders seem to demand rather than engender trust,' says New Zealand Regional Public Service Commissioner Ezra Schuster. 'I think we need to flip that dynamic,' he adds. Ezra's view is that collective strength comes from collective vulnerability – that organisations work best when people feel comfortable to say not just what they know, but what they don't know. In the leadership realm we have found that this give and take is often in the form of disclosure, sharing, asking for help and listening. Paolo Lanzarotti describes his real work as a CEO as 'guiding, asking and listening'. The leadership lesson? The best leaders are the most comfortable in displaying this vulnerability, sincerely and actively reaching out and asking for help . . . and then really listening. An incident from the life of the Nobel Laureate physicist Richard Feynman perfectly exemplifies this. He once recounted how, when he was on the committee overseeing the repair of the Three Mile Island nuclear power station that had experienced a partial meltdown and serious radioactive leak in 1979, he felt hopelessly confused by the circuit diagrams, full of complex fail-safes and control loops, produced by the engineers. They meant absolutely nothing to him. So, he innocently placed a finger on a completely random point on the diagram and asked, 'What happens if this fails?' The engineers went into a long, agitated huddle in the corner. Eventually, they came back and ruefully admitted that the whole power station would probably blow up.[21] The fault was duly rectified. As Feynman often observed: there is no such thing as a stupid question. You just need to be prepared to ask it and rely on others to provide the answer. And, of course, those who listen need the humility to take the point being made seriously rather than defensively. By the same token, the kinds of joking remonstrations that the !Kung San use to bring social rule breakers back into line that we discussed earlier depend on the recipients taking the criticism in a spirit of humility and good faith. It is a trait we should all aim to cultivate.

Proven Integrity and Shared Ethos

Shared values are a major source of trust. Words that equal deeds, plain dealing, norms based upon principles and fairness – all earn huge trust dividends. A report in the *Harvard Business Review* found that people at high-trust companies report 74 per cent less stress, 106 per cent more energy at work, 50 per cent higher productivity, 13 per cent fewer sick days, 76 per cent more engagement, 29 per cent more satisfaction with their lives and 40 per cent less burnout than in those companies where trust is low – an extraordinary productivity dividend.[22] Reflecting on the history of Mars (in 2020 rated the sixth best company to work for by *Fortune*), Jay Jakub observes how important a shared ethos is there: 'In the 1930s, when Forrest Mars Senior went to the UK and set up the Mars UK business, seven of the top ten chocolate companies in the world were UK companies. These companies were largely owned and operated by Quakers, whose success in part came from the belief that unlike chocolate company owners before them they could be trusted not to adulterate the ingredients of chocolate to get more profits. Forrest Senior was very likely influenced by this Quaker-inspired approach in the industry, hence, "Quality" became the first of the Mars five core principles along with Responsibility, Mutuality, Efficiency and Freedom.'

Airbnb have pursued a policy of 'designing for disclosure' to fast-track a sense of trust between host and guest. They realised that their business model would only work if they were able to overcome the sense of 'stranger danger' that those thinking of renting someone else's flat or house might naturally feel. Airbnb learned that some openness from the host creates a greater sense of trust from the visitor. They therefore designed a website that would encourage people to share information about themselves ('I love modern art') without falling into the trap of oversharing ('Now let me tell you about my parents-in-law . . .'). The balance they achieved by ensuring sufficient disclosure to allay 'stranger danger' fears created the trust that in turn brought business success. As one study put it, 'Unlike other more traditional accommodation providers, Airbnb offers more power to hosts in managing their bookings and deciding which guests to accept. Trust stands at the center of a host's decision to grant a guest permission to stay in their house or room.'[23]

Risk-Taking and Reciprocity

Trusting someone inevitably involves taking risks. I will do something for you in the expectation that you will pay me back eventually – but there is always the danger that you might forget to do so or might simply opt to exploit me. Some brands, however, are prepared to take such risks, utilising the display of what may prove to be unreciprocated good faith to develop consumer loyalty. UK Retailer Marks and Spencer has in the past trusted customers to bring unwanted products back without a receipt – famously to the point of being willing, without so much as a quibble, to exchange products even after they had obviously been worn. Of course, such goodwill was open to abuse, but it also inspired repeat business that outweighed the impact of the occasional instances when customers abused the company's trust. Mattress companies that promise to take back a mattress anytime within the first 100 days if it proves unsatisfactory likewise know that this display of trust is a two-way street. It gives potential purchasers the confidence to go ahead with a big-ticket item. It brings the company additional business that outweighs the fact that they will occasionally have to live up to their promise.

The Parameters of Trust

Trust involves a number of dimensions or components:

Consistency in Behaviour. *We are more likely to believe that a person, group, organisation or institution is trustworthy if their behaviour in the past reinforces this view.*

Obligation and Reciprocity. *Perhaps the single most important dimension of trust is a sense of obligation and reciprocity. 'I know that you will fulfil your obligations towards me just as I will fulfil mine towards you. We won't let each other down.'*

Common Ground and a Shared Ethos. *Trust is fast-tracked with people who share at least some of the Seven Pillars of Friendship (see p. 59). The more Pillars we share with someone, the more we are likely to trust each other. In effect, the Seven Pillars and other forms of homophily provide a quick guide to trustworthiness that circumvents the need to spend many weeks and months watching how you behave.*

Matching Words with Deeds. *Words can be blunt instruments when it comes to trust, especially when words and deeds don't match. Trust is built when there is evidence over time that you mean what you say. Turning out to have been right also earns confidence: confidence in someone's ability to predict the future or make it happen invariably earns trust.*

Humility and 'the Common Touch'. *Disclosing information freely or revealing one's hand can lead to a greater sense of trust. This 'cards on the table' approach can be effective either verbally or symbolically. Knowing when and how to seek advice engenders trust. It helps create a sense of belonging.*

Confidence. *Quiet confidence will always create a sense of trust. Over-confidence and self-assertiveness will often have the opposite effect.*

Trust from Scratch

The Oxford Strategic Leadership Programme is held at the Egrove Park campus of the Saïd Business School on the outskirts of the city of Oxford. The building is a modernist, concrete building – not exactly the Oxford of the imagination with its dreaming spires. Inside, as the programme begins (as it always does, on a Sunday afternoon) are the waiting participants, often jet-lagged and exhausted from scrambling to get away from their huge jobs for a week, missing weekend time with families who have been left in various corners of the world. There's a palpable sense of uncertainty in the room, a feeling that there must be better ways to spend a precious Sunday. People sit there with legs and arms crossed, their eyes cast down, not making contact with one another. On the face of it, it seems an inauspicious beginning.

As a team, we know we need to earn people's trust as quickly as possible. Aware that those who haven't visited Oxford before may assume that it is elitist and distant, we go out of our way to be the opposite. We learn delegates' names before they arrive (all tutors receive a photo list, descriptions and interview notes a week before the start of the programme). We make contact with them before they come – Tracey sending a personal welcoming note via LinkedIn, the tutors emailing their small groups individually to introduce themselves. The receptionists at the Business School are also given the photo list and so are able to greet participants by name as they arrive to meet the programme administrators waiting for them by the doors of the campus.

We begin as we mean to go on. We brief everyone involved in the delivery of the programme on campus, from the chef right through to the maintenance team, about the participants and the purpose of the week. Armed with this knowledge, they can act as extra pairs of eyes and ears for any signs of unhappiness, or any glitches that we might miss. One of the catering staff lent his belt to a participant who had forgotten his; one of the cleaners did the ironing for another person when he told her he'd been on international flights for the past month and hadn't been able to get home; the sommelier takes care to source wines and create menus from as many of the participants' home countries as he can; the gardener put a webcam feed up in the coffee area to show some chicks that had just hatched in a nest in the grounds. Everyone is focused on creating a sense of home, rather than institution.

As the programme starts, we seek to establish a tone that balances rigour with friendliness. We lay out very clear parameters and principles for the week but leave it to the various small groups involved to determine any 'rules' they may want for themselves (for example, choosing to respect the timings of the tutorials, no phones in sessions etc). We avoid jargon. The explicit ethos is collaborative, not competitive. The mode is mutual, reciprocal rather than broadcast. We know – and we say – that as faculty we have a whole lot to learn from every single person there. We set out to discover what that is.

We also deliberately create an early opportunity for storytelling. On the first day, we invite people to contribute to a 'Museum of Culture'. Each person brings an artefact from his or her culture, with a small handwritten description of its significance. These are displayed beautifully, as in a museum, on tables with red felt backdrops. Over a drink on the first evening, we look at the objects in this museum together. Each person has a chance to tell a story through the medium of their object about where they are from, describing the values of their culture, and its personal resonance. People also get the chance to listen to one another. Trust grows quicker, we have found, through this early disclosure. It's about making connections – finding and establishing the Seven Pillars.

We deliberately lower the risks for the participants through a manipulation of scale as the week progresses. We divide people into small Dunbar-sized groups whose composition has been carefully thought through beforehand, based on the upfront interviews. The groups are assembled not only for diversity of experience and background but also for personality type. These tutor groups meet on the first day in an exploratory way so that, from the get-go, everyone has at least five other people they know and can go and talk to.

We have developed a triage system for the first twenty-four hours or so. We keep an eagle eye out for indications of any unhappiness or any sign that an individual is hanging back on the periphery of the group. We meet as faculty regularly to discuss any early signs of problems, solitariness or mistrust. We may 'hand' participants over to one another to sit with at lunch, or chat with over coffee if we think a colleague is more suited to address an issue or a qualm – for example, if a particularly young leader is lacking in confidence, or someone who feels they have absented themselves from their business at a stressful moment. Addressing these issues directly early on helps to build the trust that oxygenates the learning.

Finally, faculty are chosen not only for their world-class expertise but also for the spirit in which they engage with the programme. They come as teachers and learners, committed to a reciprocal approach, bringing both questions and an eagerness to learn from leaders practising in the field. It is in this way that we deliberately go about constructing the shared pillars of friendship that allow trust to blossom in a way that lasts beyond the programme itself.

The lessons learned on this programme apply as much to the everyday running of committees and teams, or the induction of newcomers, as they do to the rather selective learning environment of our programme. As much as anything, they are the takeaway messages of the programme. They are the bedrock of trust.

Summary

- Trust acts as the lubricant of our social relationships, allowing us to build integrated networks both at the social and the business level.
- Friendship and business networks, as well as organisations, are social contracts held together by trust: we all agree to

abide by the unspoken rules of the game to behave honestly
and with due consideration.

- Trust, and the reputations that it gives rise to, build slowly
over time, but can be lost in an instant.
- In large groups of people, and in the absence of 'knowing'
each other, a strong sense of collective purpose and a feeling
of belonging can fast-track trust between people.
- In any social contract, there is always a strong temptation
for some individuals to act as freeriders – taking the benefits
offered by the community, but not paying all the costs.
- The double jeopardy imposed by freeriders on those who
abide by the rules of the game causes trust to be lost. As a
result, networks fragment as individuals (or businesses) seek
the shelter and security of those on whom they can feel they
can rely.
- Equally, trust should not be given away too easily. We are
seduced into placing trust in institutions, brands, technology
and data, none of which can be easily triangulated or
checked. Our pull towards simple stories can easily override
our judgement.

7.

Social Space, Social Time

'Life is probably round.'

Vincent van Gogh[1]

The extraordinary circular building designed by Herzog and de Meuron for the Blavatnik School of Government in Oxford was very much built to serve its purpose. The 'cathedral of learning', as the Royal Institute of British Architects (RIBA) described it, used the values of the School of Government as its design principles: transparency, openness and collaboration. 'It's about democracy so it's circular; political transparency, so it's glass; and Oxford, so there's stone' (as RIBA explained).[2] A very modern structure in a medieval city, it nonetheless acknowledges its environs, 'rhyming' and respecting the buildings around it through its use of stone. At the centre of the building is the Inamori Forum, a place for gathering and connection for students who come from every corner of the world.

Most of us don't have the luxury to commission a building to embody our purpose and values. We may take a floor of an existing office block, perhaps inheriting the layout from a previous tenant. Or we may simply make do with what's available – often, during the pandemic, the kitchen table or a spare bedroom. Wherever we work, our environments can either enable or diminish our ability to thrive. Strip lighting, lack of ventilation or access to green spaces, the constant whirr of machines, competing voices, hierarchical floor layouts, or the sheer daily ugliness of a poorly designed environment are some of the factors that can conspire to lower the human spirit, sap energy and create a sense of alienation. Alternatively, good design can mobilise our social brain by prioritising connection, belonging and learning, and by embodying the purpose, culture and values of the group of which we are a part.

In the previous chapters, we have argued that the world of work is a social world. Here, we focus on the work environment because this can have such a dramatic effect on the psychology and health of those who operate within it. A happy workforce is a healthy workforce because, as we saw in Chapter Three, your state of mind influences your physical as well as your psychological health. In very immediate and practical terms that means fewer days off work. There are many less obvious advantages and efficiencies too. Healthy, happy people are more focused on what needs to be done. They work more quickly. They are more willing to put in discretionary effort; they take fewer days off sick and are less likely to leave.

The Architecture of Alienation

One of Samantha's projects took her into London where she worked in an iconic building in the heart of the city. From the outside, it displayed all the power and authority conveyed by the stellar brand whose name was on the front. Inside was a different story: she felt trapped – imprisoned by the disconnect between the external view and the reality of life inside. There was a palpable gap between how it should have been (all that promise of modernity projected by glass, steel and chrome) and how it really was (constrained, staid, boring). The environment aroused a sense of rebellion and alienation, not only in her but in many who worked there – particularly, she noticed, the women.

Most towns and cities are planned and built by men with a generic (mainly male) user in mind. As the geographer Jane Darke has said, 'Our cities are patriarchy written in stone, brick, glass and concrete.'[3] There are exceptions. Many Scandinavian cities, for example, are designed to meet the broader needs of all citizens, including women and children. At night, women on board buses can ask to be dropped off at any point on the route, not just at designated stops, so that they do not have too far to walk to home and safety. In Barcelona, a group of urban designers, Punt 6, observed that the traditional town square, with its benches around the edge facing the middle, tends to get taken over by a single, dominant activity – usually football. Instead, they sought to reimagine it and found that if the space was divided up, and benches set out in different relationships to each other, then a range of interactions could take place, involving both genders and a wider range of different people.[4]

The fact remains, though, that while architects and planners generally, and rightly, place huge emphasis on physical and psychological safety and make at least a nod to inclusivity – following legal requirements for disabled ramps or ensuring the provision of changing mats in the loos – few stop to ask: how could our environment not only accommodate but also delight everyone? Most offices work according to norms set back in the 1960s when office workers were predominantly male. They therefore have a tendency to neglect what would best suit female members of staff. A 2015 study by Boris Kingma and Wouter van Marken Lichtenbelt has established, for example, that the average man likes his office temperature to be 21 degrees centigrade whereas females are more comfortable when it is set at 24 degrees.[5] In this era of flexible working, women need to be confident that there's a safe accessible entrance to the building at all times. Given the relative brevity of statutory maternity leave in many countries, they may also need somewhere where they can express milk (all too often they have to perch on the loos). Ignoring such requirements not only causes practical problems but reduces the capacity of the office to be an environment where everyone's requirements, moods and aspirations are catered for.

The modern office often fails more generally to meet the needs of those who people it. Before the invention of steel and concrete beams in the 1930s, buildings were conceived according to human proportions – measured in feet and made with hands. Expressions like 'a stone's throw away' or 'within earshot' linger on but with the advent of new technologies, the human relationship between builder and building and how we measure things has become less direct. Modern office buildings rarely display signs that someone has really cared about their fitness for human use. There is little sensitivity to form and material: no fingerprints left on the plaster or signatures carved in the wooden beams to remind people that humans were involved. Instead, many contemporary buildings are anonymous, with identikit layout and contents, and with little more thought given to their fitness for human comfort than to the average airport departure lounge. Functionality trumps aesthetics; the desire to impose order on disorderly humanity determines the layout. In the process any sense of individual identity and relationship is lost.

We somehow imagine that the buildings designed to be impressive, looming, powerful, tall and authoritative will persuade those who work within them to generate the same energy and impact. But the opposite seems to happen. The employees in those buildings often feel diminished and constrained – unable to live up to the shiny promises of a nowhere-in-particular skyscraper. Global architecture – that concocted recipe of glass, chrome and sameness that exists on a plane above the particular – merges one city into another, one building into another, and transforms an office that has personality into one that could be anyone's office. All are designed perhaps for an imagined 'everyman' who never has to experience the disjunct of travel outside their own culture.

There is a kind of urban placelessness to the downtown corporate areas of big cities, where every coffee shop looks the same, every reception area is like the one next door. Author and art historian Kyle Chayka refers to these sterile environments as 'Airspace'.[6] For his part, the American social scientist Herbert Simon remarked, 'Administrative man recognizes that the world he perceives is a drastically simplified model of the buzzing, blooming confusion that constitutes the real world.'[7] It's not surprising that planners should favour such simple, repetitive streetscapes: they make cities easier to administer and to control. But the consequence for those who use them is that they become prisoners of soulless architecture that seems somehow scared of expressing people's humanity or the meaning of the work they are engaged in. No wonder many people didn't want to come back to work at the start of what became known as the Great Resignation in early 2022. There was no pull, no emotional connection, no sense of home.

The fact is that organisations and those who build for them ignore the fundamental truth that our sense of self-worth and wellbeing doesn't just derive from *what* work we do, but *where* we do that work. Try conducting a three-day scenario planning exercise in a basement in a hotel in Chicago in February (as we once did). You can't really think about the future if you can't even see the light of day. Our environment also has to reflect what we are seeking to achieve and embody the shared purpose of those who inhabit it – you can't talk about equality in a corporate 'Town Hall' meeting if the executive floor has a different-coloured carpet to the rest of the building. Our work environments need to recreate some of the psychological safety of home and at the same time motivate people to do the best work they can. And they must be welcoming to outsiders. With their outsourced security staff and lengthy protocols of ID identification, all too many reception areas these days seem designed to have the opposite effect – to keep people out. They make the organisations they serve resemble corporate gated communities, set deliberately apart from the world with which they seek to do business.

Environments for Learning

We opened this chapter with a description of the Blavatnik School of Government in Oxford, and it's perhaps worth staying in that city a little longer to consider what it is most famous for: its college buildings. Centres of education and research for some eight centuries, they continue to thrive and to be at the cutting edge of innovation. The fact that they should have survived for so long and be able to adapt to change suggests that they must be doing something right.

It is important to understand that the colleges of Oxford and

Cambridge are not simply student halls of residence. Each is an educational institution in its own right, legally, financially and functionally separate from the university – an independence that they have all zealously guarded down through the centuries. Each college is a close-knit family of students and faculty (the 'fellows' who, formally, own the college) whose primary responsibility is to its own students. The university (which officially has no students) is a virtual body that simply sets exams and awards degrees (and these days provides the funding for central laboratories and libraries). Indeed, until only a couple of decades ago, the college heads took it in turn to act as the university's vice-chancellor, its chief executive officer – a secular form of *primus inter pares* ('first among equals', as the Pope in Rome is regularly reminded by his cardinals). The colleges are entirely responsible for teaching students, and, while conforming to a common broad plan, each does so in its own idiosyncratic way. Two students studying the same degree course at different colleges might have very different educational experiences. Alumni remain closely associated with their colleges for life, returning at intervals for college dinners to meet old friends and to share memories.

The typical number of fellows and students in a traditional Oxford or Cambridge college was around 100 – a number that gave an intimacy to the learning community by creating a sense of family. Though the colleges are now larger (typically 400–500 undergraduate and graduate students, and forty to fifty fellows), students and staff still eat together at long, narrow tables in the dining hall, deliberately designed so people can talk not only to those who sit beside them but also to those opposite too. The mixture of specialisms – linguists sit alongside medics, classicists with physicists – provides the incidental generalist education and endorphin-fuelled social connectivity that is such a powerful turbocharger to the institution's intellectual productivity. Students also play sport together, representing their college against other colleges in an immersive, physical experience where a sense of shared identity and trust is forged among individuals who know each other at the very least by sight. All colleges have a chapel, a library and gardens for more reflective pursuits. The buildings themselves, clustered around internal gardens and quadrangles (known as quads), with their cloisters and libraries and the hugger-mugger coexistence of teacher and student living on the same staircase, enable casual conversational engagement outside the formal bounds of classes and tutorials.

Although each of the thirty-nine colleges at Oxford has a shared purpose through being part of the university, individually they have their own rituals, traditions, foundation stories and idiosyncrasies. For example, the clock on Tom Tower in the middle of Christ Church college is set for five minutes and two seconds behind Greenwich Mean Time in stubborn exactitude. All Souls College has a ritual called the Mallard Song that takes place just once a century (the next is due in 2101) that celebrates the building of the college and involves processions of professors carrying flaming torches, someone carried in a chair dressed as Lord Mallard and a wooden duck tied to a pole. Such traditions may sound fanciful but they form a part of the framework of a learning environment that nurtures a sense of belonging. They provide the colleges with individual identities, reminding both the other colleges and the university administration that each is a completely independent institution. Despite this seemingly anarchic complexity, the colleges and the university work together in collaborative ventures from which all benefit in a complex give-and-take arrangement made possible by a shared sense of identity, purpose and strategic objectives.

Over the centuries of their existence, the colleges (which were founded at different times, ranging between 1249 and 2019, and vary enormously in their endowments) have slowly adapted themselves to changing conditions and financial pressures, their adaptations unhurried and considered but focused on the best interests of their individual communities and, more important than anything else, the generations of students yet to come. Though being part of these communities has always been limited to those few who have been able to pass the rigorous entrance requirements, the second secret to their success has been the international and social diversity of their faculty and students since their earliest foundation – a reminder of the importance that different cultural perspectives have to offer any organisation. Their vision of a future reflected in a family of famous alumni (often memorialised in the names of individual rooms and buildings, or as formal paintings and – latterly – photographs in the dining hall) has been the secret of their longevity – a textbook example of Owen Eastwood's approach to coaching.

Buildings and the Social Brain

In corporate environments, we don't usually see the luxury of space that Oxford colleges enjoy, but there are steps we can take to emulate them in terms of creating the conditions for innovation and learning – steps that don't have to involve more room or large budgets. One such is establishing relaxing communal spaces. A cautionary tale here reminds us of their importance. A producer in the BBC's education programmes department[8] told Robin how, a few years after she joined, her team were moved from their old ramshackle premises to a new purpose-built building. At that point, everything seemed to fall apart. What had been a close-knit, cooperative unit seemed to lose its coherence. Fresh new ideas no longer seemed forthcoming. It was some time, she said, before they realised what the problem was. In the old building, they'd had a communal room full of battered old furniture where everyone brought their lunches to eat together. Over casual conversation, someone's problem – trying to find the right person to front a programme or some half-formulated idea in need of a hook – would be solved by a serendipitous suggestion by someone from another section. In the new building, there was no central meeting place because the architects of the 1980s had deemed such things unnecessary, as being 'outside' the demands of work rather than being part of the work itself. The result was that such personal contact as occurred took place in meetings constrained by inevitable agendas. As the flow of information and ideas lost their crucial social dimension, so what had only a few months before been a highly successful unit lost both its magic and its way.

Breakthrough ideas depend upon collaboration, adjacency, assemblage, multiple perspectives . . . and serendipity. None of this can be mandated or controlled in a linear fashion, but it can be nurtured by making space for connection and for each other. Just how important this can be is well demonstrated by the UK Medical Research Council's legendary Molecular Biology Laboratory at Cambridge. The story of its creation is worth retelling. Its architects back in the 1950s argued that communal restaurants were no longer relevant in the more egalitarian post-war world. Its founder, the biochemist Max Perutz, however, disagreed. Not only did he insist that they make provision for one, but he also demanded that it had to be both cheap (if not free) and offer high-quality food. If it failed on either front, he argued, people would simply eat their sandwiches at their desks, and would never talk to each other. That he was right is, we suggest, confirmed by one bald statistic: at the last count, this lab boasted twenty-seven Nobel Prize winners.[9] To put that in a broader context: the Molecular Biology Laboratory is no larger than a single university faculty in size, yet it ranks among the top twenty-five universities worldwide in terms of the number of Nobel Prizes won.

And it is thanks to just such a serendipitous encounter that the most effective vaccines against Covid-19 were able to be developed at such speed off the back of earlier developments in mRNA research. Katalin Karikó and Drew Weissman, whose collaboration led to the development of one of the vaccines, met randomly while taking turns to use the photocopier machine at work.[10]

Just how important the kind of casual conversations that occur in communal spaces can be was demonstrated in a recent experiment with attendees at a Harvard Medical School research symposium.[11] At the start of the meeting, researchers were randomly assigned to different rooms and asked to participate in a ninety-minute unstructured brainstorming with other participants. While the baseline probability for collaboration between researchers was small, simply spending this short amount of time together in the same room increased the probability that any two attendees later submitted a joint grant proposal by almost 70 per cent. Communal space is productive space.

This apparent serendipity stems from the social, messy side of innovation. A casual remark dropped into an unplanned conversation can trigger a discussion or collaboration that solves a major problem. The relaxed exchange over lunch may, once in a crucially important blue moon, ignite the spark for a new conceptual breakthrough. We have a tendency to think of innovation as a lone activity conducted by an isolated genius. In fact, many of the great historical breakthroughs in science and engineering have come not from individuals beavering away alone in their ivory towers but from someone looking over their shoulder from another discipline and making a suggestion. The modern atomic theory of chemistry is one such well-known case. The outsider, Antoine Lavoisier,[12] noticed, with his accountant's eye, something that no one in the research community had noticed – that the equations of the existing theories of combustion didn't balance. Something was missing. Spotting that absence led to the discovery of oxygen and so to the modern atomic theory of chemistry.

You cannot force the kinds of discussions that lead to breakthroughs: they only ever occur spontaneously. But they can be physically enabled. Leaders therefore need to allow space for their corporate Cricks to find their Watsons in order for them to discover their DNA equivalent. As Professor Martin Kemp, world expert on the polymath and artist Leonardo da Vinci, remarked, 'If you keep knowledge in separate silos, what you can do with that knowledge is very limited.' This same point is made by Ian Goldin and Chris Kutarna who, in their book *The Age of Discovery,* observe that: 'When it comes to working genius, *where* you choose to plant yourself matters more than ever: for two reasons: craft and concentration.'[13] The kind of space we inhabit can enable or constrain the meeting of minds needed to invent the future.

Buildings need to be flexible, too. The architect Norman Foster, who always endeavoured to design space that enables a more 'outside-in' human interaction, sought to build in adaptability. One of his earliest buildings, the then revolutionary office block built for insurance brokers Willis Faber in the 1970s, was conceived to be 'sympathetic to human values', with open-plan spaces (the CEO demanded his own office but, when he moved in and saw the effect, he had the walls taken down), a rooftop restaurant, a swimming pool in the basement for communal activity, art incorporated into the workplace and raised floors to accommodate new technologies as they emerged. It was designed to be a building that was in conversation with its context and could change over time. Such future proofing may be something that is beyond the control of most of us, but we can still make our spaces adaptable. In his book *How Buildings Learn*, Stewart Brand[14] discusses the five layers that make up a building, from the easily changed 'stuff' (furniture, carpets, lights etc) through to the layout, the services, the 'skin' (the plaster and facings), the structure and then the site itself. We perhaps forget that we don't have to change everything – some things are very easy and cheap to adapt, such as the lighting, the built-in hierarchies of space, the echoey acoustics. Just as we can learn, so too can buildings.

In learning to adapt, however, we have to acknowledge that humans find change difficult. Seismic alterations in the way that society operates – from the massive expansion of towns and cities in Victorian times to the post-industrial landscape of much of the modern developed world – can cause a sense of dislocation and threat. In an organisational context, the arrival of hybrid working is similarly testing people's resilience and adaptability. Fear of the unknown, of routines being disrupted and anxiety over challenges that might prove too demanding all heighten the stress that people feel. And while spikes of acute stress can be productive, everyday chronic stress has powerful negative effects not only on health but also on neuroplasticity and our capacity to learn and change. Persistent high levels of the stress hormone cortisol accelerate ageing and have adverse effects on the immune system, leading inevitably to excess time off work and absenteeism.[15] Even in everyday life, we prefer constancy and the familiar – with good reason, it seems. The temptation constantly to tinker with an environment that is working well therefore needs to be resisted.

This truth also serves as a reminder that, designed correctly, the physical environment can not only stimulate creativity but allow people to relax, to reduce their levels of stress. Samantha and Tracey direct leadership programmes all over the world, but always look for a location with a heart, a gathering point for the group whether in the office or outside. It can be a fireplace, a bar, some battered old sofas, a light terrace in summer, an intimate book-lined room in winter, a garden or even a hut in the woods. Groups can work happily in the blandness of a white-boarded classroom as long as there is a totemic gathering area to go to at some point in the day – a place that encourages relaxation and sociability.

It's something that designers Clara Gaggero Westaway and Adrian Westaway noted soon after the birth of their first child when they visited the Lego offices in Denmark. The headquarters is designed to embody the Lego ethos. In fact, it looks as though it has actually been built out of Lego, with its playful sky boxes at the top of the building, complete with huge windows, natural light and views to the country beyond. Employees are invited to name meeting rooms and to decide how they want to decorate and express themselves in the 'neighbourhoods' where they work. Those spaces where they are encouraged to be noisy and to collaborate with each other are decorated in vibrant colours. In one important meeting that Clara and Adrian attended, the senior executive they met was rocking his baby in her pram with one hand as he set out the framework of a proposal with the other – a perfect blend of the relaxed and the businesslike. Of all the high-tech offices Clara and Adrian visited, this was the one, they felt, where there was nothing performative; they experienced the authentic expression of a natural, lived ethos, an environment where children mattered – and not just because their parents bought them toys. The French philosopher Gaston Bachelard wrote: 'All really inhabited space bears the essence of the notion of home.'[16] That's what the two designers felt the Lego building had achieved.

One of the truisms of life is that we spend more of our waking time at work each day than we do at home, at least during the working week. It is therefore inevitable that the workplace should evolve naturally into a parallel social community. That can have many advantages, both for the workforce and for the organisation itself. The workplace can offer important social respite and variation for us as individuals. For some it can offer a refuge from the escalating pressures of children and domestic duties – a place that allows us to step away from the frustrations of home, and commiserate with others facing similar problems or celebrate shared triumphs. For others, it can provide somewhere to escape from loneliness.

Perhaps the most important reason why a good work *social* environment is desirable, however, is that, as we saw in Chapter Three, the number and quality of friendships you have turns out to be the single most important factor influencing people's happiness, well-being, and engagement with and trust in their local community, as well as their physical and mental health (see p. 66). In this respect, it may not matter whether someone has a fulfilling home life or not, provided they have genuine friendships at work: either way, they will gain the same health benefits and function better as employees.

Many of the tech companies in California seek to be not just collections of like-minded professionals, but communities. To this end they offer perks that range from acupuncture to dog parks, stipends for travel, indoor treehouses, nap pods, paid volunteer days, Uber accounts and so on. Increasingly, even outside California, enlightened companies are offering services to their employees that go way beyond a free cup of coffee and a bike rack. They recognise that people who work long hours and can't access the services they need in the week require support beyond a desk and computer.

In this, they resemble the community models of some of the great nineteenth-century industrialists, such as the Quaker Cadbury and Rowntree chocolate barons and the Leverhulme soap-and-margarine family (now Unilever). When they built their model housing schemes for their workers, it was not just philanthropy that motivated them; they recognised that a contented, healthy workforce is a productive workforce. They provided them with schools as well as community centres where social functions could be held or clubs could meet to provide intellectual fuel for the mind. Work socials and tennis clubs might not now have the appeal they had in the 1930s, but some creative thinking about the kinds of social environments that would be attractive to employees so as to create a village environment at the heart of the organisation could turn a business round for relatively little cost. It is not enough to provide gyms and leave people to pump iron in solitude. To be effective, it needs to be a *social* activity. In Chapter Four, we extolled the virtues of choirs, and singing more generally, for creating a sense of bonding and inclusion, and noted that these have been found to work very effectively in a number of contemporary contexts. Much will, of course, depend on the urban context, commuting distances and people's family and other commitments, as well as the local cultural environment. But the effort will pay dividends in terms of employee engagement, satisfaction and health, with all the economic benefits that will flow from this.

Outside Space and the Social Brain

As the cloisters and gardens of Oxford colleges bear witness, we should not ignore the possibilities for inspiration that take root outside the built environment. Many people now practise walking meetings or hold 'walkshops' instead of workshops. The break from the office environment and rush of fresh air to the body, as well as the inspiration produced from walking in nature, contribute to fresher outcomes and unexpected results.

If you want evidence for how productive walkshops can be, you need look no further than Emmanuelle Charpentier and Jennifer Doudna, who were awarded the Nobel Prize for Chemistry in 2020 for their world-changing research that gave rise to the CRISPR gene-editing technology. The two were already distinguished scientists in their own right, but it was a casual conversation they had at a conference in Puerto Rico in 2011, followed by an animated stroll through the streets of San Juan – a city that is both old and modern, with a rich mix of culture that looks both to the sea and to the hills – that provided the inspiration for a major breakthrough in just four years. 'As they stroll along the cobbled streets, they start talking about their research. Charpentier wonders whether Doudna is interested in a collaboration – would she like to participate in studying the function of Cas9 in *S. pyogenes'* simple class 2 system?'[17]

Had Charpentier and Doudna sought to collaborate in a more conventional setting, it's hard to believe they could have made such a breakthrough so quickly. Meetings with agendas. Formal and slightly sterile rooms. The need to arrive at some kind of a decision five minutes before the end of any given session as the room has been booked by someone else. All these factors would have mitigated against creative discussion and original or imaginative thinking.

There's more solid science to back the case for walkshops. As we saw in Chapter Four, walking together is a synchronising activity that triggers the endorphin system and leads to bonding. That process provides a platform for engaged, unscripted, agenda-less, truly face-to-face interactions that are nearly impossible to mimic in either a committee room or a virtual setting online. It is not just a matter of what emerges from these random encounters that is important – it is also what is lost when interactions are held remotely or in formal meetings.

Between Home and Work: The Hybrid Office

So far we've talked about the home and office as though they are entirely separate entities. Increasingly, though, they have started to merge – a process hugely accelerated during the 2020–21 global pandemic. These days, many more people are working from home (WFH), or splitting their workdays between their house and their office. There are certainly advantages to this way of working. It enables a more relaxed morning schedule with no commute. It offers meetings at the click of a Zoom button rather than after a long walk to a meeting room on the other side of a campus. It also allows people to balance their home and work lives better, giving them the flexibility, for example, to collect their children from school instead of having to rely on grandparents, friends or after-school clubs. Improvisation teacher and facilitator Rob Poynton believes that people have become less wasteful of the face-to-face time they spend together at work as it has become more precious.

Some have suggested that hybrid working has reminded employers of the delicate balancing act many have to perform. As one chair of a financial services company put it, 'Pre-pandemic, we knew that certain people were stretched or under pressure at home but didn't directly experience it. Somehow, after two years on Zoom, being in their homes, we are more implicated – and that can't change as we move back into the office. We need to be kinder.'

But virtual and hybrid working have thrown up problems, too. When WFH was first tried in the 1990s it was found that the loss of a clear beginning and end to the working day caused some individuals to drift into working all hours, so risking burnout. Others, deprived of the company of the 'team' on a daily basis, lost motivation and commitment. As people physically shifted to their homes, the social ecosystem that the office had created was lost. Two recent studies – one carried out by Microsoft on their own staff, the other carried out on the research community at MIT (the Massachusetts Institute of Technology in Cambridge, MA) – show that, while communication with an inner core of colleagues continued virtually at the same level during the global pandemic, the casual contacts of the kind normally made around the water cooler or at meetings – the kind that, as we showed earlier, so often leads to fresh ideas and innovation – declined (Figure 7.1).[18] At the same time, it seems that more time was wasted in meetings.

It's worth noting in this context that the assumption made by many people that virtual contact via the internet has massively increased our social opportunities is a false one. Theoretically, of course, the internet has allowed us to form friendships with a more diverse range of people from a much wider range of locations than was ever previously possible. In practice, however, while there are indeed some people who list 500 or even 1,000 friends on their social

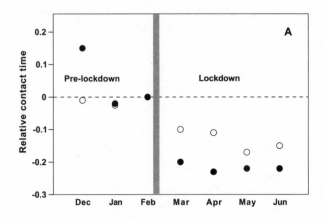

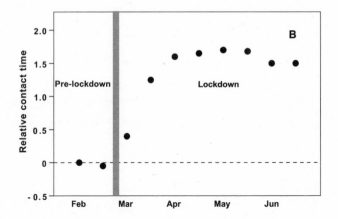

Working from Home Has Costs

Figure 7.1. A study of the Microsoft organisation revealed that lockdown in response to Covid-19 resulted in (a) a dramatic reduction in the amount of communication with both members of other groups within the organisation (unfilled symbols) and external links (weak links) (filled symbols) and, at the same time, (b) a dramatic increase in time spent in online or telephone meetings. Contact time is standardised to average pre-lockdown levels, set to zero. Redrawn from Yang et al. (2021)[19]

media pages, the average across samples that number tens of millions of users of digital media is much lower: around 170 (Table 7.1). This value is comfortably within the range of variation around the

Table 7.1. Mean number of friends that individuals have in online environments[20]

Sample	Sample size	Mean number of friends
Cellphone calling network (Europe)	26,680	134
Cellphone calling network (China)	15,209	141
University email network	35,600	250
Facebook friends (worldwide)	1,000,000	150–250
Facebook friends (student sample, UK)	339	175
Facebook friends (UK, two adult samples)	3,375	169
Facebook friends (US sample)	61,000,000	149
AVERAGE: Overall		174
Facebook only		173

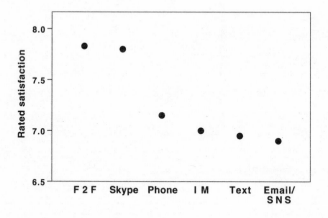

The Medium Matters

Figure 7.2. Level of satisfaction with interactions with five best friends when using different media in everyday spontaneous interactions. F2F = face to face; IM = instant messaging. Source: Vlahovic et al. (2012)[21]

150 friends and family that we typically have in our offline social networks (see Figure 2.1). In fact, an analysis of some 61 million Facebook accounts yielded an average number of friends listed of exactly 149.[22]

It seems that our social world is not actually increased by social media. Those who have more than a couple of hundred 'friends' on their social media accounts are simply extending their online social world into the layers of acquaintances and tribe members (the 500 and 1,500 layers of the Dunbar Graph in Figure 2.3) in just the way we naturally do in our everyday offline world. This doesn't make them friends in any meaningful sense, however. If anything, they are more like anonymous Twitter followers. It seems that the constraints on our social world are not the technological limitations of face-to-face communication so much as our mind's capacity to handle relationships. What this highlights is that the internet is full of traps for the unwary, not least because our inability to inhibit behaviour effectively causes us to act first and think afterwards (see p. 178).

More importantly, perhaps, the evidence suggests that we do not always find the digital world as satisfactory as the face-to-face world for building and maintaining friendships (Figure 7.2). Even though video-embedded media (Skype, Zoom, Teams) are clearly more satisfying than text-based media, or even phone calls, our recent experience of Zoom suggests that these online environments all work best with established relationships. None of them are especially satisfactory for building new relationships with strangers. In the online world, and most obviously so with text-based media, we don't get to see the fine details of an individual's behaviour – those subtle, difficult-to-cheat non-verbal signals that allow us to judge their honesty and character (see p. 130).

It may be an egregious mistake to assume that broader work relationships of the type so important for creativity and personal wellbeing will thrive in the virtual office. Some leaders are acutely aware of this and have worked hard to create online the natural social connections that take place in the physical office. Ezra Schuster,

Social Dangers in the Digital World

It goes without saying that one of the biggest dangers of the text-based digital world (emails, Facebook, texts, SMSs) is hitting the <SEND> button without reading what you have written first. What sounds fine in speech often comes across as nonsense if it is written down just as we speak it. More important, however, is the fact that, when we first articulate an idea in our minds, our half-formed thoughts might express our inner feelings of the moment but can inadvertently come across as rude, aggressive, unkind, overly familiar, distasteful or just plain muddled. As we speak, we often reformulate what we say in response to our listeners' reactions.

In a conventional conversation, our words literally disappear into thin air – if we are lucky, before the other person has fully registered exactly what we said. In text-based media, there is no such escape: it is there to read and reread for all time, a permanent record – as many unfortunates have found to their subsequent cost.

In a survey carried out in collaboration with the Holocaust Memorial Day Trust, one of our studies[23] found that as many as 50 per cent of the people sampled had at some point in the past regretted what they had said in an email, half of them because they later realised it would have upset the person it was sent to. Younger people (age eighteen to twenty-five) were two-and-a-half times more likely to press <SEND> without reading over what they had written than those over fifty-five years in age. Men of all ages were worse at this than women: only 25 per cent admitted to checking an email before sending it, compared to 40 per cent of women.

Regional Public Service Commissioner at the Ministry of Health in New Zealand, refers to a Samoan notion of *teu le va* or 'nurturing the space'. During the pandemic, he was 'Zooming like nobody's business, investing in relationships, nurturing them' and providing safety in virtual forums 'for people to connect and to talk about what is really important, to be free and frank'. The need to maintain the social channels between home and work was just as important as the need to maintain formal business channels.

The head of HR at Dr Yoge Patel's Blue Bear Systems, who Yoge describes as a 'bubbly personality who nonetheless has the steeliness to get to the human story behind the story', took it upon herself to contact all employees personally each week during the 2020 lockdowns in the UK so as to make a human connection, to listen for any distress, to do what she could for their wellbeing, to visit them virtually in their homes. Regular contact like this is necessary because, even in the best of times, friendships and even work relationships decay rapidly in the absence of continued social investment (Figure 2.5).

Simultaneously, WFH initiatives have highlighted what the physical office environment can and should achieve. It's the place where real human exchange, as opposed to simply sharing information, needs to take place. Dr Yoge Patel sees huge opportunities for her employees through working from home: 'I love the idea that they may be able to eat lunch with their small children or spend their breaks with an elderly parent.' But she leaves the choice between home working and coming to the office to her employees, for she recognises that, for some, working from home is a 'lonelier and diminished experience'. Back in the 1990s, when WFH was first tried, one very large multinational designed a new, purpose-built complex that allowed them to combine three separate campuses that, for reasons of history and accident, were some miles apart. The new complex housed boutique shops, a first-class restaurant, cafés, gyms, relaxation spaces . . . everything you could possibly want to make the business day go more smoothly. The plan was to do away with separate offices, give everyone a laptop so they could work from home and simply have workstations scattered throughout the building where people could hot-desk and plug in when they needed to come in. The planners invested a great deal of time talking everyone through the new designs. They had anticipated that it would be the older staff who would be most resistant on the grounds that they would be too attached to their private offices, ready support and the habitual rhythms of office life. They were completely taken aback to find that the older generations were absolutely delighted with the new arrangements. It was the younger ones that vehemently objected: they came in to work, they said, to meet their friends. Work was the context for their social life. It hadn't occurred to anyone that this might even be relevant. Post-pandemic this basic truth is more apparent than ever.

The fact that the workplace is an important source of friendships, especially for younger people, should remind us that, even before the 2020 pandemic, we were facing a pandemic of loneliness among the younger generation moving to their first job in a new city. Unfamiliar with where to go to meet like-minded people, their only source of social life is the office. Yet most of those they share an office with will already have busy social and family lives, and will lack the capacity to befriend newcomers. As a result, many newcomers are tipped headlong into a downward spiral of loneliness, with all the consequences that brings of depression, illness and time off work (see p. 66). Those who move with families are somewhat buffered against this, but younger singles will not have that advantage and, being young, many are likely to lack the resilience that age and experience bring to cope with dislocations of this kind. In the contemporary globalised world of work, this problem will be exacerbated for those moving from another culture, since they face a double disadvantage – becoming familiar with a new community and a new culture at the same time. Providing contexts in which newcomers can meet people from the wider organisation rather than just their particular office will widen their opportunities to find others with whom they share their Seven Pillars, who may in turn provide them with a gateway into the wider social world outside work. A Zoom meeting is not a helpful environment in which to make friendships within the organisation or the local community.

As we move into a future where WFH will be a constant, prescient companies will think carefully about what they can do to provide more social connection for their employees. One company distinguishes 'head-down working' – you can do it anywhere you like – from 'collaborative tasks', where coming into the office is advocated, with some mandated whole-office gatherings at various punctuation points during the year. Others have sought to turn their workplaces into 'attractors', offering interesting talks at lunchtime, drinks after work etc. Before the pandemic hit, many felt that, in order to learn, they had to leave the confines of the office – to go on a learning retreat of some sort away from the day-to-day bustle of the office. These 'off-sites' deliberately changed the rhythm and location of work, creating a jolt, or feeling of surprise (the most efficient emotion for learning), as well as the stickiness that comes from disrupting the habitual (the fact is that we remember locations much more readily than we remember time – 'where' always trumps 'when'). Post-pandemic, there is a new-found recognition that people expect more than work when they're at work.

There is one final issue with hybrid working that often seems to get overlooked: not everyone's job can be done from home. Those whose jobs require them to be physically present, those who serve in cafeterias and restaurants, those who make the products on the factory floor, or who treat patients in hospitals or teach in schools or fly the planes we travel in, cannot do their job at home. For businesses that live mainly online, this may not be an issue. But many will have both kinds of job types and there is a danger of creating a divisively two-tier workforce – those who can work from home and those (often low-paid) who have to come in to work every day whether they like it or not. There's a hidden danger here of reinforcing the old inequalities between management and the factory floor, of stirring up old resentments of the 'haves' by the 'have-nots'.

Time Matters

If place exerts a powerful psychological influence on us, so does time. How we experience it, allocate it and use it is key to our well-being and productivity. Unfortunately, it's another aspect of the life of the organisation that all too often gets ignored. The typical modern corporation behaves as though time is infinitely expandable, piling up more and more work as it embraces the latest thinking or exciting initiative. The Japanese have a word for dying from overwork ('*koroshi*'). They may be the only people to encapsulate the phenomenon in this way, but they are certainly not the only people to experience it. Organisations are notoriously poor at stopping things and metaphorically clearing out the cupboards to make time and space for the new. As a result, the modern executive is overloaded and often works sub-optimally in a state of chronic stress, housed in an 'always on' environment, running to stand still.

It may be an old cliché that you can't look after others if you fail to look after yourself, but clichés tend to be true. It is the job of leaders to be time lords – to know the difference between stretch and stress; to help their people to box off time for themselves; to pause, reflect and take time, particularly for holidays. Too often, their holidays are spent worrying about the business. But the business will still be there when they get back. Barings Bank did not crash in the 1990s because the board were all away on holiday. It crashed while everyone was at their desks, but not paying attention to what was going on in one corner of the organisation. Like any other scarce resource, time needs to be maximised, considered and treated as if it were precious. Effective use of work time does not equate to presenteeism – the idea that you have got to be in the office in order to be productive. A focus on impact rather than process may lead you to spend your time in very different ways. If you're responsible for innovation and good ideas happen while you are running, then running should be part of your work. If you are responsible for customer satisfaction, then most of your time should be spent out listening to customers, rather than in internal meetings. If you're responsible for strategy, you need long periods of reflection with nothing in your diary, opportunities to learn from other industries, to collaborate, to experiment and prototype the future. All these activities are 'time in' – not 'time out'.

This valuing of time is important not only organisationally but also personally. The modern US practice of moving away from any set holiday entitlement to allowing people to take 'as much holiday as they like' has generally had the opposite effect, perhaps deliberately so. Such a policy needs an explicit, communicated credo around the importance of taking of holidays. If they remain frowned upon – and rarely taken by bosses – people can be scared to take any holiday at all if it runs against the corporate ethos. If they then leave the company, their formal entitlement invariably disappears with their contracts. Discouraging people from taking holiday is counterproductive. Human beings need recovery time in order to thrive. In the same way, they need time during the day to relax. And they need time to plan. A relentless emphasis on short-term targets, deadlines and KPIs (Key Performance Indicators) keeps leaders busy with managing the present. However, it puts the future at risk.

This tendency to focus on the short term derives from one of our most robust psychological traits: our very strong tendency to discount the future – in other words, our inability to stop ourselves from grabbing the biggest slice of cake now when we could have the whole cake later if we wait (see p. 184). Short-term, private greed nearly always trumps longer-term public benefit, and especially so when the short-term payout is high for those who negotiate it.

Research by Alex Hill, Professor of Operations Management at London's Kingston University, shows how detrimental our short-term view of the world is to the long-term success of organisations.[24] He notes how more than three quarters of the companies on the London FTSE 100 index have disappeared over the past thirty years. When he compared a sample of businesses that had survived for more than a century with ones that had not, he found that one thing seemed to be especially important: their size. Those that survived were small, invariably employing fewer than 300 full-time staff (even if they had a very large number of temporary part-time staff in addition). They typically had a core of stable staff who had been there for a long time and were deeply steeped in the corporate philosophy, and a CEO who had been in post for more than a decade (with a policy of overlapping successors – implying that CEOs retired

Discounting the Future

In the famous Stanford Marshmallow Experiment, the psychologist Walter Mischel tested children's ability to delay gratification. He asked them not to eat a marshmallow on the table while he was out of the room, promising a much larger reward later if they were able to do so. Young children are not especially good at resisting temptation, although they get better at it as they grow up.[25] In follow-up studies, the researchers found that children who were unable to resist temptation had poorer educational attainment at school and were more likely to become obese. This worrying finding has since been confirmed in much larger-scale studies. One study carried out in New Zealand, which followed 1,000 children from birth well into adulthood, found that children who were better at resisting temptation when they were young were much less likely to get into trouble with the law as teenagers or as adults.[26]

The ability to inhibit instinctive responses in the interests of greater longer-term benefits plays a crucial role in allowing us to manage both our relationships and our communities. Failing to do so results in communities fragmenting, thereby undermining the very benefits for which they were formed in the first place.

However desirable a long-term strategy might be, it is often undermined by our tendency to discount the future – to live now and hope we can pay later. The tendency to do so is what gives rise to the Tragedy of the Commons. The temptation to graze an extra cow on the public common land will, if everyone does it, result in the land being overgrazed and no longer able to support the village. But, individually, we are always tempted to do it because in the short run we gain an extra benefit for our family: we hope that everyone else in the village will adhere to the village grazing rules and won't notice our rule-bending. It is this temptation, played out on an international scale, that has caused the overfishing of the world's oceans and the deforestation that has blighted the tropical forests of the Amazon, central Africa and southeast Asia.

rather than being forced out). They were also characterised by a family ethos, a long-term vision and a sense of social purpose, as well as stability of location.

It's another reminder that the bigger organisations become, the more they sow the seeds of their own demise. It also shows how intricately interwoven the various aspects of the social brain are. The size of groups, the nature of their interactions, where and how they meet and for how long all have a bearing on their ultimate success.

Summary

- Organisations function more efficiently when their workforce is happy and engaged. Creating a sense of community is central to this.
- Spaces influence our mood and productivity as much as people do. Creating the right environment is more important for businesses than having the right 'mission statement'.
- Casual meetings are often the single most important source of innovations. Creating opportunities where these can occur (over coffee, lunch or a beer after work) is crucial.
- New joiners, especially if they come from abroad, can experience difficulty finding friends outside the work environment; enabling them to establish themselves in the wider community may both smooth the transition to a new job and minimise undesirable consequences in terms of depression and ill-health.
- Hybrid work patterns need to be managed carefully: there is a risk of people losing contact with both the organisation's sense of community and its sense of purpose. Working from home also risks people missing out on casual contacts that later turn out to be formative.
- Online meetings rarely provide the kind of social environment in which new meaningful relationships can easily be built up.

8.

The Social Brain at Work

'The stars we are given. The constellations we make.'

Rebecca Solnit[1]

A large part of the unique gifts and capabilities we possess as human beings involves our sophisticated powers of connection and our social abilities. It is surprising then that, even today, in the twenty-first century, the dominant metaphor for the organisation is still the machine. Leaders may talk about being 'people-focused' but you only have to read their annual report or strategy document to spot the tell-tale words: 'leverage', 'top-down', 'bottom-up', 'centralised', 'decentralised', 'reporting lines', 'well-oiled', 'nuts and bolts', 'spanner in the works'. This is the vocabulary of the finite, complicated – but not complex – controllable system. It is a linguistic bulwark against anxiety. Even the World Economic Forum's widely cited phrase 'The Fourth Industrial Revolution', used to describe the digitally enabled period we are living through, follows this notion.

Machines are narrowly brilliant. Speak to any leader, however, and they will tell you that the hardest part of their role is leading people in all their illogical, creative, emotional, different guises. In comparison to unleashing people's social powers, the technical stuff is easy. The metaphors we've reached for in this book are more natural, but bring with them a degree of complexity that can defy the simple mechanistic models we so often use. Human talent, after all, does not conform to a grid but is more organic and shape-shifting. Equally, the line between employee and 'line manager' is rarely straight. The imaginative construct we hold for the organisations within which we work is key to how we're expected to behave in – and relate to – them.

The simple fact is that no organisation functions in the – perhaps reassuringly – predictable way that a machine does. Give a diverse group of people a challenge and a deadline but no org plan or set of instructions and they'll still miraculously rise to the occasion. Cooperation and a solution will emerge as if by magic. They won't need to be imposed. It's not just that the machine metaphor is incorrect, either. It's also harmful. In its construction of a world of predictable, robotic performance, it creates an assumption that, if human efforts fall short, the problem must lie with the individual concerned, not the system. In reality, people are the round pegs being squeezed into square holes. The problem lies with the square holes – the way in which organisations are structured and conceived.

This essential truth has become ever more apparent in recent years as new forces have started to shape society. The unstructured working conditions of the gig economy have left people feeling untethered. The global pandemic left many isolated. Young people feel insecure and powerless amid such complex mega-challenges as climate change, and such local pressures as a shortage of housing. This, surely, is the moment to gather up the hem of organisations from below – to think in smaller, more human scales, rather than monoliths, so that we can unleash the potential of the 7 billion people on this planet in all their human differences, circle by circle, to do what only human beings can do: create a better future.

Unfortunately, a combination of time pressure and poor office layout has caused far too many leadership teams to become hidden away in the 'C' Suite. There they lose contact with the 'ground floor and the edges' where the production work is actually being done. As the Mandarin saying has it: 'Heaven is high and the emperor far away.' Those who pay scant attention to the day-to-day dynamics of human relationships, and the human biology that informs them, or are too far removed to understand what's actually going on, will find leadership very challenging. It becomes rather like the push-me/

pull-you sensation that Arctic explorers call 'negative drift' where the ice floes underfoot are moving one way, while your dogsled pulls the other – at best you remain on the same spot while simultaneously finding yourself exhausted. In our work with and in organisations over many years, we have discovered that it's the leaders who understand these force shifts and who also lead for these dynamics that find leadership both productive and rewarding.

In this final chapter we first summarise the implications for organisations of Robin's work on groups and group size. We then suggest some practical steps that leaders should consider taking to adapt to a social brain way of management and day-to-day working. Finally, we show how the various facets of the social brain we've discussed in earlier chapters can be brought together to form what we call the Thrive Model™, which is composed of six key elements: connection, culture, values, belonging, learning and purpose.

The Social Brain in Action

Managing Organisational Size and Structure

Organisation size and spread is a key challenge for any human-shaped organisation. It's a particular problem because organisations measure success through growth and expansion and so assume that bigger must equal better. As we have seen, the Dunbar Number of 150 represents the natural limit on the number of meaningful social relationships that an individual can manage at any one time, while the Dunbar Graph identifies the size and character of the sub-groups that make up the Dunbar Number as well as its higher-level clusterings. In a traditional hierarchical structure, the only real way for a leader to deal with very large numbers of employees is to categorise and caricature them: they are simply too numerous to allow for any kind of real personal relationship. Groups of workers necessarily become depersonalised with labels such as 'Marketing' or 'the US office' or 'High Potentials'. They are literally 'human resources', averaged out and little different from the raw materials delivered to the factory door. Leaders themselves are so distanced from the people with whom they work that they, too, become depersonalised: employees project their own ideas onto the person of the leader and make assumptions about them that more often reflect their own local hopes and fears rather than the real character of the person at the helm. These are hardly ideal conditions for the creation of trust and social capital. Of course, the fact that many organisations number many more than 150 exacerbates the problem proportionately.

Humans evolved to thrive in small groups where each member knows all the others, and where bonds of trust are accordingly

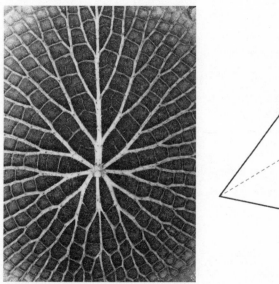 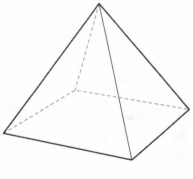

Alternative Ways to Envisage Organisations

Figure 8.1. Left: The ribs on the underside of a waterlily leaf[2] form a fractal pattern that provides the metre-diameter leaf with strength while at the same time distributing the weight so as to give it buoyancy. Right: The pyramidal shape of traditional management structures. The shape of adaptive organisations that will thrive in a fast-paced future will be inspired by more natural honeycombs, fractals, ripples and lattices, not the brittle, inflexible pyramids of old.[3]

created. To replicate this universal biological need in large groups requires thinking in circles – fives, fifteens, fifties, one hundred and fifties, and beyond: numbers that are governed by the peculiarly stable 'rule of three', like a three-legged stool of solidity. As groups grow, they tend to move quickly from one of these numbers to the next because these particular group sizes seem to be especially stable. If they don't make the jump quickly enough, difficulties and fractures are likely to emerge. Leaders need to be mindful of what it takes to build trust in large organisations and to develop strategies to manage growth in their various units so that they don't inadvertently fall down the cracks between the Dunbar layers. Instead of relying on the metaphor of a management pyramid, imaginative constructs of large organisations should take their inspiration from nature: the floret of a Romanesco broccoli, a snowflake or the veins on the underside of a giant waterlily leaf (Figure 8.1). As it happens, the peculiar strength and flexibility of the architecture of the giant waterlily leaf is being used to inspire floating buildings resilient enough to withstand the rigours of climate change.[4]

Matching Group Size to Task

The Dunbar Graph, with its ripple structure, usefully shows what size of group is best suited to the task in hand. When quick decisions are needed or frequent meetings required, groups of four or five work best. When open-ended brainstorming is needed, where outside sources of information are required or will prove useful, then groups of twelve to fifteen work best; because the timetables of a larger number of people have to be coordinated here, such groups will necessarily meet less often. Groups that perform a particular function within an organisation (usually referred to as departments) are most likely to work best when they are either fifty or 150 in size. The way in which information flows around the system seems to be optimised at group sizes of fifteen, fifty, 150 and 500. There is something inherently unstable about groups of intermediate size, as the Hutterite example we considered in Chapter Two suggests. Left to themselves, groups will migrate quickly to the next number; if they don't, they are likely to fracture prematurely into two.

If we follow these number-based principles and think carefully about what we want individual groups to achieve, we are in a position to match task to group and group to task more effectively. Crisis-handling groups and creative teams operate best if they are kept small. Because they don't have to keep taking time out to debrief each other, they can function at speed. And because they are not frequently having to stop to ask, 'Well, what does X actually mean by Y?', they can mentalise the task in hand and achieve a state of creative 'flow'. Larger groups, by contrast, work well for brainstorming and complex decision-making, particularly if they draw on a diverse range of voices. They are, however, less likely to reach a consensus fast. Either way, it's essential not to allow a group to grow larger than its function strictly demands. Management by large committees invariably either ends up stuck in a cycle of irreconcilable views or becomes a rubber-stamping body. For the individuals involved, it is an unsatisfying and frustrating use of their time.

The temptation to increase the size of a group or committee is often driven by a desire to be inclusive, or by the understandable fear that people might end up feeling excluded. But adding voices to the group simply to keep them happy is an organisational trap. It rapidly diminishes effectiveness, as well as wasting the time of those who don't actually need to be there. What's more, the combination of an unnecessarily large number of people and a limited amount of time tends to result in only the loudest voices being heard. Its effect is entirely counterproductive.

Mastering Group Dynamics

As an organisation grows, each circle of its Dunbar Graph develops a different set of needs and consequent dynamics, and therefore requires different kinds of leadership. Groups of up to five need no leader. The average pop group is an obvious example: the group is small enough to allow its members to mentalise, to understand what

Matching Team Size to Task

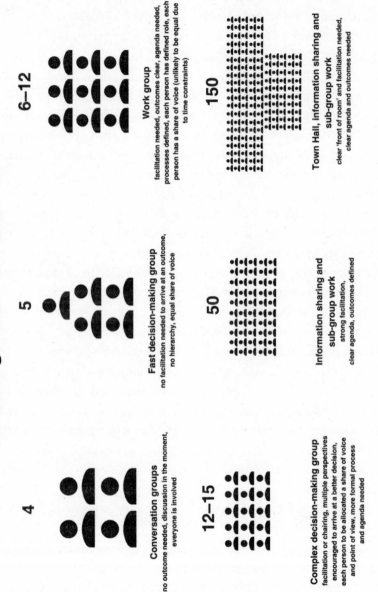

4

Conversation groups
no outcome needed, discussion in the moment, everyone is involved

12–15

Complex decision-making group
facilitation or chairing, multiple perspectives encouraged to arrive at a better decision, each person to be allocated a share of voice and point of view, more formal process and agenda needed

5

Fast decision-making group
no facilitation needed to arrive at an outcome, no hierarchy, equal share of voice

50

Information sharing and sub-group work
strong facilitation, clear agenda, outcomes defined

6–12

Work group
facilitation needed, outcomes clear, agenda needed, processes defined, each person has a defined role, each person has a share of voice (unlikely to be equal due to time constraints)

150

Town Hall, information sharing and sub-group work
clear 'front of room' and facilitation needed, clear agenda and outcomes needed

Figure 8.2. Different kinds of task need to be carefully matched to group size. Failure to do so will inevitably result in inefficiencies that make the group's decision-making processes less effective.

each is thinking about the others' thinking. It is a great structure for improvisation. The volatility of some pop groups notwithstanding, groups of this size generally have staying power because members become closely bonded through frequent meetings and the deep-down familiarity this creates. When a small group works really well, the intensity of their cooperation can present a provocative challenge to the norms and ways of working of the wider group, and so drive new initiatives and fresh ideas. The high-performing 'fives' don't need to take minutes of meetings, for example, and often disregard set processes, finding that they get in the way. If they are to thrive, these highly productive, creative small groups often need protection and the permission to operate differently, more than they require bringing into line. They tend to be groups that are agile, time-efficient and creative. When they work well, they work really well. Disrupt them at your peril.

Groups of fifteen or so need a chair – or facilitator – to provide structure and to allow for equal participation and airtime. Whereas groups of five can be fairly static in their make-up, groups of fifteen are at their best when their membership is more dynamic, when individuals are swapped in and out as a changing world or evolving business environment demands. Given that leaders spend about 60 per cent of their time with members of this group they need to be alive to the opportunities and challenges involved. Opportunities arise from bringing in fresh voices and new perspectives. Challenges come either when the changes made to the composition of the group are too radical; or when new members are added but it's felt that it would be too awkward to remove existing people to make room for them. The latter scenario is common in organisations that are conceived as pyramids: since they work on the principle that people either move up or down, taking an individual away from a particular group is invariably viewed as an act of demotion. In flatter, more project-based structures, by contrast, leaders can feel free to be more nomadic, acting as attractors to teams according to capability and changing business need. It's these flatter structures that tend to produce more agile, adaptive leadership teams.

These two inner, intimate circles of relationship – the group of five and the slightly larger group of fifteen (which includes the five) – are characterised by a deep sense of obligation and loyalty. It's what makes them so powerful – and, at the same time, makes changing their make-up so difficult. The late Paul Robertson, lead violinist and founder of the Medici Quartet, talked of the trauma when one member of the quartet left. He reflected on how long it took the players who were left to recover, just as it takes a family time to get over a ruction. Managing exits and entrances so that overall team performance is maximised is an often-avoided task. After all, we prefer to stick with who and what we know. One reason why organisations are often so willing to bring in management consultants is that they introduce expertise from the world outside that allows action – sometimes radical action – to be recommended in a way that absolves the board from blame. At the same time, of course – and perhaps most importantly – involving management consultants allows the settled world at the top of the organisation to remain unchanged. This is dangerously wrong-headed. It allows a culture of complacency and dependency to grow, rather than one that encourages vibrancy and individual development.

Groups of fifty need an explicit leader and a greater degree of structure than the two smaller ones. There is too much going on and too many mindstates involved for people to self-organise. This size is often a tipping point for start-ups. It can represent the moment at which the founders are no longer able to hold their governing idea in their head, or balance the imperative for momentum with the need to preserve the relationships that originally made the business so successful. The cognitive load is simply too big. By the time 150 is reached, a degree of stratification is required – sub-leaders and sub-sections take on some of the leadership burden (as in an orchestra). Now a leader must lead *through* others. More explicit shared purposes and values become even more important, as well as regular two-way communication. Autocrats and micromanagers don't choose this route – but then their focus doesn't generally lie with human thriving.

Beyond about 150, any leader has reached the limit of both their cognitive powers and the time they have available for the members of their tribe. At this level, there is an inevitable symbolic element to their role. They become a screen or avatar onto which employees and stakeholders project their hopes and fears. This is the point at which, to quote Bill Gore, 'We' becomes 'Us and Them', and a new, quite different conception of the organisation emerges. Leaders can continue to be relational in style, but only by working through groups of roughly fifteen, and by judicious zooming in and zooming out as required.

When an organisation gets significantly larger than 150, the same principles continue to apply. Introducing internal structuring along the ripple lines of the Dunbar Graph will help to ensure both cohesion and information flow. The rule of three continues beyond 150 to groupings of 500, 1,500 and 5,000 in the same ripple series (Figure 2.3). With these larger groupings, it becomes more and more necessary to have some kind of 'totem pole' on the 'village green' as a focus for organisational loyalty and action. These 'totem poles' work best if they create a meaningful sense of the organisation as family and provide some kind of social purpose or value, preferably with an inspiring foundation story.

Leadership and the Social Brain

Building Leadership Capability

If organisations are best served by a ripple structure, then that suggests that leadership needs to be similarly flexible and non-monolithic. This requires an effective distributed form of leadership – and, in turn, that means cultivating leadership capability at all levels. The ability to develop leaders – lots of them – right through the organisation, regardless of tenure or position, is one of the most important capabilities for anyone keen to foster a thriving environment. These will be the people who lead the sub-sections of the orchestra, the teams of fifteen who share a purpose and a sense of values. Effective management depends on trusted people at all levels who can relate to and activate their own networks to build the future. These leaders need facilitative skills, the ability to empathise with others and exercise judgement to make decisions.

Too many corporate cultures promote people who have mastery of a particular discipline – in other words those who can provide technical answers – rather than those who are curious, ask new questions and can bring the outside in. Leadership is seen as primarily positional rather than for what it is, a means whereby a better future can be ushered in. Provided that there is a clearly articulated purpose and shared values, a more distributed leadership structure can deliver and be accountable for a relational organisation at vast scale without threatening to fracture the supply line or causing outposts to splinter off in a way that was the undoing of empires of old.

With our combined fifty years of working with leaders from all over the world, we see leadership in terms of task and relationship, rather than position. The leadership task is to develop a widely understood purpose and a set of values that bring people together in a shared culture. It is also to engage relentlessly with the changing needs and ideas of stakeholders – to listen, evaluate, connect, encourage, to stop and confront difficulty where necessary. It's exhausting work that's never completely mastered. In terms of relationship, the leadership pronoun is 'we' rather than 'I': an acknowledgement that achievement is the result of a collective effort and not something for the leader to glory in alone. A Social Brain Leader is one who can inspire, earn trust, manage distance and sustain growth – of people as well as enterprise. This requires flexibility of mind and spirit, attention to the big picture as well as the ability to swoop into detail when needed, especially when it comes to people. The technical stuff can largely be outsourced to others.

The bigger an organisation gets the more leaders are needed. Spend your time and attention on cultivating leadership. Ramatu Abdulkadir, public service supply chain leader in Kaduna Province, Nigeria, sums it up in the following terms: 'In supply chain management, most of the focus is on technology, the platform, software and so on. The human aspect of the work is downplayed. My real work, though, is generally about human beings. As long as people are not engaged or their hearts are not in the right place, all the technology in the world can't help you. We must build leaders. We have to build people who build systems, not the other way round.'

Creating the Best Teams

A high-functioning team that is more than the sum of its parts is the holy grail of any business. All too often, however, this basic truth gets forgotten at times of change. HR departments and leaders can often fail to appreciate the dynamics that made a particular group successful, and think instead in terms of individuals when they make decisions about promotion or staffing. In so doing, they neglect to consider how plucking out one of the members of that group to be placed somewhere else within the organisation might impact on the other members. They may also fail to consider what the impact might be on the individual concerned: it is not uncommon for someone who has been hugely successful as a member of one group to fail when removed from it. The footballer Ashley Cole, for example – one of the finest full backs of modern times – was mocked on social media in 2014 when the press photograph of his new transfer team, Roma, showed him standing apart from the rest, 'lurking' rather than in the centre of the action.[5] Given that his talent was undisputed, his lacklustre performance on the pitch was put down to his inability to bond with his new team members. In fifteen months or so, he had decided to move on.

This sense of dislocation is different from a common phenomenon whereby someone is promoted beyond their abilities (the so-called 'Peter Principle'). But the Peter Principle can mask a similar underlying cause: failure to thrive due to being promoted out of a supportive team. All leaders are incomplete; they need others to magnify their strengths and compensate for their weaknesses.

The market is awash with tools that are supposed to enable effective team development: the MBTI (Myers–Briggs Type Indicator currently used by eighty-nine out of the Fortune 100 companies) has been around since the 1940s. However, these tools tend to focus on how each individual can help the group. Few tools look at the world through the other end of the telescope and consider how the group helps the individual. Some industries have, nonetheless, understood that there is an efficient, almost instant alternative to hiring a talented individual or buying a whole company in order to grow capability. The so-called 'lift-out', where companies buy intact teams that are already up and running and ready to go, has become a feature particularly of investment banks, consultancies, medical specialists, advertising agencies and other professional service firms. It can also, of course, be a potent way to hollow out the competition. The investment bank HSBC was left with no one but a graduate trainee to take charge of analysing media equities after its entire team of analysts decamped for competitor ABN AMRO.[6]

Leading in Complex Environments

The 'feel' of a place, its ethos, structure, rituals, stories, habits and shared practice – its culture, in other words – is a crucial bellwether for the social health of any organisation. Walk into the reception and you can sense the tone of the place; look around and you can quickly notice what matters – and what doesn't. We are naturally attracted to hierarchy and status but, just as our tendency towards homophily needs at times to be disrupted, so too does our desire to be safely part of a system geared to status. In complex systems (and it could be said that all groups with the scope to behave naturally form complex systems), good ideas come from the edge, not the centre, since people located there tend to have more direct experience of how the future is unfolding. The bank clerk is the first to notice how customer interactions are shifting, the shoe salesperson sees first what styles are flying off the shelves – and through chatting with customers, she hears why. Local interaction at all levels of an organisation is its lifeblood.

A vibrant organisation is always in the process of self-reorganising and adapting to new patterns as they emerge. Rigid organisation charts – even though they appear to offer reassuring clarity – can be a static cage. An organisation's culture arranged on Dunbar Graph principles, by contrast, is inherently dynamic. Individuals come and go, moving through the layers as their friendship needs and opportunities for connection change. In this at least, it can serve as an effective foundational model for resilience. By using the circles of its ripple structure to better understand the underlying links between time and relationship, leaders can bring air and life into their organisations through judicious intervention. Sometimes, that requires the current processes and structures to be disrupted, or new voices to be listened to and cultivated. In one of our interviews, a recently retired CEO of a leading organisation reflected on one of the changes he would have made during his tenure if he'd known then what he now knew: 'As time went by, I realised I was increasingly only listening to a couple of people when seeking counsel. I was in a comfortable echo chamber of my own making – in retrospect I would have changed that and brought in different, more diverse opinions.' Shakespeare understood the need for the disruptive voice. His 'wise fools' – in *King Lear* and *Twelfth Night*, for example – were employed both to bring in ideas from the outside and to speak truth to power without fear or favour.

Twenty-first-century leaders who find ways to bring challenging voices into the inner sanctum, to spend their allotted 60 per cent of time and attention with a changing group of fifteen or so people at the centre, are more likely to succeed. This is especially true if they enable a similar natural movement of small relational groups, powered by a shared purpose, all the way through the organisation. It may seem counterintuitive but the most time-efficient act is to create deliberative systems by inviting in alternative viewpoints, even disagreement, at key moments of decision-making, particularly at the start of projects. Once a project is underway, it is much more expensive to unravel. And it becomes harder and harder to hear – or even want to hear – critical voices.

In place of a positional leader presiding over the rest from atop the pyramid, the conception then must be of a leader working through and with others, being legitimately part of the team while still setting the direction; doing different, but not necessarily more important work. Here it is a matter not only of how those in leadership positions (and we reiterate here that those are not only at the top) use the scarce resources of time and attention. Having an eye to the macro and the micro, the horizon and the ground, at the same time involves both being on the dancefloor and at times 'getting on the balcony' to quote the Harvard academic Ron Heifetz.[7] These foundational groups of fifteen – fanning out into fifties, one hundred and fifties and beyond – are the building blocks of human exchange. Each cluster benefits from the luxury of trust and personal relationship; each cluster connects its influence with another: this is the contagious way that movements work. Authors and social movement starters Jeremy Heimans and Henry Timms, in their book *New Power*, use the metaphor of water or electricity to represent this kind of power: the leader is there to channel and direct it, not to hoard it or hand it out as though it were money.[8] Power is never the property of an individual. In their (and our) conception of power, leadership itself lies within the personal relationship between leader and follower, not in the position or the person or their traits. An autocrat who gives an order that is not followed is not a leader, nor is the person who starts a Mexican wave at a football ground if no one raises their arms in response. 'A good leader makes a good follower', to quote the famed psychoanalyst Wilfred Bion.[9] Organisations with a 'social brain' are relational in construct. They make space for individuals, and they grow big by staying small, accreting small units. They pay attention to the space between people.

Managing Time and Attention

Having a strong, shared purpose determines where you – and others in your organisation – spend your time and attention. 'Leadership has got bigger,' one CEO we talked to reflected post-pandemic, 'but our days and our capacities have not.' The most frequently overheard lament is that there is precious little time to think about the future, to focus on the hard stuff or to meet the people waiting at the gates. Days are filled with the urgencies of business as usual and the punctuation of meetings, not to mention meetings about meetings. Leaders feel more like the slaves of time than timelords. But perhaps that's because they've been paying attention to and spending time on the wrong things.

Social Brain Leaders will find ways to recapture their diaries by first acknowledging that time and attention are the most precious resources they – and arguably their organisations – have. Rather than replacing eight hour-long meetings with sixteen half-hour ones, they instead recognise that more busyness is not necessarily good business. Just as the paradox of scaling an organisation involves growing big by staying small, so the paradox of managing time in order to achieve a purpose involves doing less in order to achieve more.

Leaders we have worked with have tried different strategies. One senior executive from a large mobility company made it known that Wednesday mornings were 'no meeting' mornings. This space in the middle of the week allowed her to tackle more complex thought-hungry problems on those days. The experiment worked so well that she later encouraged her whole team to adopt the habit. Another chief information officer realised that he was generally less productive straight after lunch. Very little attention is paid to our natural circadian rhythms when planning the timing of important meetings, never mind the fact that some of us are morning people and others are evening people[10] and work better at different times of day. He therefore decided that he would go to the gym three times a week at lunchtime – and use the time he spent there to exercise, recharge his batteries and reflect. The endorphins created by this new regimen sharpened up his thinking and allowed him to focus better, to be more relaxed and to embrace the afternoon with an elevated mood. Initially, he felt guilty about doing something that felt self-indulgent. Only later, when he realised how much more productive and purposeful he now was in the afternoons, did this experiment settle into a long-term habit.

Another simple strategy is to institute the discipline of fifty-minute or even twenty-five-minute meetings. One large bank in the UK has a pre-arranged setting that encourages colleagues to have twenty-five-minute meetings where decisions need to be made, with time set aside *between* each meeting to allow for a coffee or tea break. Ten minutes, or even five minutes, won back from the time in a meeting can be put to good use – to put into action something from the discussion (not to squeeze in another mini meeting!), or just to have a coffee and reflect. It may take a while for these experiments to become a discipline, but persevering with them will allow you to make time for thinking about the future. One group of managing directors from a global organisation discovered that each one of them in their own territories essentially spent several hours each Monday morning first being reported to and then reporting the territory's figures back to the central hub. When they computed the collective amount of leadership time spent in directing and redirecting information alone rather than working on the future together, they were shocked. What else could they have been more profitably doing?

The Thrive Model™

Most leaders are understandably tempted to reach for the latest model, technology or framework to provide an apparently solid structure in uncertain times. In so doing they tend to ignore our inherited biological forces rumbling under the surface, pulling at our human fabric. It is always easier to pay attention to the surface appearance, to what can be easily measured: targets, costs and physical output numbers. What is far less easy to measure – but is nonetheless the key ingredient for those measurable outcomes – is the interplay within groups and between individuals, and the forces that drive those interactions. Dynamics such as these, operating in the unnamed spaces between, are the unseen and constant forces that enable or, alternatively, disrupt, even derail, organisational life. They have been the focus of this book.

In the course of our research, we talked to many people leading organisations, large and small. What emerged from these conversations was a clear picture of the ideal conditions for human thriving within a modern organisation. These are captured in the Thrive Model™

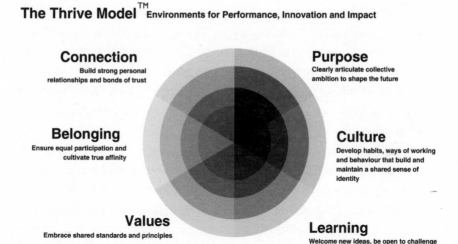

The Thrive Model™ Environments for Performance, Innovation and Impact

Connection
Build strong personal relationships and bonds of trust

Purpose
Clearly articulate collective ambition to shape the future

Belonging
Ensure equal participation and cultivate true affinity

Culture
Develop habits, ways of working and behaviour that build and maintain a shared sense of identity

Values
Embrace shared standards and principles

Learning
Welcome new ideas, be open to challenge and opportunity

The Thrive Model™

Figure 8.3. Organisations only flourish when people do. There are six dimensions to an environment that enables this flourishing. These dimensions are most generative where relationship is strongest, at the centre of the circle. As the layers radiate outwards, the effects diminish.

in Figure 8.3. This ideal environment is a place where there are clear, shared values and purpose, the opportunity for everyone to find meaning in their work and to learn and develop, somewhere where there is the possibility for human connection and friendship, a shared sense of belonging and a culture that celebrates all of these qualities. This section describes ways in which leaders can optimise the possibilities for more human-shaped work. Some of the strategies involved are simple to turn into action, some are more complex. All require leaders' time and attention.

We will now look at each in turn.

Connection: Building Friendship and Trust

Having the time and the space to make friends at work is an important element of building connection. As we indicated in Chapter Three, the Seven Pillars of Friendship (shared interests, worldview, sense of humour, musical taste, language, education, where the teenage years were spent) provide a foundation for relationships, particularly in fragile times or periods of transition. They also ensure the growth of trust. But if there is no time at work to find out about one another and build common ground, these shared pathways will never be built.

Tracey once spent some time working with a global consulting firm. One evening on a late, shared taxi ride back from a client, three members of the long-established team revealed that earlier in their careers they had been a PhD art historian, an army officer and a nuclear submarine pilot. Until that moment, even though they had worked together for many months, none had known about the very different paths the others had once pursued or thought that their former experiences might offer inspiration for the present. They hadn't taken time to get to know each other, let alone to make friends.

Yet the advantages of making friends at work are huge. Those who do so are less likely to leave and more likely to feel a sense of wellbeing. The Seven Pillars are particularly important in a hybrid working environment where it's not possible to spend time together around the coffee machine or walk to meetings. To know that there are, say, four other rock climbers in the company or to meet up with the three others who went to school in the same town can bring both reassurance and an instant sense of trust. The problem is that discovering this bond can take months, sometimes years, at the best of times; it takes disproportionately longer under hybrid working conditions. Designing in social time, even during virtual meetings, is very important for building these bonds of connection and trust. Margaret Heffernan, CEO and author, in a conversation with a group of senior leaders from across the world attending the OSLP, finished her session with one simple reminder: 'The most important thing you can do as a leader is to keep connected – with your family, with your friends. This is the most important part of life.'

The number and quality of friendships you have has a bigger effect on your health than any of the factors that your doctor usually worries about: your weight, how much exercise you take, what you eat, what pills you are prescribed, or the quality of the air you breathe. Friends exert powerful influence over health choices as well.[11] The best way to lose weight is to spend time with slim friends. Want to give up smoking? Forget nicotine patches; spend more time with non-smoking friends. If there is no time or space for friendship or conversation with medical staff while you are in hospital . . . well, it doesn't take a genius to figure out what the consequences will be. There is currently a crisis of mental health in work settings and a great deal of time and effort is being spent on gym memberships, mindfulness, meditation, in-house psychologists etc, all of which may well be positive developments – but without friendship there is a danger that they merely paper over the cracks.

Of course, overemphasis on the Seven Pillars can also produce an unhealthy, siloed culture. The job of a leader is to enable friendships to develop at work, but also at times to disrupt the cosiness of natural bonds so as to get people to build new points of connection from which they will benefit. The most generative relationships are often those that emerge out of difference. They are also the most productive and efficient in terms of outcomes, the serendipitous source of innovation and new directions. The skill of bringing people together to solve problems productively and to see disagreement in the room as an asset (in the short term at least) is one of the foundational skills of a Social Brain Leader.

Belonging: Creating a Sense of Kinship

In order to thrive, human beings need to feel that they belong to a tribe or group that gives them a voice, ensures that they are heard and so brings meaning to their lives. A sense of belonging is a huge factor in employee wellbeing and retention. Feeling left out, overlooked or excluded creates anxiety and stress, and results in underperformance. Owen Eastwood gives the example of a highly successful football manager wanting to give feedback – or criticism – to a young player. He always prefaced the feedback by reminding the young man why he was recruited, what stood out about him, what particular promise he showed, why he absolutely belonged to the team. In this way, the positive hormones that come from a sense of inclusion were activated and the developmental feedback was more easily absorbed.

A sense of belonging is a reciprocal thing. It's not enough simply to be invited into an organisation, to be hired or recruited; people also need to be recognised and welcomed as members of a family if they are to feel that they belong. When an organisational culture works best, the organisation belongs to the people as much as they belong to 'it'. Like family bonds, a strong group culture depends on a shared language, rituals, artefacts, stories, memories, experiences and, importantly, values. It is hard to feel at home in a sterile environment, or to feel part of an organisation that hasn't taken the trouble to find out who you are. Crucially a sense of belonging also comes from sharing a purpose and collective meaning, some worthwhile direction and focus that can be experienced by all. This does not derive simply from a written mission statement or stated purpose. It is formed by the culture of the organisation, its aspirations, its practices and rituals, which in turn come from its people and their personalities, past, present and future. This sense of shared endeavour is often difficult to put down on paper, but, just as we gauge someone's personality in the first minutes after we meet them, so we can sense purpose and ethos in the style and ambience of an office or a shopfloor. It is present in the way you are greeted (or not) as you walk through a building; it is communicated in the feel of the place and the people. Feeling is data when it comes to culture. Lovelyn Nwadeyi, social justice activist, extends this idea: 'It isn't enough to be passive recipients of an existing culture, rather the power lies in collectively crafting the language that is used in organisations to build this feeling of belonging and access.'

Why is the notion of belonging so powerful? The word 'diversity' implies deviation from the norm, and 'inclusion' an invitation by a more powerful group to a less powerful outsider. The notion of belonging doesn't take sides. Both incumbents and newcomers belong without any powerplay. The Dunbar Graph with its clear delineation of human cognitive and time constraints emphasises a problem for hierarchical organisations that focus on diversity and inclusion rather than belonging. If I bring someone new into my close group of fifteen, then an incumbent will necessarily have to swap out (due to limits of time and brain size). This inevitably involves feelings of exclusion (sometimes resentment) and loss of status for the incumbent. These feelings can provoke a backlash and even more deeply entrenched feelings of 'us and them'. By contrast, if the focus lies in helping everyone to feel included – from the most traditional, establishment figure through to the newest recruit from a completely different background – there is no divisive 'us and them'.

A sense of belonging should begin the moment a new member of staff steps through the door and every moment thereafter. All too often, the actual process of inducting new staff is the element of the recruitment process that gets overlooked. It is, however, the part that merits most attention. A proper welcome is remembered.

Well executed, these transitional rituals help newcomers to become productive as fast as possible and, crucially, to feel they want to be a member of a community that recognises them as an individual, rather than just another employee. The 2022 UN women representative for the Netherlands, Enaam Ahmed Ali, recounts how, a few weeks into her job at the bank where she works, on the first day of Ramadan her manager beckoned her aside, away from the team, to ask if there was anything the manager or the team could do – or should be doing – differently to help her feel comfortable. The key element here was the preparedness for the institution itself to adapt to the new individual, rather than the other way around, and the care they showed to ensure that her first experiences should be good ones.

It's not only beginnings that merit more attention than they usually receive, but also endings. People retire from organisations, taking their accumulated knowledge, stories and the richness of their experience with them. Organisations say goodbye to them without sufficiently honouring what these individuals have done, or seeking to capture what they have learned to be shared with others. One company we worked with had a flexible approach to retirement and those who choose to leave. They keep contact with their alumni, take pride in 'preserving lifelong relationships'. The firm 'leaves the door open' for rehiring people who have left earlier in their careers. This company is something of an outlier. Instead, all too often, the door closes on a life of work – and that's it. And with that is often lost a wealth of knowledge and experience.

Purpose: Creating Collective Meaning

None of the group practices enumerated above are sufficient in themselves unless there is a shared meaning and purpose to work. People want more from their labours than for work to be an end in itself – for it to be merely a means of survival. Groups of human beings left to their own devices tend to create meaning and momentum together. However minor the role an employee plays, it is important for them to understand the contribution they are making to the broader purpose of the organisation and, ideally, to society. Having an organisational purpose that is sincerely meant and authentically adopted throughout the organisation is royal jelly for employees. Creating individual meaning at work is made easier when there is a connection back to the organisational purpose. Human beings have a highly developed capacity to learn and experiment and when the organisational purpose encourages the freedom for individual expression, this learning and experimentation is folded back into organisational performance and innovation. Several years ago, historian Theodore Zeldin undertook a research project with IKEA to explore the possibilities for fostering learning in their stores. He transformed their Liverpool store into a cultural learning hub where customers were given the chance to talk to one another and with the salespeople over supper with menus of conversation. In this way purely transactional exchanges were replaced with much more human, developmental connections.

In a similar vein but for different reasons, social entrepreneur Thami Schweichler, CEO of Makers Unite in Amsterdam, helps refugees and newcomers with a refugee background become socially connected in the Netherlands. He views the act of creating something together as central to the business of integration and as such always begins the process of connection by fostering the co-creation of projects between locals and newcomers. This experience of creating together not only fast-tracks meaningful connections but also supports the critical process of learning about each other in a safe and productive space.

This ambition is not always as easy as it sounds, particularly when new initiatives or ways of working are introduced. Take, for example, the experience of one CEO we worked with who had the laudable ambition of cutting his company's dependence on plastics. He launched a series of experiments and innovations to achieve his goal, but was frustrated to find that they made slow progress. It was only when he set out to establish why this was that he discovered that in seeking to change a purpose he had ignored a process and the human ecosystem that surrounded it. His initiative involved upfront investment and an acceptance that sales would be flat for a while. Company bonuses, however, were predicated on growth. It wasn't until he realigned remuneration so that it wasn't directly linked to output that he started to make progress with a programme that, on the surface, had nothing to do with the obstacle that had stood in its way. This kind of double-loop learning – where the system 'learns' as well as the people within it – is increasingly important in large organisations where IT systems, global protocols and 'plumbed-in' ways of working can rumble on unseen in the background, thwarting the tides of change.

Keeping corporate and individual purpose aligned, then, demands constant attention if inertia or resistance are to be avoided. After all, our natural human tendency is to stick with the status quo. We'll stay with the same bank, even though their customer service is dismal. We'll holiday in the same place as we have for the past five years, even though we know the weather tends to be dire. We'll drink the same brand of tea without stopping to ask ourselves whether there might be a better one out there. In the same way, in a work environment we'll stick with projects that have overrun, traditional ways of working that no longer serve, contracts that are not delivering, and expectations that can no longer be honoured because, at one level, it's the easiest route. We find it particularly difficult to let people go. Our natural desire to maintain existing bonds overrides a realisation that perhaps a particular person is no longer a good fit within the organisation. Leaders often find it most difficult to end things with a colleague who is a consistently high performer, even if their behaviour (often not measured) is in conflict with the organisational values. But when loyalties no longer match espoused values and purpose, action needs to be taken. Organisations where poorly behaved colleagues are accommodated or seen to be favoured gradually weaken outwards from the core.

A good leader will know when to call a halt. But they will also know how to do it. A brutal approach can cause huge damage both internally and externally, as was the case recently with a British ferry company that informed staff via video that they no longer had a job and would be replaced by agency workers. The best practitioners take time to honour the past, to remember what was achieved and, where appropriate, to mark the end with appropriate ritual. A restatement of purpose requires careful handling.

Values: Tight Principles, Loose Rules

Too often a company's values are stated on its website but go unlived by senior management and largely unnoticed by employees. They also tend to be too generic and too numerous to be memorable. Yet, as the Dunbar ripple structure shows, groups function best when they strongly share particular values. Shared values guarantee that choices are not made that compromise the integrity of the organisation. They ensure coherent decision-making. And they allow for that decision-making to be devolved to like-minded people across the organisation, so avoiding logjams and delay and ensuring that individuals feel empowered. It's not for nothing that Debra France at Gore believes in the rule of 'tight principles and loose rules'. 'Shared values become a form of governance that is fueled by the passion and commitment of each person who shares a belief in that principle. When Gore associates discuss what must be tight and what can be loose, they realize that they want to be tight about the shared principles of freedom, fairness, commitment and waterline, while remaining loose about *how* we will live these principles. This allows teams around the world and in different cultures to carefully consider: what does "fair" mean for these associates? What does "freedom" look like for different associates in different professions or careers? Are we truly supporting every associate in making his or her own commitments? Are we expecting every associate to make the decisions they have the knowledge and understanding to make, while seeking the counsel of others to ensure those decisions are the best for the entire community?'

Like the principles designed by Forrest Mars Senior that live on in Mars more than sixty years later, the Gore principles continue to 'guide us in the decisions we make, in the work we do and in our behavior toward each other, our partners and our customers.'[12]

Because the decisions an organisation makes stem from its values, every decision feeds back into those values. For Professor Ngaire Woods, Dean of the Blavatnik School of Government in Oxford, this loop offers an opportunity. Every decision, she says, even a very minor one, is an opportunity to communicate values. Take her example of whether or not faculty should be allowed free coffee. A 'yes' could provide the opportunity to underline the value of academics coming together, exchanging ideas and spending time with each other to improve their teaching and research. A 'no' could emphasise the importance of their scholarship fund and the need for every penny going towards the education of those who don't have the means to come to Oxford.

For her part Professor Ruth Chang, Chair of Jurisprudence at the University of Oxford, talks of the way in which, when faced with a hard decision – that is, one where there is no obvious right or wrong, or better or worse – we have a tendency either to hope we can wait until a clear answer presents itself or allow ourselves to drift into taking one path or another. Her view is that if our values are sufficiently strong, we won't waver between different options but instead will make a firm commitment to the path that matches our values most closely. The decision-making data come from within. Any subsequent obstacles or setbacks that may then occur will become challenges to be overcome rather than evidence that we made the wrong choice. What's more, we will be shaping the future, rather than allowing the future to shape us.

Learning: Listening and Getting People to Listen

In order to communicate with others, we spend much of our time polishing our PowerPoint slides and seeking to get the accompanying presentation just right. We may also adopt an open-door policy or, on a larger scale, decide to hold 'Town Halls'. But if we can't be confident that people have actually understood what we've said, all such approaches offer little more than 'box-ticking' comfort. The fact is that the message given is never as important as the message received.

Getting a message across, however, requires great care and attention. People tend to remember the words *they've* spoken, rather than what others have said. When we think others are listening, it's quite likely that what they're actually doing is preparing their next remark. Encouraging listening to learn, rather than listening to respond (waiting for a break in the talk to say what you were going to say anyway) is hard to achieve.

There are, however, various techniques we can draw on that will help. In the first place, we should consider manner as much as we do matter. Tone and gesture, along with an awareness of acoustics and setting, are, as the linguist Albert Mehrabian[13] found, more important than the words themselves. We also have to listen as much as – if not more than – we speak. Leadership expert Jennifer Garvey Berger says that the test of an effective leader is not how much people appreciate them, but how much people come to appreciate themselves in their leader's presence. The creation of this kind of environment requires time for creative listening as well as time for people to speak their minds. As, by their very nature, none of these listening capabilities draw attention to themselves, they are all too easily overlooked and their importance underestimated. Too often we feel we have to impress by being the centre of attention. But, as the Chinese proverb has it, 'Speech is silver, but silence [listening] is gold.'

Another communication tool that is still underused by those in senior positions is the narrative or story. Storytelling has been practised throughout history to bind communities together and help make sense of things. It is a form of broadcast that is inclusive. It connects teller to hearer. At the same time, by engaging emotionally with the hearer and requiring them to interpret what is being said, it transforms them from passive bystander into active participant. Storytelling, in other words, is a relational form of communication – the relating of a story literally gets us 'related'. Presentations that consist entirely of facts and figures will be swiftly forgotten. Presentations that contain stories will not.

Similarly, memorable is what for want of a better term can be labelled as playfulness. As we pointed out in Chapter Three, a sense of humour is one of the Seven Pillars of Friendship, but in the West we tend still to be dominated by a Protestant work ethic that regards fun as frivolous. Work is work, after all. Surely it's inappropriate to throw back your head and laugh when you're in the office? Yet, as we showed in Chapter Four, a sense of humour and – more generally – a sense of playfulness are vitally important. The synchrony of laughter, of music and dancing, and of eating and drinking together, not only bonds groups, but invites people to be curious and to explore. And it sticks in the memory. Charlotte Murphy and colleagues discovered that 'high-curiosity states can improve memory of information beyond the target of a person's curiosity, even when that information is completely incidental to the topics that piqued an individual's curiosity'.[14]

A company we work with always sends out a professionally produced, convincing April Fool on 1 April each year. Why divert creative time and energy to something that is little more than a joke? Because it communicates a whole lot about the values, tone and confidence of the company. It brings people together. And it's memorable. Well-judged humour is productive.

As a rule, we feel most comfortable listening to and learning from like-minded individuals. They make life easier: we don't have to interrupt the conversation by having to explain the joke, decode the acronym or provide the one outsider in the group with background information that everyone else knows. They can also be genuinely beneficial. Like-minded people are able to discuss deep issues more easily and reach decisions faster precisely because they share the same knowledge base or because sharing the same frame of reference minimises the risk of misunderstandings. There are times when homogenous teams are necessary, for example when deep technical expertise is required – simply because they will get the job done better and more quickly.

In other contexts, however, echo chambers can hamper progress and lead to faulty decision-making and blinkered judgment. They inhibit us from learning. If habitual assumptions or the same voices dominate, an organisation can quickly get out of step with the changing context. It's the problem faced by every autocrat in history, whether in the palace or the boardroom. If colleagues can't or won't pass on the bad news or say the unpalatable, the juggernaut will continue inexorably on its way to the cliff edge. In a 2016 study,[15] psychologists David Rock and Heidi Grant found that diverse teams not only enhanced productivity but also fostered innovation and decision-making. These teams were more likely to make fact-based decisions and to be more objective as well as being less conformist than homogenous groups. A more diverse board is more likely to have different sources of knowledge and experience. It will be more likely to include individuals who are willing to question received wisdom and settled habits, and to offer new perspectives.

Diverse teams produce better results. Economist Tim Harford quotes a study by academics Katherine Phillips, Katie Liljenquist and Margaret Neale that showed how groups containing an outsider proved better at solving a murder mystery puzzle than those made up of friends.[16] Interestingly, groups that comprised friends complacently assumed that they had performed better; groups with an outsider, though more proficient, both felt uncomfortable and underestimated their ability to succeed. McKinsey's 2020 *Diversity Wins* study, which looked at 1,000 large companies, concluded that the greater the representation of diverse groups (they looked both at gender and ethnicity), the higher the likelihood of outperformance, matched against industry norms.[17] Interestingly, diversity of ethnicity had an even greater positive impact on performance than diversity of gender, probably because, in this context, two genders were more likely to be from the same cultural background and share the same perspectives.

Diversity, then, involves not just issues of equality and justice but more creative working and better decision-making. Take gender, for example. In their book *Boys Will Be Boys*, finance professors Brad Barber and Terrance Odean found that men tended to lose more on the stock market relative to women because they traded too often.[18] They concluded that the reason for this was that men were prone to overconfidence. In such contexts, women's tendency to greater caution would have offered an important countervailing force. The Austrian physicist Stefan Thurner found similar gender differences in the online game world *Pardus*.[19] Because they were less prone to risky decisions, women players were often more successful. In addition, their trades were more gender-biased and reciprocal than men's were, with a stronger preference for homophily and stability. For an insightful view of the world, you need the views of both genders.

We need to embrace the fact that genders do differ from one another, not in terms of intelligence but, as we emphasised in Chapter Five, in terms of social style. Put at its simplest: the male social world tends to be more club-like, whereas the female one tends to be more dyadically focused and personalised. This difference between the genders influences attitudes, conversational styles and responses to social circumstance as well as to threats – and is instrumental in the striking tendency for conversations to segregate by gender.[20] Both genders can learn to adjust to the other's social or conversational style, but, like learning a new language as an adult, the adjustment is never perfect, often tiring and sometimes irksome – to both parties. It is important to remember that one style is not better than the other, but rather that they are simply different ways of achieving the same end, namely building networks of psychological and social support. They are two ends of a continuum on the same distribution, with a degree of overlap in the middle, complementing each other in ways that can often enhance problem-solving by simultaneously adding balance and difference.

Diversity is about different personality types, too. Krešimir Josić, at the University of Houston, has found that the best decisions tend to come from a mix of impulsive and cautious people.[21] More generally, we need people of different ages, worldviews and capabilities, all drawn from different disciplines, if we're to explore different ways of doing things and come up with new ideas. Leonardo da Vinci thought in a whole range of different ways on paper, moving from equations through to sketches, to mirror writing, to architectural models, to figures as he grappled with a single issue. Few individuals have his flexibility of mind, but we can take a leaf out of his book if we bring together people who, jointly, incorporate his multistranded way of thinking and doing.

Diverse groups, however, require enlightened leadership if the best is to be gained from them. There is no point having the most diverse committee if some voices remain unheard or fail to get sufficient airtime. It's also crucial to understand that each of us is diverse. As Walt Whitman put it, we all contain multitudes.[22] Leadership approaches that assume that a particular person will always react in a particular way miss out on a nuanced appreciation of that person's complexity. We are all hard to categorise if we are fully known and have proper attention paid to us.

Culture: Ritual and Environment

Organisational cultures that are well understood and 'felt' by newcomers and existing members alike are made up of a collection of prompts. These cultural prompts have different qualities – some are clear and overt (a sign outside a coffee shop clarifying that all are welcome conveys a sense of belonging), but some of these prompts are fainter and less explicit, in what Edgar Schein[23] has described as 'occurring below the surface'. Like an iceberg, culture includes that which is seen above the surface (the artefacts) as well as the assumptions and behaviours that are subconscious or 'below the surface'. While organisational cultures are always adjusting and shifting in step with the external context and the changing make-up of the group, successful cultures (and by successful we mean supportive of the purpose and strategy of the organisation) are those that have a consistent thread running through them like a stick of rock. Cultural consistency emerges from the stories told, the rituals practised, the collectively resonant symbols and habits of the group. The culture is underpinned by shared values, expressed in a language broadly understood by all. The processes and ways of working designed into the system support rather than undermine the culture and, crucially, the leaders embody it not only in the way they talk but also in the way they act.

A culture that encourages homogeneity at all costs, though, is to be assiduously avoided. Cultish, inward-looking sameness where management is a secretive clique sequestered on the fifth floor, drinking their own Kool-Aid, far beyond the reach of the ordinary men and women below, is dangerous in the extreme. The mavericks, eccentrics and creatives – so vital to an innovative culture – will often be rejected by such a group in the interests of self-protection and efficiency. The shadow side of belonging needs to be actively worked *against* in generative cultures, just as some of the positive natural inclinations of the desire to belong need to be worked *with*. Whistle-blowers, for example, find it hard to be heard in groups where there is a homogeneity of view.

CEO and author Margaret Heffernan has written extensively on this subject. She cites the well-known case of Enron's Sherron Watkins.[24] When Watkins discovered accounting irregularities that baffled her, she wrote to Kenneth Lay, who was Enron's chairman at that time, articulating her worries, hoping that he would know how to remedy them. Instead, the first thing he did was to seek legal advice on getting her fired. In the end, Watkins never went public with her concerns. Her letter came to light during the investigation in the wake of the company's bankruptcy. Watkins had simply hoped to fix the problems before the company failed, but the culture (and leadership) turned away and could not hear what she had to say.

When it comes to the physical environment within which people can thrive, it needs to be recognised that this doesn't just happen by chance: it needs to be designed. The sort of workspace one finds at Airbnb, which is consciously based on the home, is rare. Far too often, people settle for an office set-up that is sterile and bland. And yet environment is crucial. At its best it can create a culture where people feel safe, and also unsafely safe: safe enough to speak up, sufficiently unsafely safe that they will take risks together and invent. They will also be able to enjoy spaces that encourage them to make serendipitous connections with one another. The global pandemic has shown that while Zoom and Teams are great for sharing information, it takes physical proximity to engender trust and encourage creativity.

Just as you might match team with task, matching environment with team is equally important. How many times has the long, immovable board table prevented real equality of exchange, the dark basement without views to the outside world prevented imaginative thinking about the future, the team 'get-together' in a conference room lacked hearth and warmth – or a delicate exchange with a foreign partner taken place in a restaurant with dreadful acoustics? In human-shaped organisations, even micro-decisions about environment can have a huge impact. Light and health consultant Dr Shelley James would say that a good place to start would be to bring in more natural light, a still largely unappreciated driver of productivity, wellbeing and sharpened attention.

Where and how things happen influences outcomes almost as much as the things themselves. A Colombian colleague told us about the historic peace negotiations that were held between FARC rebels and the government in the most unpromising of environments: in the jungle, in the heat, amid clouds of mosquitoes, and with a wind so strong that it kept blowing papers away. Not surprisingly, the talks fell apart. Most office environments are not quite that bad, but many are not conducive for productive working. The design of meeting rooms naturally seems to create a formal hierarchy – an inevitable consequence of who sits at the head of the table. Mixing up where the chief executive sits in smaller meetings can shake up the dynamics.

One government leader who had a tricky issue to work through with a large team, for example, convened a breakfast meeting in a room with small round tables, where unexpectedly good coffee and croissants were served, and where a small-group conversational format was applied. Simply changing the usual set-up altered the day-to-day mood and helped to bring about a positive outcome. Eating a meal together before, rather than after, an important meeting is always a game-changer – but one that's rarely planned for. The endorphins produced by the shared meal, the structure and orchestration of the meal, as well as the social time spent together positively affect the outcome. A small, intimate room or a conversational walk in the park can be what's needed for a sensitive topic. Culture and environment are inextricably tied together.

Finally . . .

Much of this book may appear to be no more than common sense. We find it hard to function well in big groups. Feeling left out is a miserable experience. It's good if we like our colleagues, and so on. But the research that underpins this common sense has not generally been acted upon in organisations, perhaps because it feels too intuitive, too soft, too 'nice to have' rather than 'essential to DO'. Over the years, we have worked with thousands of leaders from across the world. Only the best of them see their organisations in these very human terms and seek to engage with these very human issues.

In the nineteenth century, water and air were taken for granted and their properties little understood. It's only today, with both under threat, that we realise how vital they are and legislate to protect them. Today, we either take the social nature of organisations for granted, or don't give it a thought. The time has come, though, when more and more people are being forced to realise just how key the social organisation is to our health and performance. Robin has been at the forefront of this new science of understanding something very old – our evolutionary inheritance. Samantha and Tracey have worked extensively with teams to understand the benefits of putting the science into practice.

We are, nonetheless, optimists. We believe that with more

confidence in ourselves as human beings, more focus on the dynamics of relationship and on our ability to learn and adapt, groups can be enabled to be much more than the sum of their parts. The realisation of this optimistic vision will require mature, self-aware leadership at all levels within organisations. It will require grown-ups at the helm with a long-term focus that incorporates the past, even the distant past, as well as the future. It will also require people who can both capitalise on and work against our more primal selves. Some of the conclusions we draw are hard to implement, particularly those that address the underlying design of organisations. Some are easy, cheap and simple to incorporate. A meal together, a walking meeting, ten minutes shaved off a call for a more personal check-in – these quickly and automatically change the hormonal mix within which we operate, making work feel more like play. The pay-off from the various insights we offer could be the creation of organisations in which the next generation will thrive – where work is decent, purposeful and to be enjoyed, and where each person gets to express their individual talent in work that matters. The creation of environments within which everyone can thrive – from the most junior to the chair – is the job of leadership. These environments will need leaders who are prepared to spend their time and attention creating opportunities for connection and learning, who foster a sense of belonging and enable people to find meaning and purpose in their work within a culture that reinforces these human needs and gifts.

On the ground floor of the Ashmolean Museum in Oxford is a Stradivarius violin in a glass box. It was donated to the museum on one condition – that it was never played. How much of a loss to music is that? Yet so many of the human gifts that our biology has given us remain boxed inside boxy organisations. Our imagination, our social selves, the sophistication of our communication, our capacity for joy remains 'unplayed' without enlightened leaders with the courage to set it free. As the historian Theodore Zeldin has remarked, 'Can we not have more experiments to offer something better to young people? Isn't this the ultimate purpose of organisations?'

The territory of leadership is swampy ground – it requires courage and the ability to ask for help in order to negotiate a pathway. Those who imagine the ground beneath their feet is solid are probably managing the present, not leading into the future. A sense of humility and acknowledgement of the need for others are essential qualities right the way through any growing organisation, not just at the top.

Afterword

Our work always involves hypotheses, experiments, close observation, behavioural prototyping and learning at pace from mistakes. As we've developed our thoughts and ideas, we've road-tested them on a whole range of colleagues and other professionals, who have offered us invaluable feedback. Some have asked, 'So how do we begin? Where should we take our first steps towards greater thriving at work?'

In response, we offer you here some ideas for those first steps – some practical approaches and behavioural experiments that you might try (which have worked for us and we believe will work for you too). You will find that some suggestions are very simple: for example, beginning a tricky meeting with a shared meal, rather than going out together after it's all over – a simple shift that can transform outcomes hugely. Some of our suggestions are more challenging, involving changes in perspectives and attitudes. These are not quick fixes; they require a more considered, longer-term response.

Leading by Numbers

- If you are leading a growing business, then always have the Dunbar graph at the front of your mind. Make sure that you understand the dynamics and implications of each group size (five, fifteen and fifty) and be particularly sensitive to the relational challenges that occur once a group reaches 150.
- Given that you typically spend 60 per cent of your social time and attention on an inner circle of fifteen, it's crucial to make sure that all those fifteen are relevant to the tasks in hand. Don't let freeloaders keep their seat at the table and don't be

tempted to add new voices without being prepared to swap out old voices to make room.

- Each team size has its own strengths and dynamics. It's therefore essential to map team to task. Ask yourself, for example, whether your creative teams are too large to move fast and whether your strategy teams are too small to allow for fresh viewpoints.
- If you detect stress or conflict within your organisation, check the numbers. Are group sizes too big? Are people being required to sustain more departmental relationships than is humanly possible?
- Value the emotional data gathered from the 'social brain' as much as traditionally extracted quantitative data.

A Sense of Belonging

- If you detect tensions between departments and units within your organisation – a sense of 'us' and 'them' – find people who can work across these divisions to reconnect groups and act as bridges between them.
- Design in beginnings and endings. Use the rituals of welcome and farewell for new joiners and leavers.
- Every organisation has a foundation myth or story. Make sure that yours is inclusive and makes people feel welcome. Does it require updating?
- Test your organisational language, including acronyms. Make sure the language that is most often used reflects the desired culture and doesn't exclude or complicate a collective sense of belonging.
- Look at your broader ecosystem: the people (contract workers, supply-chain workers etc) who are not employees but on whom you nevertheless depend heavily. Find ways to give them a sense of belonging.

Bonding

- Actively make time for people to get together and benefit from such synchronous activities as eating, drinking, walking together, laughing and sharing stories.
- Scrutinise meetings that occur on a regular basis. Do they actually fulfil a definite purpose (practical, strategic or social) or are they just calendar fillers?
- Find time – and space – for building friendships. Encouraging people to eat together, establishing places where they can gather and chat, will pay dividends.
- While it's important to create a socially relaxed environment, there are times when a degree of stress or surprise can spark creative ideas. For example, the simple act of moving a regular meeting to an unexpected environment can disrupt habitual dynamics and jolt members into new ways of interacting.
- Find out what people really feel about working for – and with – your organisation. Ask them.

The Medium and the Message

- If you have an important message to share, always map it out first and consider what impact it will have: huge damage can be caused by a thoughtless use of language or an inappropriate tone. Rehearse in front of a mirror or video yourself. Make sure that your body language accords with what you are seeking to say.
- Check how effective a conversationalist you are by asking others to offer feedback. What should you STOP doing? What should you START doing? What should you CONTINUE doing?

- We tend to focus on what we have to say and how others react to the message we are imparting. Next time you're in a meeting, stand back a little and seek to assess the mood of the room, people's body language, and the tone they adopt when speaking. You will quickly establish whether the group functions well together or whether work is required to make it gel.

The Size of Trust

- A trust environment is built through give and take and a willingness to express vulnerability. Asking for help not only makes practical sense, it also creates bonds of trust.
- Learn to spot the 'freeriders' within your system – people who exploit others' goodwill and trust. It's also important to identify those who display 'Dark Triad' traits (narcissism, Machiavellianism and psychopathy). All need to be dealt with swiftly, as their effects can be deeply corrosive.
- Make sure that the people you listen to, especially at times of decision-making or stress, are not simply those who will tell you what you want to hear. You need to ensure that they are people you can trust. The two groups are not interchangeable.

Social Space, Social Time

- Never underestimate the impact of physical environment (space, light, layout and location) on people's sense of wellbeing and their creativity.
- Creativity demands diversity. Make sure that you draw on as wide a range of voices as possible, and that group sizes are calibrated so as to allow all opinions to be aired.
- Give individual groups the time, budget and permission to build their own sense of belonging and team identity.

Acknowledgements

With thanks to our wonderful friendship layer who have been supportive and encouraging. To Jack Barron, Lia Rockey and Harry Camilleri for early editing help, to Kitty Camilleri for her work on graphics, referencing and permissions, to all our interviewees for their time, wisdom and patience, to Gavin Weeks who has been an invaluable sounding board, to the team at Thompson Harrison for their ongoing support, to Donald Winchester at Watson Little for his advice and advocacy and finally to Nigel Wilcockson at Penguin Random House for his valuable guidance on structure and coherence.

Notes

1. Introduction

1 Phelan, James, 'Rhetorical literary ethics and lyric narrative: Robert Frost's "Home Burial"', *Poetics Today*, 25.4, pp. 627–51, 2004.

2 Santayana, George, *The Life of Reason: Or, The Phases of Human Progress*, one-volume ed. (London: Constable & Co., 1954).

3 French, Robert B. & Simpson, Peter, 'The "work group": redressing the balance in Bion's Experiences in Groups', *Human Relations*, 63.12, pp. 1859–1878, 2010.

4 Flik, H., *Ameba Concept . . . Organizing around Opportunity within the GORE Culture* (Putzbrunn, West Germany: W. L. Gore & Associates GmbH, 1990).

5 Bion, W. R. et al., *Experiences in Groups: And Other Papers* (Abingdon: Taylor & Francis, 1991).

2. Leading by Numbers

1 Schumacher, E. F., *Small Is Beautiful: A Study of Economics as if People Mattered* (London: Vintage, 1993), p. 58.

2 Mandelbrot, B., *The Fractal Geometry of Nature* (New York: W. H. Freeman, 1983).

3 Dunbar, R. I. M., 'Coevolution of neocortex size, group size and language in humans', *Behavioral and Brain Sciences*, 16, pp. 681–735, 1993.

4 Dunbar, R. I. M., 'Coevolution of neocortex size, group size and language in humans', *Behavioral and Brain Sciences*, 16, pp. 681–735, 1993.

5 Dunbar, R. I. M., 'The social brain hypothesis', *Evolutionary Anthropology*, 6, pp. 178–190, 1998.

6 Dunbar, R. I. M., 'Structure and function in human and primate social networks: implications for diffusion, network stability and health', *Proceedings of the Royal Society, London*, 476A, 20200446, 2020.

7 Mandelbrot, B., *The Fractal Geometry of Nature* (New York: W. H. Freeman, 1983).

8 Dunbar, R. I. M., *Friends: Understanding the Power of Our Most Important Relationships* (London and New York: Little, Brown, 2021).

9 Dunbar, R. I. M., 'The anatomy of friendship', *Trends in Cognitive Sciences*, 22, pp. 32–51, 2018.

10 Tett, G., 'Silos and silences: why so few people spotted the problems in complex credit and what that implies for the future', *Financial Stability Review*, 14, pp. 121–129, 2010; Tett, G., *The Silo Effect: Why Putting Everything in Its Place Isn't Such a Bright Idea* (London: Hachette, 2016); Johnson, G., 'Organizational structure and scalar stress', in *Theory and Explanation in Archaeology*, ed. C. Renfrew, M. Rowlands & B. A. Segraves (New York: Academic Press, 1982), pp. 389–421.

11 Dunbar, R. I. M. & Sosis, R., 'Optimising human community sizes', *Evolution and Human Behavior*, 39, pp. 106–111, 2017.

12 Dunbar, R. I. M. & Sosis, R., 'Optimising human community sizes', *Evolution and Human Behavior*, 39, pp. 106–111, 2017.

13 Bretherton, R. & Dunbar, R. I. M., 'Dunbar's number goes to church: The social brain hypothesis as a third strand in the study of church growth', *Archives of the Psychology of Religion*, 42, pp. 63–76, 2020; Dunbar, R. I. M., *How Religion Evolved and Why It Endures* (London: Pelican and New York: Oxford University Press, 2022).

14 West, B., Massari, G. F., Culbreth, G., Failla, R., Bologna, M., Dunbar, R. I. M. & Grigolini, P., 'Relating size and functionality in human social networks through complexity', *Proceedings of the National Academy of Sciences, USA*, 117, pp. 18355–18358, 2020.

15 West, B., Massari, G. F., Culbreth, G., Failla, R., Bologna, M., Dunbar, R. I. M. & Grigolini, P., 'Relating size and functionality in human social networks through complexity', *Proceedings of the National Academy of Sciences, USA*, 117, pp. 18355–18358, 2020.

16 Morgan, Gareth, *Imaginization: New Mindsets for Seeing, Organizing and Managing* (San Francisco: Berrett-Koehler, 1997).

17 Dunbar, R. I. M., 'Structure and function in human and primate social networks: implications for diffusion, network stability and health', *Proceedings of the Royal Society, London*, 476A, 20200446, 2020.

18 Sutcliffe, A. J., Dunbar, R. I. M., Binder, J. & Arrow, H., 'Relationships and the social brain: integrating psychological and evolutionary perspectives', *British Journal of Psychology*, 103, pp. 149–168, 2012.

19 Bretherton, R. & Dunbar, R. I. M., 'Dunbar's number goes to church: The social brain hypothesis as a third strand in the study of church growth', *Archives of the Psychology of Religion*, 42, pp. 63–76, 2020; Dunbar, R. I. M., *How Religion Evolved and Why It Endures* (London: Pelican and New York: Oxford University Press, 2022).

20 Wang, P., Ma, J. C., Jiang, Z. Q., Zhou, W. X. & Sornette, D., 'Comparative analysis of layered structures in empirical investor networks and cellphone communication networks', *EPJ Data Science*, 9:11, 2020.

21 Webber, E. & Dunbar, R. I. M., 'The fractal structure of communities of practice: implications for business organization', *PLoS One*, 15: e0232204, 2020.

22 Mandelbaum, D. G., *The Plains Cree: An Ethnographic, Historical and Comparative Study* (Regina, SK: University of Regina Press, 1979); Crowshoe, R. & Manneschmidt, S., *Akak'stiman: A Blackfoot Framework for Decision-Making and Mediation Processes* (Calgary, AB: University of Calgary Press, 2002).

23 Dunbar, R. I. M., 'Constraints on the evolution of social institutions and their implications for information flow', *Journal of Institutional Economics*, 7, pp. 345–371, 2011.

24 Tamarit, I., Cuesta, J., Dunbar, R. I. M. & Sánchez, A., 'Cognitive resource allocation determines the organisation of personal networks', *Proceedings of the National Academy of Sciences, USA*, 115, 1719233115, 2018; Tamarit, I., Sánchez, A. & Cuesta, J. A., 'Beyond Dunbar circles: a continuous description of social relationships and resource allocation', *Scientific Reports*, 12, pp. 1–11, 2022.

25 Dunbar, R. I. M., 'Sexual segregation in human conversations', *Behaviour*, 153, pp. 1–14, 2016.

26 Buys, C. J. & Larson, K. L., 'Human sympathy groups', *Psychological Reports*, 45, pp. 547–553, 1979.

27 Sutcliffe, A. J., Dunbar, R. I. M., Binder, J. & Arrow, H., 'Relationships and the social brain: integrating psychological and evolutionary perspectives', *British Journal of Psychology*, 103, pp. 149–168, 2012.

28 Microsoft Work Trend Index Annual Report 2021, www.microsoft. com/en-us/worklab/work-trend-index, 2021.

29 Webber, E. & Dunbar, R. I. M., 'The fractal structure of communities of practice: implications for business organization', *PLoS One*, 15: e0232204, 2020.

30 Dunbar, R. I. M., 'Virtual touch and the human social world', *Current Opinion in Behavioral Sciences*, 44, pp. 14–19, 2021; Dunbar, R. I. M., *Friends: Understanding the Power of Our Most Important Relationships* (London and New York: Little Brown, 2021).

31 Roberts, S. B. G., Dunbar, R. I. M., Pollet, T. V. & Kuppens, T., 'Exploring variations in active network size: constraints and ego characteristics', *Social Networks*, 31, pp. 138–146, 2009.

32 Granovetter, M. S., 'The strength of weak ties', *American Sociological Review*, 78, pp. 1360–1380, 1973.

33 Dunbar, R. I. M. & Sosis, R., 'Optimising human community sizes', *Evolution and Human Behavior*, 39, pp. 106–111, 2017.

34 'Bill Gore on: Freedom Vs. Organisation', *The Electronic Engineering Times*, p. 86, 1984.

35 Bartleby, 'The number of the best', *The Economist*, 434, p. 53, 2020.

36 Sutcliffe, A. J., Dunbar, R. I. M., Binder, J. & Arrow, H., 'Relationships and the social brain: integrating psychological and evolutionary perspectives', *British Journal of Psychology*, 103, pp. 149–168, 2012.

37 Webber, E. & Dunbar, R. I. M., 'The fractal structure of communities of practice: implications for business organization', *PLoS One*, 15: e0232204, 2020.

38 Hall, J. A., 'How many hours does it take to make a friend?' *Journal of Social and Personal Relationships*, 36, pp. 1278–1296, 2019.

39 Sutcliffe, A. J., Dunbar, R. I. M., Binder, J. & Arrow, H., 'Relationships and the social brain: integrating psychological and evolutionary perspectives', *British Journal of Psychology*, 103, pp. 149–168, 2012.

40 Burt, R. S., 'Decay functions', *Social Networks*, 22, pp. 1–28, 2000.

41 Dunbar, R. I. M. & Sosis, R., 'Optimising human community sizes', *Evolution and Human Behavior*, 39, pp. 106–111, 2017.

42 Latané, B., Williams, K. & Harkins, S. 'Many hands make light the

work: the causes and consequences of social loafing', *Journal of Personality and Social Psychology*, 37, pp. 822–832, 1979.

43 Hoegl, M., 'Smaller teams – better teamwork: how to keep project teams small', *Business Horizons*, 48, pp. 209–214, 2005.

44 Erhart, S., Lehment, H. & Vasquez-Paz, J. L., 'Monetary policy committee size and inflation volatility', *Kiel Working Papers 1377* (Kiel Institute for the World Economy, 2007).

45 Bartleby, 'The number of the best', *The Economist*, 434, p. 53, 2020.

3. A Sense of Belonging

1 Faulkner, W., *As I Lay Dying* (London: Vintage, 2004).

2 World Happiness Report, https://worldhappiness.report/ed/2021/, 2021.

3 Madsen, E., Tunney, R. J., Fieldman, G., Plotkin, H. C., Dunbar, R. I. M., Richardson, J-M. & McFarland, D. J., 'Kinship and altruism: a cross-cultural experimental study', *British Journal of Psychology*, 98, pp. 339–359, 2007.

4 Heffernan, M., *Women on Top: How Women Entrepreneurs Are Rewriting the Rules of Business Success* (London: Penguin Books, 2008).

5 Felin, T., 'When strategy walks out the door', *MIT Sloan Management Review*, 58:1, 2016.

6 Dunbar, R. I. M., *Friends: Understanding the Power of Our Most Important Relationships* (London and New York: Little, Brown, 2021).

7 Dunbar, R. I. M., 'The anatomy of friendship', *Trends in Cognitive Sciences*, 22, pp. 32–5, 2018.

8 Dunbar, R. I. M., *Friends: Understanding the Power of Our Most Important Relationships* (London: Little, Brown, 2021).

9 Sorniotti, A. & Molva, R., 'A provably secure secret handshake with dynamic controlled matching', *Computers & Security*, 29, pp. 619–627, 2010.

10 Curry, O. & Dunbar, R. I. M., 'Do birds of a feather flock together? The relationship between similarity and altruism in social networks', *Human Nature*, 24, pp. 336–347, 2013.

11 Floccia, C., Butler, J., Girard, F. & Goslin, J., 'Categorization of regional and foreign accent in five-to-seven-year-old British children', *International Journal of Behavioral Development*, 33, pp. 366–375, 2009.

12 Launay, J. & Dunbar, R. I. M., 'Playing with strangers: which shared traits attract us most to new people?', *PLoS One*, 10: e0129688, 2016.

13 Mann, A., 'Why we need best friends at work', www.gallup.com/workplace/236213/why-need-best-friends-work.aspx, 15 January 2018.

14 Baym, N. et al., 'What a year of WFH has done to our relationships at work', *Harvard Business Review*, 22 March 2021.

15 Holt-Lunstad, J., Smith, T. & Bradley Layton, J., 'Social relationships and mortality risk: a metaanalytic review', *PLoS Medicine*, 7: e1000316, 2010.

16 Santini, Z., Jose, P., Koyanagi, A., Meilstrup, C., Nielsen, L., Madsen, K., Hinrichsen, C., Dunbar, R. I. M. & Koushede, V., 'The moderating role of social network size in the temporal association between formal social participation and mental health: a longitudinal analysis using two consecutive waves of the Survey of Health, Ageing and Retirement in Europe (SHARE)', *Social Psychiatry and Psychiatric Epidemiology*, 56, pp. 417–428, 2021.

17 https://www.night-club.org/

18 Coleman, J. S., *Foundations of Social Theory* (Cambridge, MA: Harvard University Press, 1994).

19 Pettinger, L., 'Friends, relations and colleagues: the blurred boundaries of the workplace', *Sociological Review*, 53, pp. 37–55, 2005.

20 Harrison, D. A., Price, K. H., Gavin, J. H. & Florey, A. T., 'Time, teams, and task performance: changing effects of surface- and deep-level diversity on group functioning', *Academy of Management Journal*, 45, pp. 1029–1045, 2005.

21 Baldwin, J. & Mead, M., *A Rap on Race* (London: Corgi, 1972).

4. Bonding

1 Wang, P., 'Sky Earth Human: Five Poems', *Chinese Literature Today*, 7:1, pp. 70–75, 2018.

2 Loh, H. H., Tseng, L. F., Wei, E. & Li, C. H., 'Beta-endorphin is a potent analgesic agent', *Proceedings of the National Academy of Sciences, USA*, 73, pp. 2895–2898, 1976.

3 Mozzanica, N., Villa, M. L., Foppa, S., Vignati, G., Cattaneo, A., Diotti, R. & Finzi, A. F., 'Plasma α-melanocyte-stimulating hormone, β-endorphin, met-enkephalin, and natural killer cell activity in

vitiligo', *Journal of the American Academy of Dermatology*, 26, pp. 693–700, 1992; Puente, J., Maturana, P., Miranda, D., Navarro, C., Wolf, M. E. & Mosnaim, A. D., 'Enhancement of human natural killer cell activity by opioid peptides: similar response to methionine-enkephalin and β-endorphin', *Brain, Behavior, and Immunity*, 6, pp. 32–39, 1992.

4   Dunbar, R. I. M., Frangou, A., Grainger, F. & Pearce, E., 'Laughter influences social bonding but not prosocial generosity to friends and strangers', *PLoS One*, 16, e0256229, 2021.

5   Cohen, E. E. A., Ejsmond-Frey, R., Knight, N. & Dunbar, R. I. M., 'Rowers' high: behavioural synchrony is correlated with elevated pain thresholds', *Biology Letters*, 6, pp. 106–108, 2010; Tarr, B., Launay, J., Cohen, E. & Dunbar, R. I. M., 'Synchrony and exertion during dance independently raise pain threshold and encourage social bonding', *Biology Letters*, 11, 20150767, 2015.

6   Cohen, E. E. A., Ejsmond-Frey, R., Knight, N. & Dunbar, R. I. M., 'Rowers' high: behavioural synchrony is correlated with elevated pain thresholds', *Biology Letters*, 6, pp. 106–108, 2010.

7   Cohen, E. E. A., Ejsmond-Frey, R., Knight, N. & Dunbar, R. I. M., 'Rowers' high: behavioural synchrony is correlated with elevated pain thresholds', *Biology Letters*, 6, pp. 106–108, 2010.

8   Dunbar, R. I. M., Teasdale, B., Thompson, J., Budelmann, F., Duncan, S., van Emde Boas, E. & Maguire, L. 'Emotional arousal when watching drama increases pain threshold and social bonding', *Royal Society Open Science*, 3, 160288, 2016.

9   Tuckman, B. W., 'Development sequence in small groups', *Psychological Bulletin*, 63, pp. 384–399, 1965.

10 Kristiansen, P. & Rasmussen, R., *Building a Better Business Using the Lego Serious Play Method* (Hoboken, NJ: John Wiley & Sons, 2014).

11 Kristiansen, P. & Rasmussen, R., *Building a Better Business Using the Lego Serious Play Method* (Hoboken, NJ: John Wiley & Sons, 2014).

12 Dunbar, R. I. M. et al., *Friends on Tap: The Role of Pubs at the Heart of the Community* (St Albans: CAMRA, 2016); Dunbar, R. I. M., Launay, J., Wlodarski, R., Robertson, C., Pearce, E., Carney, J. & MacCarron, P., 'Functional benefits of (modest) alcohol consumption', *Adaptive Human Behavior and Physiology*, 3, 118–133, 2017.

13 Dunbar, R. I. M., *Eating Together,* Report for The Big Lunch Company, 2016; Dunbar, R. I. M., 'Breaking bread: the functions of social eating', *Adaptive Human Behavior and Physiology*, 3, pp. 198–211, 2017; 'Social eating helps connect communities', www.edenprojectcommunities. com/blog/social-eating-helps-connect-communities, 2017.

14 www.edenprojectcommunities.com/blog/the-big-lunch-is-good-for-business

15 Dunbar, R. I. M., 'Breaking bread: the functions of social eating', *Adaptive Human Behavior and Physiology*, 3, pp. 198–211, 2017.

16 https://en.wikipedia.org/wiki/Radio_calisthenics

17 Bannan, N., Bamford, J. & Dunbar, R. I. M., 'The evolution of gender dimorphism in the human voice: the role of *octave equivalence*', *Current Anthropology* (in press).

18 Weinstein, D., Launay, J., Pearce, E., Dunbar, R. I. M. & Stewart, L., 'Group music performance causes elevated pain thresholds and social bonding in small and large groups of singers', *Evolution and Human Behavior*, 37, pp. 152–158, 2016.

19 Pearce E., Launay, J., MacCarron, P. & Dunbar, R. I. M., 'Tuning in to others: exploring relational and collective bonding in singing and non-singing groups over time', *Psychology of Music*, 45, pp. 496–512, 2017.

20 www.beatingtime.org

21 Vaag, J., Saksvik, P. Ø., Theorell, T., Skillingstad, T., & Bjerkeset, O., 'Sound of well-being – choir singing as an intervention to improve well-being among employees in two Norwegian county hospitals', *Arts and Health*, 5, pp. 93–102, 2013.

5. The Medium and the Message

1 Jalāl al-Dīn Rūmī, *Selected Poems*, trans. C. Banks; with J. Moyne, A. J. Arberry & R. Nicholson (London: Penguin, 1999).

2 Milmo, D., 'Better.com boss apologises for firing 900 staff on Zoom call', *Guardian*, 8 December 2021.

3 Stiller, J. & Dunbar, R. I. M., 'Perspective-taking and memory capacity predict social network size', *Social Networks*, 29, pp. 93–104,

2007; Powell, J., Lewis, P. A., Dunbar, R. I. M., García-Fiñana, M. & Roberts, N. 'Orbital prefrontal cortex volume correlates with social cognitive competence', *Neuropsychologia*, 48, pp. 3554–3562, 2010.

4 Lewis, P. A., Rezaie, R., Browne, R., Roberts, N. & Dunbar, R. I. M., 'Ventromedial prefrontal volume predicts understanding of others and social network size', *NeuroImage*, 57, pp. 1624–1629, 2011; Lewis, P. A., Birch, A., Hall, A. & Dunbar, R. I. M., 'Higher order intentionality tasks are cognitively more demanding', *Social, Cognitive and Affective Neuroscience*, 12, pp. 1063–1071, 2017.

5 Stiller, J. & Dunbar, R. I. M., 'Perspective-taking and memory capacity predict social network size', *Social Networks*, 29, pp. 93–104, 2007; Launay, J., Pearce, E., Wlodarski, R., van Duijn, M., Carney, J. & Dunbar, R. I. M., 'Higher order mentalising and executive functioning', *Personality and Individual Differences*, 86, pp. 6–14, 2015.

6 Dunbar, R. I. M., Duncan, N. & Marriot, A., 'Human conversational behaviour', *Human Nature*, 8, pp. 231–246, 1997; Dahmardeh, M. & Dunbar, R. I. M., 'What shall we talk about in Farsi? Content of everyday conversations in Iran', *Human Nature*, 28, pp. 423–433, 2017.

7 Dunbar, R. I. M., Duncan, N. & Marriot, A., 'Human conversational behaviour', *Human Nature*, 8, pp. 231–246, 1997.

8 Dunbar, R. I. M., 'Sexual segregation in human conversations', *Behaviour*, 153, pp. 1–14, 2017.

9 Dunbar, R. I. M., Duncan, N. & Nettle, D., 'Size and structure of freely forming conversational groups', *Human Nature*, 6, pp. 67–78, 1995.

10 Krems, J., Neuberg, S. & Dunbar, R. I. M., 'Something to talk about: are conversation sizes constrained by mental modeling abilities?', *Evolution and Human Behavavior*, 37, pp. 423–428, 2016.

11 Krems, J., Neuberg, S., & Dunbar, R. I. M., 'Something to talk about: are conversation sizes constrained by mental modeling abilities?', *Evolution and Human Behaviour*, 37, pp. 423–428, 2016.

12 Nauta, S., 'How to ensure that the future of work is fair for all', *The Economist*, 8 November 2021.

13 Coates, J., *Women, Men and Language: A Sociolinguistic Account of Gender Differences in Language* (London: Routledge, 2015).

14 Grainger, S. & Dunbar, R. I. M., 'The structure of dyadic conversations and sex differences in social style', *Journal of Evolutionary Psychology*, 7, pp. 83–93, 2009.

15 Dunbar, R. I. M., 'Sexual segregation in human conversations', *Behaviour*, 153, pp. 1–14, 2016.

16 Stiller, J. & Dunbar, R. I. M., 'Perspective-taking and memory capacity predict social network size', *Social Networks*, 29, pp. 93–10, 2007; Powell, J., Lewis, P., Dunbar, R., García-Fiñana, M. & Roberts, N., 'Orbital prefrontal cortex volume correlates with social cognitive competence', *Neuropsychologia*, 48, pp. 3554–3562, 2010.

17 Machin, A. & Dunbar, R. I. M., 'Sex and gender in romantic partnerships and best friendships', *Journal of Relationship Research*, 4, e8, 2013.

18 David-Barrett, T., Rotkirch, A., Carney, J., Behncke Izquierdo, I., Krems, J., Townley, D., McDaniell, E., Byrne Smith, A. & Dunbar, R. I. M., 'Women favour dyadic relationships, but men prefer clubs', *PLoS One*, 10, e0118329, 2015; Dunbar, R. I. M., *Friends: Understanding the Power of Our Most Important Relationships* (London: Little, Brown, 2021).

19 Roberts, S. B. G. & Dunbar, R. I. M., 'Managing relationship decay: network, gender, and contextual effects', *Human Nature*, 26, pp. 426–450, 2015.

20 Benenson, J. F. & Wrangham, R. W., 'Cross-cultural sex differences in post-conflict affiliation following sports matches', *Current Biology*, 26, pp. 2208–2212, 2016; Benenson, J. F., Markovits, H., Thompson, M. E. & Wrangham, R. W., 'Under threat of social exclusion, females exclude more than males', *Psychological Science*, 22, pp. 538–544, 2011; Benenson, J. F., Markovits, H., Fitzgerald, C., Geoffroy, D., Flemming, J., Kahlenberg, S. M. & Wrangham, R. W., 'Males' greater tolerance of same-sex peers', *Psychological Science*, 20, pp. 184–190, 2009; for a general summary, see: Dunbar, R. I. M., *Friends: Understanding the Power of Our Most Important Relationships*, Chapter 13 (London: Little, Brown, 2021).

21 Pearce, E., Wlodarski, R., Machin, A. & Dunbar, R. I. M., 'Exploring the links between dispositions, romantic relationships, support networks and community inclusion in men and women', *PLoS One*, 14: e0216210, 2019.

22 Roberts, S. B. G. & Dunbar, R. I. M., 'Managing relationship decay: network, gender, and contextual effects', *Human Nature*, 26, pp. 426–450, 2015.

23 Ballakrishnen, S., Fielding-Singh, P. & Magliozzi, D., 'Intentional invisibility: professional women and the navigation of workplace constraints', *Sociological Perspectives*, 62, pp. 23–41, 2019.

24 Heilman, M. E. & Okimoto, T. G., 'Why are women penalized for success at male tasks?: The implied communality deficit', *Journal of Applied Psychology*, 92, pp. 81–92, 2007; McGinn, K. L. & Tempest, N., 'Heidi Roizen', Harvard Business School Case, 800–228, 2000 (revised 2010); Corell, S., 'Creating a level playing field', Stanford Michelle R. Clayman Institute for Gender Research, 2013.

25 Judge, T. A. & Cable, D. M., 'The effect of physical height on workplace success and income: preliminary test of a theoretical model', *Journal of Applied Psychology*, 89, pp. 428–441, 2004.

26 Schumacher, A., 'On the significance of stature in human society', *Journal of Human Evolution*, 11, pp. 697–701, 1982.

27 Pawlowski, B., Dunbar, R. I. M. & Lipowicz, A., 'Tall men have more reproductive success', *Nature*, 403, p. 156, 2000.

28 Schick, A. & Steckel, R. H. 'Height, human capital, and earnings: the contributions of cognitive and noncognitive ability', *Journal of Human Capital*, 9, pp. 94–115, 2015.

29 Jacobi, T. & Schweers, D., 'Justice, interrupted: the effect of gender, ideology, and seniority at Supreme Court oral arguments', *Virginia Law Review,* 103, 1379, 2017.

30 Mehrabian, A., *Nonverbal Communication* (Chicago: Aldine-Atherton, 1972).

31 Galinsky, A. D., Magee, J. C., Inesi, M. E. & Gruenfeld, D. H., 'Power and perspectives not taken', *Psychological Science*, 17, pp. 1068–1074, 2006.

32 Galang, C. M. & Obhi, S. S., 'Social power and frontal alpha asymmetry', *Cognitive Neuroscience*, 10, pp. 44–56, 2019.

33 Dunbar, R. I. M., Robledo del Canto, J.-P., Tamarit, I., Cross, I. & Smith, E., 'Nonverbal auditory cues allow relationship quality to be inferred during conversations', *Journal of Nonverbal Behavior*, 46, pp. 1–18, 2022.

34 Dunbar, R. I. M., Robledo del Canto, J.-P., Tamarit, I., Cross, I. & Smith, E., 'Nonverbal auditory cues allow relationship quality to be inferred during conversations', *Journal of Nonverbal Behavior,* 46, pp. 1–18, 2022.

35 Johnson-Laird, P. N., 'Mental models and human reasoning', *Proceedings of the National Academy of Sciences, USA*, 107, pp. 18243–18250, 2010.

6. The Size of Trust

1 Shakespeare, W. & Fletcher, J., *Henry VIII*.

2 Gebbia, J., 'How Airbnb Designs for Trust', TED Talk, March 2016.

3 Kähkönen, T., Blomqvist, K., Gillespie, N. & Vanhala, M., 'Employee trust repair: a systematic review of twenty years of empirical research and future research directions', *Journal of Business Research*, 130, pp. 98–109, 2021.

4 Gilbert, P., *The Compassionate Mind* (London: Robinson, 2013).

5 Gray, D. J. P., Sidaway-Lee, K., White, E., Thorne, A. & Evans, P. H., 'Continuity of care with doctors – a matter of life and death? A systematic review of continuity of care and mortality', *BMJ Open*, 8, e021161, 2018.

6 Dunbar, R. I. M., *How Religion Evolved and Why It Endures* (London: Pelican and New York: Oxford University Press, 2022).

7 Hogan, R., *Personality and the Fate of Organizations* (London: Erlbaum, 2007).

8 Dunbar, R. I. M., *How Religion Evolved and Why It Endures* (London: Pelican and New York: Oxford University Press, 2022).

9 Bateson, M., Nettle, D. & Roberts, G., 'Cues of being watched enhance cooperation in a real-world setting', *Biology Letters*, 2, pp. 412–414, 2006.

10 Nettle, D. & Dunbar, R. I. M., 'Social markers and the evolution of reciprocal exchange', *Current Anthropology*, 38, pp. 93–99, 1997.

11 Serota, K. B., Levine, T. R. & Boster, F. J., 'The prevalence of lying in America: three studies of self-reported lies', *Human Communication Research*, 36, pp. 2–25, 2010.

12 Gai, P. & Kapadia, S. 'Contagion in financial networks', *Proceedings of the Royal Society, London*, 466A, pp. 2401–2423, 2010; Glasserman, P. & Young, H. P., 'Contagion in financial networks', *Journal of Economic Literature*, 54, pp. 779–831, 2016; Benoit, S., Colliard, J. E., Hurlin, C. & Pérignon, C., 'Where the risks lie: a survey on systemic risk', *Review of Finance*, 21, pp. 109–152, 2017.

13 Iñiguez, G. et al., 'Effects of deception in social networks', *Proceedings of the Royal Society, London*, 281B, 20141195, 2014.

14 Caballero, R. & Simsek, A., 'Fire sales in a model of complexity', *Journal of Finance*, 68, pp. 2549–2587, 2013.

15 McGregor, D., *The Human Side of Enterprise* (American Management Association, 1957); Schein, E., 'Douglas McGregor: theoretician, moral philosopher or behaviorist?', *Journal of Management History*, 17, pp. 156–164, 2011.

16 Cosmides, L., 'The logic of social exchange: has natural selection shaped how humans reason? Studies with the Wason selection task', *Cognition*, 31, pp. 187–276, 1989.

17 Pötsch, H. D., 'There was a tolerance for breaking the rules', news conference, 10 December 2015.

18 Losada, M. & Heaphy, E., 'The role of positivity and connectivity in the performance of business teams: a nonlinear dynamics model', *American Behavioral Scientist*, 47, pp. 740–765, 2004.

19 Alderwick, H., 'Is the NHS overwhelmed?', *BMJ*, 376, O51, 2022.

20 Heffernan, M., *Uncharted: How Uncertainty Can Power Change* (New York: Simon & Schuster, 2021).

21 Feynman, R. P., *Surely You're Joking, Mr. Feynman?* (London: Vintage, 1985).

22 Zak, P. J., 'The neuroscience of trust: management behaviors that foster employee engagement', *Harvard Business Review*, Jan/Feb 2017.

23 Wang, Y., Asaad, Y. & Filieri, R., 'What makes hosts trust Airbnb? Antecedents of hosts' trust toward Airbnb and its impact on continuance intention', *Journal of Travel Research*, 59, pp. 686–703, 2020.

7. Social Space, Social Time

1 Day, J. A., 'Vincent van Gogh painted with words: the letters to Emile Bernard', *Choice: Current Reviews for Academic Libraries*, 45, p. 1149, 2008.

2 www.architecture.com/awards-and-competitions-landing-page/awards/riba-regional-awards/riba-south-award-winners/blavatnik-school-of-government

3 Kern, L., *Feminist City: Claiming Space in a Man-Made World* (New York: Verso, 2020).

4 Renau, V., 'Designing contemporary living spaces: a feminist perspective in urbanism coming from Col·lectiu Punt 6 in Barcelona', *Pad* 13.18, pp. 241–58, 2020.

5 Kingma, B. & Marken Lichtenbelt, W. van, 'Energy consumption

in buildings and female thermal demand', *Nature Climate Change*, 5, pp. 1054–1056, 2015.

6 'Airspace', *The Digital Human*, BBC Sounds, 15 February 2019.

7 Simon, Herbert A., *The Sciences of the Artificial*, 3rd ed. (Cambridge, MA and London: MIT Press, 1996).

8 Dunbar, R. I. M., *Grooming, Gossip and the Evolution of Language* (London: Faber, 1996).

9 www2.mrc-lmb.cam.ac.uk/achievements/lmb-nobel-prizes/

10 Kolata, G. & Mueller, B., 'Decades of discoveries before "miraculous" sprint to a vaccine', *New York Times*, 16 January 2022.

11 Boudreau, K., Ganguli, I., Gaule, P., Guinan, E. & Lakhani, K., 'Colocation and scientific collaboration: evidence from a field experiment', Harvard Business School Working Paper, No. 13–023, 2012.

12 Lavoisier identified and named oxygen and hydrogen, and his experiments laid the foundations for the modern atomic theory of chemistry. Unfortunately, he had the bad luck simply by virtue of being employed by the king to manage the French army's gunpowder production to be on the wrong side of the French Revolution; as a result, he lost his head on the guillotine, prompting one contemporary observer to lament that science had lost one of its greatest geniuses while his head was still full of novel insights.

13 Goldin, I. & Kutarna, C., *Age of Discovery: Navigating the Risks and Rewards of Our New Renaissance* (London: Bloomsbury, 2016).

14 Brand, S., *How Buildings Learn: What Happens After They're Built* (London: Phoenix Illustrated, 1997).

15 Bauer, M. E., 'Stress, glucocorticoids and ageing of the immune system', *Stress*, 8, pp. 69–83, 2005; Aschbacher, K., O'Donovan, A., Wolkowitz, O. M., Dhabhar, F. S., Su, Y. & Epel, E., 'Good stress, bad stress and oxidative stress: insights from anticipatory cortisol reactivity', *Psychoneuroendocrinology*, 38, pp. 1698–1708, 2013.

16 Bachelard, G., *La Poétique de l'espace* (Paris: Presses Universitaires de France, 1967).

17 https://www.nobelprize.org/prizes/chemistry/2020/popular-information/

18 Yang, L., Holtz, D., Jaffe, S., Suri, S., Sinha, S., Weston, J. et al., 'The effects of remote work on collaboration among information workers',

Nature Human Behaviour 6, pp. 43–54, 2022; Carmody, D., Mazzarello, M., Santi, P., Harris, T., Lehmann, S., Abbiasov, T., Dunbar, R. I. M. & Ratti, C., 'The effect of co-location of human communication networks', *Nature Commuter Sciences*, 2, pp. 494–503, 2022.

19 Yang, L., Holtz, D., Jaffe, S., Suri, S., Sinha, S., Weston, J. et al., 'The effects of remote work on collaboration among information workers', *Nature Human Behaviour* 6, pp. 43–54, 2022.

20 Dunbar, R. I. M., 'Structure and function in human and primate social networks: implications for diffusion, network stability and health', *Proceedings of the Royal Society, London*, 476A: 20200446, 2020.

21 Vlahovic, T., Roberts, S. B. G. & Dunbar, R. I. M., 'Effects of duration and laughter on subjective happiness within different modes of communication', *Journal of Computer-Mediated Communication*, 17, pp. 436–450, 2012.

22 Bond, R. M., Fariss, C. J., Jones, J. J., Kramer, A. D., Marlow, C., Settle, J. E. & Fowler, J. H., 'A 61-million-person experiment in social influence and political mobilization', *Nature* 489, pp. 295–298, 2012.

23 Dunbar, R. I. M., *Speak Up, Speak Out*, Report for the Holocaust Memorial Day Trust, 2012.

24 Hill, A., Mellon, L. & Goddard, J., 'How winning organizations last 100 years', *Harvard Business Review*, 27 September 2018.

25 Mischel, W., *The Marshmallow Test: Understanding Self-Control and How to Master It* (New York: Random House, 2014).

26 Moffitt, T., Caspi, A., Rutter, M. & Silva, P., *Sex Differences in Antisocial Behaviour: Conduct Disorder, Delinquency, and Violence in the Dunedin Longitudinal Study* (Cambridge: Cambridge University Press, 2001); Moffitt, T. E., Arseneault, L., Belsky, D., Dickson, N., Hancox, R. J. et al., 'A gradient of childhood self-control predicts health, wealth, and public safety', *Proceedings of the National Academy of Sciences, USA*, 108, pp. 2693–2698, 2011.

8. *The Social Brain at Work*

1 Solnit, R., *Storming the Gates of Paradise: Landscapes for Politics* (Berkeley, CA: University of California Press, 2007).

2 Photo taken by Chris Thorogood, Deputy Director and Head of Science at the University of Oxford Botanic Garden and Arboretum. Used with permission.

3 Adobe stock credit/ ONYXprj/ Image248671547

4 Thorogood, C. J., 'The University of Oxford Botanic Garden: sharing the scientific wonder and importance of plants with the world', *Curtis's Botanical Magazine*, 38, pp. 438–50, 2021.

5 Sheen, T., 'Ashley Cole is mocked by Roma captain Francesco Totti during official team photo', *Independent*, 1 August 2014.

6 Groysberg, B. & Abrahams, R., 'Lift outs: how to acquire a high-functioning team', *Harvard Business Review*, December 2006.

7 Heifetz, R. & Linsky, M., 'A survival guide for leaders', *Harvard Business Review*, June 2002.

8 Heimans, J. & Timms, H., *New Power: How Power Works in Our Hyperconnected World and How to Make It Work for You* (New York: Doubleday, 2019).

9 Bion, W. R. et al., *Experiences in Groups: And Other Papers* (London: Taylor & Francis Group, 1991).

10 Roy, C., Monsivais, D., Bhattacharya, K., Dunbar, R. I. M. & Kaski, K., 'Morningness–eveningness assessment from mobile phone communication analysis', *Scientific Reports*, 11, 14606, 2021.

11 Christakis, N. A. & Fowler, J. H., *Connected: The Surprising Power of Our Social Networks and How They Shape Our Lives* (New York: Little, Brown Spark, 2009).

12 https://www.gore.com/about/our-beliefs-and-principles

13 Mehrabian, A., *Nonverbal Communication* (Abingdon: Routledge, 2017).

14 Murphy, C., Dehmelt, V., Yonelinas, A. P., Ranganath, C. & Gruber, M. J., 'Temporal proximity to the elicitation of curiosity is key for enhancing memory for incidental information', *Learning & Memory*, 28, pp. 34–39, 2021.

15 Rock, D. & Grant, H., 'Why diverse teams are smarter: diversity as a tool in enhancing profitability, efficiency and quality of decision-making', *Harvard Business Review*, 4 November 2016.

16 Harford, T., 'Diversity means looking for the knife in a drawerful of spoons', *Financial Times*, 7 September 2017.

17 Dixon-Fyle, S., Dolan, K., Hunt, V. & Prince, S., *Diversity Wins: How Inclusion Matters*, McKinsey Report, May 2020.

18 Barber, B. & Odean, T., *Boys Will Be Boys: Gender, Overconfidence and Common Stock Investment* (California: Graduate School of Management, University of California, 1998).

19 Szell, M. & Thurner, S., 'How women organize social networks different from men', *Scientific Reports*, 3, p. 1214, 2013.

20 Dunbar, R. I. M., 'Sexual segregation in human conversations', *Behaviour*, 153, pp. 1–14, 2016.

21 Karamched, B., Stickler, M., Ott, W., Lindner, B., Kilpatrick, Z. P. & Josić, K., 'Heterogeneity improves speed and accuracy in social networks', *Physical Review Letters*, 125, 21, p. 218302, 2020.

22 Whitman, W., *Song of Myself*. A Facsimile of the Original, 1855 Edition of the Poem (Philadelphia: Masterbooks, 1973).

23 Schein, E., *Organizational Culture and Leadership* (Hoboken, NJ: John Wiley & Sons, 2016).

24 Heffernan, M. *Wilful Blindness: Why We Ignore the Obvious at Our Peril* (London: Simon & Schuster, 2012).

Appendix

List of Contributors

Interviewee, Specialism,
Role

Ramatu Abdulkadir, supply chain leader
Head of Pharmacy Department, National Ear Care Centre, Kaduna
State, Nigeria

**Enaam Ahmed Ali, the 2022 UN special representative for women
and climate for the Netherlands**
Sustainability Lead at Rabobank

Jane Byam Shaw OBE, NGO founder
Trustee of The Felix Project

Prof. Ruth Chang, Professor of Law
Chair of Jurisprudence at the University of Oxford

Lynda Chen, advisory board member
Senior China Advisor of the Economics of Mutuality Foundation

Prof. Justin Cobb, orthopaedic surgeon
Professor of Orthopaedic Surgery at Imperial College

Dr Oliver Cox, architectural historian
Head of Academic Partnerships at the Victoria and Albert Museum

Owen Eastwood, performance coach
Author of *Belonging: The Ancient Code of Togetherness*

Debra France, retired global leader of learning and development, W. L. Gore and Associates
Executive Coach and Learning Leader

Clara Gaggero Westaway and Adrian Westaway, award-winning inventors and designers
Co-founders at Special Projects

Dr Jennifer Garvey Berger, leadership expert and adult developmentalist
CEO of Cultivating Leadership

Prof. Paul Gilbert, author and Professor of Clinical Psychology
Author of *The Compassionate Mind*

Peter Hanke, conductor and musician
Associate Fellow at Oxford Saïd Business School

Dr Kirsten Harrison, city strategy and urban development expert
Urban Development Consultant

Prof. Margaret Heffernan, Chief Executive Officer and author
Professor of Practice at the University of Bath

Prof. Cecilia Heyes, Professor of Psychology
Fellow of All Souls, Oxford

Dr Kim Howard, psychologist and organisation development expert
Head of Human Capital at FirstRand Corporate Centre

Melanie Howard, innovator
Chair at Future Foundation

Piers Ibbotson, speaker, coach and facilitator
Associate Professor at the Warwick Business School

Prof. Claus Jacobs, Professor of Strategy
KPM Centre for Public Management, University of Bern

Atul Jaggi, company president
President and Deputy Managing Director at Gabriel India Limited

Dr Jay Jakub, author, public speaker and strategic advisor
Chief Advocacy Officer at the Economics of Mutuality Foundation and
a former Senior Director at the Mars, Incorporated corporate think
tank Catalyst

Dr Shelley James, light and health consultant
Founder of Age of Light Innovations

**Prof. Martin Kemp, world expert on the polymath and artist
Leonardo da Vinci**
Professor Emeritus at Trinity College, Oxford

Paolo Lanzarotti, Chief Executive Officer
CEO of Asahi Europe and International

Alison McDowell, digital identity expert
Director, Beruku Advisory

Gareth Morgan, academic and author
Professor Emeritus of Organisation Studies at the Toronto Schulich
School of Business

Lovelyn Nwadeyi, social justice activist
Inclusion Strategy Manager EMEA, Netflix

Dr Yoge Patel, Chief Executive Officer
CEO of Blue Bear Systems and CASSIMA

Sharon Peake, occupational psychologist and gender equality expert
Founder and CEO, Shape Talent

Robert Poynton, improvisation teacher and facilitator
Co-founder of Yellow

Nick Rust OBE, Chief Executive Officer
Chair of the Starting Price Regulatory Commission Ltd

Ezra Schuster, educator
Regional Public Service Commissioner at the Ministry of Health, New
Zealand

Thami Schweichler, social entrepreneur
Managing Director of Makers Unite

Dr Reima Shakeir, author and lecturer
Adjunct Assistant Professor of Business and Society and Organisational
  Communication, NYU Stern School of Business

Dave Snowden, systems thinker, consultant and author
Founder of Cognitive Edge and Cynefin Company

David Storey, Senior Executive
Partner at EY

Graham 'Skroo' Turner, Chief Executive Officer
CEO of the public company Flight Centre Travel Group

**Lieutenant General Sir Tyrone Urch KBE, retired three-star
  lieutenant general**
Brigadier, British Army and Commander of the Home Command

Sue Wixley, community activist
Head of Communications at Clean Air Fund

Prof. Ngaire Woods, Professor of Global Economic Governance
Dean of the Blavatnik School of Government, University of Oxford

Prof. Theodore Zeldin CBE, professor, historian and author
President at Oxford Muse Foundation

Index

Italic page numbers refer to Figures.

AB InBev (brewing conglomerate) 69, 99
Abdulkadir, Ramatu 196–197, 247
ABN AMRO (investment bank) 198
actors *see* theatre, productions
adrenalin 90, 93
Ahmed Ali, Enaam 208, 247
Airbnb (online accommodation platform) 49, 136, 152–153, 218
alcohol consumption 66–67, 69, 96
All Blacks (rugby team) 51, 74
All Souls College, Oxford 165
altruism:
    and group size 22, 34, 39, 79
    and kinship 22, 39, 51–52, *53–54*
    and tribes 71
Amazon (corporation) 72
Amish communities 23–24
Amsterdam 209
    diamond market 137
Anabaptist Christian sects 23–24, 31, 34, 190
ANC (African National Congress) 54, 55, 105
anti-social behaviour *see* Dark Triad (personality types); freeriders
apartheid 54, 105
apes *see* monkeys and apes
architecture and built environment 155, 159–172, 179–180, 190, 218–220
    see also housing; office design

Arctic exploration 188
Ariane de Rothschild Fellowship 101–102
Armies:
    structure and organisation 21, 29–30, 52, 75–76, 93–94
    training 75–76, 93–94
Ashmolean Museum, Oxford 221
atomic theory 168, 241
Australopithecines 11, 12

Bachelard, Gaston 170
badges, and tribal identity 71, 72
Baldwin, James 73
Barber, Brad 216
barber's shop quartets 101
Barcelona 161
Barings Bank 182
BBC, education programmes department 166
Beating Time (charity) 105
behaviourism, early-twentieth-century 3–4
Benton, Marie 105
Better.com (financial technology company) 110
Big Lunch, The (communal eating events) 96–97
Bion, Wilfred 16, 200
'birds of a feather effect' *see* homophily
Blackfoot people (*Siksika*) 29

Blavatnik School of Government,
Oxford 159, 163, 212
Blue Bear Systems Research Ltd 116, 179
BMW (motor manufacturer) 63, 64
board meetings *see* meetings
body language 112–113, 119, 129,
131–132, 135, 177, 225–226
Botsman, Rachel 142
brain damage, and social
relationships 22–23
brain size:
and evolution 11, 12
and group size 8–9, 20–21, 22–23,
47, 207
and social time 8
Brand, Stewart, *How Buildings Learn* 169
buildings *see* architecture and built
environment; housing; office
design
Burt, Ronald 42
Buurtzorg (homecare nursing
company) 149–150
Buys, Christian 32
Byam Shaw, Jane 97, 247

Cadbury, John 171–172
Cambridge University, colleges 164–165
CAMRA (Campaign for Real Ale) 96
Chang, Ruth 212, 247
change, implementing 110, 197
Charpentier, Emmanuelle 172–173
Chayka, Kyle 162
Chen, Lynda 97, 247
Cheyenne people (*Tsêhéstáno*) 29
Chicago 163
bankers 41, 42
children:
and bonding 95
childcare 32, 150, 161, 174
friendship groups 57

and kinship 51, 60
and play 95, 170
and temptation 184
worldviews 134
choirs 95, 103–106, *103–104*, 172
Christ Church, Oxford 165
church congregation sizes 20, 21, 24–25
climate change 187, 190
Cobb, Justin 115–116, 247
Cole, Ashley 197
Coleman, James 68
committees:
chairing 120, 122, 127, 157, 173, 193, 217
size 42–44, *44*, 120–122, 191
see also meetings
Communities of Practice (CoPs)
28–29, 33
conductors (music) 17–19, 106, 129, 150–151
congregations *see* church
congregation sizes
Convergence Theory (linguistics) 129
conversation 117–134
and bonding 97, 98–99
and friendship 61, 65, *126*
and gender 117, 118–119, 123, *126*, 135
and group size 19, 32, 117–122, *118*,
128, 135
and homophily 61
and language 112, 123, 134–135, 178
and social media 178
Cooper, Charlotte 133
CoPs *see* Communities of Practice
cortisol 8, 90, 107, 169
Covid-19 pandemic 15, 39, 97, 106, 118,
167, 178, 187, 219
lockdowns 13–14, 33, 69, *175*, 179
working from home 15, 33, 50, 69,
107, 137, 159, 173–175, *175*, 179–181
see also Great Resignation (2022)
Cox, Chris 37

Cox, Oliver 247
Cree people (*Paskwâwiyiniwak*) 29
Cynefin Company (action research
    and development hub) 45, 133–134

da Vinci, Leonardo 168, 217
dancing 34, 76, 87, 88, 90, 101–102, 107–108
Dark Triad (personality types)
    139–141, 226
Darke, Jane 160
de Blok, Jos 149–150
deforestation 184
Denisovans 11
depression (illness) 66–67, 90, 96, 180, 185
dialects 58–60, 72, 110
diamond trade 137
diversity:
    of opinions and thinking 64, 70,
        78, 128, 199, 217, 226
    in teams and groups 65, 102, 128,
        133, 165–166, 207, 215–217, 226
doctors:
    general practitioners 138–139
    surgeons 115–116
    see also NHS (National Health
      Service)
dopamine 87, 90
Doudna, Jennifer 172–173
Dunbar Graph 7, 26–39, 27, 46, 58, 117,
    136, 177, 188, 190–191, 195, 199, 207
Dunbar Number 7, 19–23, 34–35, 50, 188
    discovery of 20–21
    layered structure 26–31, 47, 190

Eastwood, Owen 45–46, 51, 73–74, 133,
    139, 151, 166, 206, 247
eating and drinking, social 34, 87, 90,
    96–99, 106, 107–108, 220
    see also alcohol consumption
echo chambers 57, 199, 215

Edward, Harry 133
email 20, 33, 77, 112, 176, 178
endorphins 8–9, 76, 85–92, 87, 91,
    96–98, 101, 103, 106–107, 149
engagement:
    employee 65, 105–107, 152, 172
    and social groups 6, 24, 34, 60–61,
      64, 96–97
Enron (energy company) 218
epinephrine *see* adrenalin
evolution 10–13
exercising, communal 100–101
EY (professional services network)
    54, 106

Facebook (social media application)
    21, 37, 69, 176, 177, 178
family *see* kinship
family histories, tracing of 51, 73
FARC (Colombian guerrilla
    movement) 219
Faulkner, William, *As I Lay Dying* 49
feasting *see* eating and drinking, social
Felix Project, The (food charity) 97
Feynman, Richard 151–152
Flight Centre Travel Group 38–39
football 45, 115–116, 161, 197, 206
Foster, Norman 168
foundation and identity stories 71,
    73–74, 132–134, 165, 195, 224
'Fourth Industrial Revolution' 186
France, Debra 36, 76–77, 146–147, 211, 248
freeriders 42, 142, 143–144, 144,
    146–148, 158, 223, 226
Friendship, Seven Pillars of 57–63, 59–60,
    63, 69, 77, 109, 154, 156, 180, 204–205
friendship groups, in workplace 41,
    42, 65–70, 66–67, 77–78, 124–125,
    204–206, 225
Frost, Robert, 'Home Burial' 1

Gabriel India Ltd (automobile parts manufacturer) 97–98
Gage, Phineas 22–23
Gaggero Westaway, Clara 44–45, 170, 248
Galang, Michael 129
Galinsky, Adam 129
gaming, online 28, 71, 216
gardens and outside space 164–165, 172–173
Garvey Berger, Jennifer 46, 65–67, 127, 213, 248
gender differences:
   and conversation 117, 118–119, 123, 135
   and friendship 53–54, *53*, 57, 124–125, 126
   and mentalising 116, 117, 123
   and social style 123–128, 216
   and work environment 160–161
genealogy 51, 73
Gilbert, Paul 138, 248
Goldin, Ian 168
Gore, Willard (Bill) and Vieve 9, 35, 143
   Gore management model 9–10, 35–36, 76–77, 146–147, 211–212
gossip 128, 147–148
Grant, Heidi 215
Gray, Sir Denis Pereira 139
Great Resignation (2022) 163
grooming:
   humans 85
   monkeys and apes 8–9, 84–87
grooming-at-a-distance behaviours 86–87, *88*
group size:
   and altruism 22, 34, 39, 79
   and brain size 8–9, 20–21, 22–23, 47, 207
   business management models 9–10, 35–39, 44–47, 116

   and committees 42–44, *44*, 120–122, 191
   and conversation 19, 32, 117–122, *118*, 128, 135
   and decision-making 29, 32, 42–44, 47, 120, 190, 191, 192, 199–200
   and efficiency 44–47, 48, 191, 193, 199–200
   and endorphin production 86–87
   and evolution 10–13, *12*
   and information flow 25–26, *25*, 30–31, 43, 190–191, 195, 200
   and kinship 50–51
   and leadership 191–197
   management of 188–195, *189*, *192*, 223–224, 226
   and mentalising 113–119, *114*
   monkeys and apes 10, 20–21, 86–87
   Oxford Strategic Leadership Programme example 5–7
   and social time 8, 14, 21–22, 39–41, *40*
   and trust 19, 28, 35–36, 45, 136–139, 142, 144–145, *145*, 157
   see also Dunbar Graph; Dunbar Number; scalar stress problem
Gulbenkian Museum, Lisbon 102

Hamlet (Shakespeare) 94, 121
Hanke, Peter 17, 19, 106, 129, 150–151, 248
Hanks, Tom 50
Harford, Tim 215
Harrison, David 70
Harrison, Kirsten 248
Harvard Medical School 167–168
health:
   and bonding 105, 107
   and endorphins 86
   and friendship 66–67, 205
   and trust 139
   and work environment 160, 169–170, 171–172

healthcare 14–50, 105, 115–116, 138–139, 149
Heaphy, Emily 148
heart attacks 66–67
Heffernan, Margaret 54, 149–150, 205, 218, 248
Heidelberg Folk 11–12
Heifetz, Ron 200
height, and success 127
Heimans, Jeremy 200
Heineken (brewing company) 64
Herzog and de Meuron (architects) 159
Heyes, Cecilia 141, 248
hierarchical management structures 10, 29–30, 75–77, 109, 188–190, *189*
 see also pyramidal management structures
Hill, Alex 183
Hogan, Robert, *Personality and the Fate of Organizations* 141
holidays 182, 183, 210
Holocaust Memorial Day Trust 178
homophily 4, 51, 57–64, 78, 154, 216
 disruption of 4, 70, 78, 198, 199
hormones:
 and ill-health 169
 and social behaviour 8–9, 79–80, 85–92, 107–108
 see also endorphins
hospitals 105, 149
 operating theatres 115–116
hot-desking 15, 49, 179
housing:
 shortages 187
 workers' 171–172
Howard, Kim 37–38, 99, 134, 248
Howard, Melanie 67–68, 248
HSBC (investment bank) 198
humour, sense of 59, 60, 61, 69, 147, 214
 see also jokes and joking

hunter-gatherer societies 12–13, 21, 28, 29, 33, 34, 50, 134, 147
Hutterite communities 23–24, 31, 34, 190
hybrid working 14, 107, 169, 173–181, 185, 204–205
 see also working from home

Ibbotson, Piers 41, 94–95, 133, 248
identity stories *see* foundation and identity stories
IKEA (retailer) 209
Improbable (tech start-up) 99
India 97–98
induction programmes 56, 72, 74, 157, 207–208
initiation ceremonies 74

Jacobs, Claus 95–96, 248
Jaggi, Atul 97–98, 248
Jakub, Jay 37, 152, 249
James, Shelley 219, 249
Japan 100, 182
jogging 86, 92
jokes and joking 50, 61, 68, 109, 115, 147, 152
 see also humour, sense of
Josić, Krešimir 216–217
judiciary 127–128

Karikó, Katalin 167
Kemp, Martin 168, 249
Key Performance Indicators (KPIs) 183
Kingma, Boris 161
kinship:
 and altruism 22, 39, 51–52, *53–54*
 biological 51–52, *53–54*, 61–62, 63, 64
 development of sense of 51–56, 63–64, 75–76, 77, 185, 206–208, 224
 and trust 63–64, 76
 see also homophily

KPIs *see* Key Performance Indicators
!Kung San people 147, 152
Kutarna, Chris 168

language, shared:
    and friendship 58–60, 109–110
    and tribes 70, 71, 72–73, 109
language, words and meaning
        110–113, 123, 128–132, *130*, 133,
        134–135, 154, 178, 213
    see also mentalising
Lanzarotti, Paolo 151, 249
Larson, Kenneth 32
Latané, Bibb 43
laughter 87, 88, 90, 92, 94, 98, 107
    see also humour, sense of; jokes and
        joking
Lavoisier, Antoine 168, 241
Lay, Kenneth 218
Lego Group (toy manufacturer)
        95–96, 170
Leverhulme, William Lever, 1st
        Viscount 171–172
liars and lying 141, 144–145, *145*, 147
Liljenquist, Katie 215
Liminal Space, The (consultancy)
        67–68
lockdowns (during pandemic) 13–14,
        33, 69, *175*, 179
Losada, Michael 148

Machiavelli, Niccolò 140
Machiavellianism 139–140, 141, 143, 226
machine model of organisations 3–4,
        14, 186–187
Magna (car components company) 35
Makers Unite (creative agency) 209
Malone, Gareth 104
Mandela, Nelson 54
Mandelbrot, Benoit 19

Māori culture 51, 56
Marken Lichtenbelt, Wouter van 161
Marks and Spencer (retailer) 153
Mars (confectionery and food
        company) 37, 63, 64, 152, 211
Mars, Forrest, Sr 152, 211
Massachusetts Institute of
        Technology (MIT) 174
    Sloan School of Management 146
maternity leave 161
    re-entry after 74
matriculation ceremonies,
        university 74
MBTI *see* Myers–Briggs Type Indicator
McCord, Patty 37
McDonalds (fastfood chain) 49
McDowell, Alison 249
McGregor, Douglas 146
meals *see* eating and drinking, social
Medical Research Council Molecular
        Biology Laboratory, Cambridge
        167
Medici Quartet 194
meetings:
    organisation of 29, 120, 172–174,
        190, 193, 201–202
    social dynamics of 112–113
    see also committees; virtual
        meetings
Mehrabian, Albert 128–129, 213
mentalising 113–121, *114*, 123, 135, 191–192
Mercedes (motor manufacturer) 64
Merkel, Angela 131
Microsoft (technology company) 174, *175*
    Work Trend Index 32–33, 65
    see also Teams
military:
    organisation 21, 29–30, 52, 75–76,
        93–94
    training 75–76, 93–94

Milton, John, *Paradise Lost* 83
mirroring 123, 129
Mischel, Walter 184
MIT *see* Massachusetts Institute of
    Technology
model housing, for workers 171–172
monetary policy committees
    42–43, 44
monkeys and apes:
    bonded relationships 84–87, 107
    and evolution 11, 12
    group size 10, 20–21, 86–87
    kinship 50
    social grooming 8–9, 84–87
Morgan, Gareth 249
    Imaginization 26
Murphy, Charlotte 214
music 106, 221
    conductors 17–19, 106, 129, 150–151
    musical tastes 59, 60, 62, 63, 204
    see also singing
music groups:
    size and organisation 17–19,
        150–151, 191–193, 194
    see also choirs
Myers–Briggs Type Indicator (MBTI)
    198

narcissism 116, 139–140, 141, 226
National Health Service *see* NHS
National Trust 71
Nauta, Sacha 122–123
Neale, Margaret 215
Neanderthals 11–12
Netflix (streaming company) 37
New Zealand 55–56, 151, 178, 184
    All Blacks (rugby team) 51, 74
    see also Māori culture
newcomers 56, 72, 157, 180, 207–208,
    209

    see also induction programmes
NHS (National Health Service) 97,
    148–149
night work 67–68
Ninety-One (investment
    management company) 38, 99
Nobel Prize 151, 167, 172
nurses 115–116, 150
Nwadeyi, Lovelyn 206, 249

Obhi, Sukhvinder 129
Odean, Terrance 216
office design 49–50, 159–160, 161–163,
    169–172, 179–180, 187, 218–220
Olympic Games 133
online gaming 28, 71, 216
online meetings *see* virtual meetings
orchestras, size and organisation
    17–19, 194
organisational size 183, 188–190
OSLP *see* Oxford Strategic
    Leadership Programme
out-groups 4, 36, 71
outside space *see* gardens and outside
    space
overfishing 184
Oxford Muse Foundation 97
Oxford Strategic Leadership
    Programme (OSLP) 3, 95–96,
    98, 100–101, 155–157
    group size 5–7, 128, 156
Oxford University:
    boat crews 91–92, 91
    colleges 163–166, 172
    matriculation ceremonies 74
    meals 98–99, 164
    see also Blavatnik School of
        Government; Saïd Business
        School
oxytocin 87–88, 89

pain:
    management 85, 89–90, 98
    thresholds 53, 86, 87, 88, 91–92, 91,
        101, 103
pandemic *see* Covid-19 pandemic
Patel, Yoge 116, 179, 249
Peake, Sharon 125–126, 249
performance indicators *see* Key
    Performance Indicators
personal development, prioritisation
    over group development 80–81
Perutz, Max 167
Peter Principle 197–198
Pettinger, Lynne 68
Phillips, Heather 105
Phillips, Katherine 215
Plato 95
play and playfulness 82, 83, 84, 95–96,
    147–148, 214, 221
plays *see* theatre, productions
pop groups *see* music groups
Pötsch, Hans Dieter 147
PowerPoint presentations 109, 122,
    133, 212
Poynton, Robert 132, 174, 249
prehistory, social groups in 10–13,
    38, 50
prisons and prisoners 102–104, 105
psychopathy 140–141, 226
Punt 6 (urban designers) 161
pyramidal management structures
    189, 190, 193, 200
    see also hierarchical management
    structures

Quakers 152, 171

refugees 102, 209
religion 62, 63, 140
    rituals 76, 88, 106

remote working *see* working from
    home
retirement 100, 208
rituals:
    non-religious 29, 51, 56, 71, 73–74,
        88, 98–99, 165
    religious 76, 88, 106
    see also grooming
Robertson, Paul 194
Rock, David 215
Roman army 30
rowing (sport) 91–92, 91, 101
Rowntree, Henry Isaac 171–172
rugby 51, 74, 115–116
rule-breaking 35, 142, 144, 145–147, 152,
    158, 184
Rumi 109
Rust, Nick 249

SABMiller (brewing company) 69,
    73–74, 99
Safebook (online security software) 59
Saïd Business School, Oxford 7, 155
    see also Oxford Strategic
    Leadership Programme (OSLP)
Salisbury, Chris 139
Samoa 74, 178
San Juan, Puerto Rico 173
Santayana, George 4
scalar stress problem 23–26
Schein, Edgar 217
schools:
    bonding exercise in girls' school
        81–83
    results league tables 81
Schumacher, E.F. 17
Schuster, Ezra 55, 151, 177–178, 249
Schweichler, Thami 209, 250
sea shanties 101
serotonin 90

Seven Pillars of Friendship 57–63, *59–60*, 63, 69, 77, 109, 154, 156, 180, 204–205
Shakeir, Reima 250
Shakespeare, William 82, 120, 199
    Hamlet 94, 121
share-trading 28, 144–145, 216
Shenzhen 100 stock exchange 28
short-term contracts 74
short-term targets 183, 184
silos 23, 25, 35, 48, 57, 62, 70, 78, 143, 168, 205
Simon, Herbert 162
singing 34, 87, *88*, 90, 101–106, *103–104*, 107–108, 172
    see also choirs
Skype (telecommunications application) *176*, 177
smoking, giving up *66–67*, 205
Snowden, Dave 45, 133–134, 250
Social Brain Hypothesis 8–9, *20–21*
social grooming *see* grooming
social group size *see* group size
social media *20*, 21, 37, 57, 69, 174–177, *176*, 178
social time 181–183
    and brain size 8
    and group size 8, 14, 21–22, 39–41, *40*
    and kinship 52
    and leadership 201–202
    and meetings 205
    and office design 50, 180
    and trust 47
Solnit, Rebecca 186
Sotomayor, Sonia 128
South Africa x, 53, 105–106, 134
    National Peace Accord (NPA; 1991) 54–55
spider plants 26
Spielberg, Steven, *The Terminal* 50
sponsors (voluntary role) 76–77

sports teams 73, 133, 139, 164, 206
    see also football; rowing (sport); rugby
Stanford Marshmallow Experiment 184
Starbucks (coffeehouse chain) 72
stock exchanges 28
    see also share-trading
Storey, David 54–55, 106, 250
storytelling 34, *88*, 132–134, 135, 156, 213–214
    see also foundation and identity stories
Stronach, Frank 35
supply chain management 197
support cliques 27, 31–32, 39
Supreme Court, US 127–128
surgeons 115–116
sympathy groups 27, 32–33, 39
synchrony, behavioural 76, 90–93, 95, 101–102, 106–107, 135, 214, 225

Teams (business communication platform) 33, 177, 219
temptation, resisting 184
Tenovus Cancer Care (charity) 105
Terminal, The (film; 2004) 50
testosterone 89
theatre:
    audiences 92, 108
    productions 92, 94
    see also Shakespeare, William
'theory of mind' 113–115
Theory X and Theory Y managerial styles 146–147, 148
Three Mile Island nuclear power plant accident (1979) 151–152
Thrive Model™ *viii*, 188, 202–220, *203*
Thurner, Stefan 216
time management 181–183, 187, 201–202
Timms, Henry 200
Tragedy of the Commons 184

tribal communities 29, 38, 70–72, 147
tribes (social and organisational
     groups) 38, 70–77, 71, 83, 110,
     136–137, 177, 195, 206
trust 136–158, 226
    and bonding 55, 79–80, 81, 83,
        94–95, 107, 142, 157
    and communication 23, 115, 131, 154
    and friendship 59–62, 60, 67, 154,
        156–157
    and group size 19, 28, 35–36, 45,
        136–139, 142, 144–145, 145, 157
    and kinship 63–64, 76
    and social time 47
Tuckman group model 94
Turner, Graham 'Skroo' 38, 250
Twitter (social networking
     application) 177

Unilever (corporation) 64, 171–172
urban development 13, 137, 160–163,
     171–172
    see also architecture and built
        environment; villages
Urch, Sir Tyrone 30, 52, 93–94, 250

van Gogh, Vincent 159
vasopressin 89
video-embedded media *see* Skype;
     Teams; Zoom
villages:
    development of 13, 34
    size 13, 20, 21
    social organisation 13, 21,
        132–133, 134

virtual meetings 13, 110, 123, 174, 177,
     178, 180, 185, 205, 219
Virtual Reality (VR) 116
Volkswagen (motor manufacturer) 147

walkshops (walking meetings)
     106–107, 172–173
Walmart (retail corporation) 63
Wang, Ping 79
Warwick Business School 94–95
waterlily leaves 189, 190
Watkins, Sherron 218
website design 153, 211
Weissman, Drew 167
West, Bruce 25
Westaway, Clara Gaggero and Adrian
     44–45, 170, 248
WhatsApp (messaging application)
     13, 102
Whitman, Walt 217
Willis-Faber Building, Ipswich 169
Wixley, Sue 13–14, 250
W. L. Gore and Associates *see* Gore
     management model
Woods, Ngaire 212, 250
working from home (WFH) 15, 33, 50,
     69, 107, 122–123, 137, 159, 173–181, 175
    see also hybrid working
World Economic Forum 186
World Happiness Report (2021) 50

Zeldin, Theodore 97, 109, 209, 221, 250
zero-hours contracts 74
Zoom (videoconferencing application)
     13, 110, 123, 174, 177, 178, 180, 219